...aile Munna
Ballymun
Tel: 8421890

True
Colours

Barry Geraghty

with Niall Kelly

Gill Books

D0277123

Gill Books
Hume Avenue
Park West
Dublin 12
www.gillbooks.ie

Gill Books is an imprint of M.H. Gill and Co.

© Barry Geraghty 2020
978 07171 8988 5

Print origination by O'K Graphic Design
Copy-edited by Jane Rogers
Proofread by Neil Burkey
Printed by CPI Group (UK) Ltd, Croydon, CRO 4YY

This book is typeset in 11.5/17 pt Sabon.

The paper used in this book comes from the wood pulp of managed forests.
For every tree felled, at least one tree is planted, thereby renewing natural
resources.

All rights reserved.

No part of this publication may be copied, reproduced or transmitted in any
form or by any means, without written permission of the publishers.

A CIP catalogue record for this book is available from the British Library.

5 4 3 2 1

To Paula, Síofra, Órla and Rían

Withdrawn from Stock
Dublin City Public Libraries

Prologue

t starts in the weighroom, before you even set foot on the track. Everything has to be calm. Nice and calm. The best jockeys are like the church mouse. You want to be so quiet on a horse that he hardly even knows you're there. From the moment you sit up on him, every change has to be a subtle one. Every move has to be a gentle one. Racehorses want to race. It doesn't take much to set them off. If your backside so much as brushes off the saddle as he canters off to go down to the start – boom, lights on. And that's when you find yourself in trouble.

A horse feeds off your emotion. If you're nervous, if you're tense, if you're wound up, he knows. The adrenaline is pumping but you have to control it. If your heart is thumping and your pulse is racing, a horse will feel it. They're not mind readers; they just notice the little things, a slight shift in your balance, your fingers gripping the reins a tiny bit tighter than you think. Keep your hands soft, your touch light, a nice gentle hold. You're not trying to start a row. You're not trying to start a fight. You don't want your horse taking you on, because if he takes you on, there's only going to be one winner. If you're relaxed, you'll hear him breathing, exhaling, almost like a sigh. He's trusting you. He's relaxing too.

You want to get to the start early, quietly. If you're late into the parade ring, you'll be late to the start, and if you're late to the start, you'll be out of position before the white flag is raised and

1

Leabharlanna Poiblí Chathair Baile Átha Cliath
Dublin City Public Libraries

it's time to jump off. Position is everything. From the moment the race starts, you're constantly working on where you are, where you want to be. The computer is going. You're scanning everything. Are we going fast enough, too fast, just right? Where's that lad going? Am I on the best ground here or should I move out – is that bit better? How's the favourite getting on? How about now? And over and over again.

And as you're watching, you're listening. The sounds of the race, the clatter of hooves, the *whoosh* as we brush through the top of a fence, it's so familiar that it's white noise, in the background but not intruding. You're listening for something else, some bit of information. The bang of a horse as he steps through a hurdle. The gurgle of another one that's struggling to fill his lungs, hanging on to his last bit of energy even though from the outside he looks as though he's still full of running. Someone might say something: a bit of slagging after a mistake; a half a chat, trying to suss out your strategy; a shout for a bit of space when things get tight. Most of the time there's no need to shout. You're close enough to practically whisper. The noise of the crowd only travels so far from the stands. When you're out in the country, it's near silence, and if you're on a horse that's running keen, raised voices aren't going to help him settle. Silence is golden.

There are days when the ground comes back at you like bullets, flicking off the top of the sod as the horse in front gallops through. There are days when it comes sod and all, two fists full like a punch in the face. You drop your eyes, tuck in your chin and try to take it on your shoulders instead. When the first set of goggles are covered in muck, you pull them down and move on to the second pair; when the second pair are covered, the best you can do is try to give them a wipe with your glove; when your glove is covered, you're on your own.

All the while you're watching, judging, calculating. The distance to the fence. The length of your stride. How much your horse has already given you. How much more he can give. You might be tanking along or you might be hanging on for dear life. You plot your course and you make your move.

When you turn into the home straight, with the finish line in sight, you wait for the right moment. You wait and you wait. You know it when it comes. All the lights turn green, and you go.

At least that's how it should happen.

April 2019

The problem with the Topham Chase, I'm reminded again as the tape goes up, is that it's a cavalry charge. Twenty-seven horses, stretched out across the track pretty much in a single line, haring down to the first fence. It's the day before the Grand National and the Topham, which is run over the same iconic Aintree fences as the National, serves as a sort of mini dress rehearsal. In a race like this, you want to be riding a horse that understands the situation, one that won't take too many risks on you. Because, over these fences, it's rare for a mistake to go unpunished.

The horse I'm on, Peregrine Run, isn't a big, flashy horse or a flamboyant jumper. He's nimble, the type of fella who will bring me right in tight to the base of the fence and then pop up over it, rather than trying to take off when we're still a couple of yards away and soar through the air in full flight. One of his nice, measured short strides isn't going to be much good to us at the first fence, though. We're slow getting away at the start and if we're too conservative at the first, we'll pretty much surrender any chance of momentum and position, probably land dead last, and our race will be as good as over after 10 seconds.

I give him a little squeeze to let him know that we need to really go at this first fence, attack it, and land on the front foot on the other side. When we get there, he puts in such a big jump that it nearly takes us both by surprise and from that point on, the careful, cautious approach that we were both expecting goes out the window. When the next fence comes, he goes for another big jump. The same thing again at the one after that. I wait a few fences for him to get it out of his system, but he's not too interested in the way things are normally done. This is the new way and he's enjoying it, and all I can do is get myself on the same page, ride the race he's insisting on riding, go with him and hope for the best. I give him a squeeze at the next – all right so, if you're going for it, let's go for it – and he goes again without a second of hesitation, taking it on like a big horse.

Once we've jumped the first few fences, the horses tend to find their natural position in the race. Some want to be right up the front, others want to hang towards the back where there's a little bit more room; I'm a bit like Goldilocks for now, happy enough to be somewhere in the middle. Just right. We've 18 fences to jump in total and already there have been a couple of fallers. For those horses and their jockeys, the race is already over.

You expect falls in a race like this, but when it happens, it happens so quickly, with so much else going on around you at the same time, that it's hard to pick up on the detail. We're well into the second half of the race when we come to jump the Canal Turn, one of the famously tricky fences. The name is a bit of a giveaway – the fence is on a bend in the track, and most jockeys want to take the shortest route, so we tend to bunch towards the inner. I don't notice the horse in front of us as he makes a mistake. When you land over a fence behind a faller, your horse will always try to avoid another horse or jockey, but he can only do that if he sees them. And you can only steer him around if you see them. You never know what might be waiting for you around the corner out of sight as you jump the Canal Turn. Both of you might not even realise that there's someone there on the ground until it's already too late. Out of the corner of my eye, I think I spot the pink silks of the jockey we've just galloped over. I think they're the colours that Fish – Mark Enright – was wearing. I don't know for certain. That's racing. It's nobody's fault, but that doesn't stop me blaming myself. We jump the next few fences without any incident, thankfully, and I put it out of my head for now. We've still got a race to run and I can't afford to dwell on it.

We're still up there with the leading dozen as we come down to jump the third last, but I know that we're not going to win the race. Peregrine Run is not showing any immediate signs of giving up on me, but I can tell that he doesn't have a huge amount left in reserve, and there are four or five others in front of us still going better. Maybe now is the time to play it safe with a short one, I think, but if he hears me think it, he ignores it just as quickly. Halfway through another big one, our last big one, his heart's not really in it and I know we're not going to make it. He comes down on top of the fence and I feel him stumble on landing as he tries to shoot his front legs out into position in time to save us both. It's too little too late. Momentum has already dug in its claws. He goes down and as I'm launched left and over his shoulder, I brace for impact.

I'm already on the other side of the fence by the time the final few stragglers reach it and clamber up and over. Away in the distance, the leader turns the screw and ups the pace at the front again but anything that's coming from behind me at this stage might as well be in a different race. They're tired and in survival mode, but they still manage to breeze past me like I'm not even there – thankfully. Peregrine Run is long gone, back on his feet and galloping off alone to finish the job we had started together. I slowly sit up so that I can look down at my leg. It's bent inwards two inches above the ankle. It was an easy fall for both of us, relatively speaking, but it's not always the fall itself that does the most damage; it's the traffic coming from behind that you have to worry about. As the horse rolled left, he rolled me with him and pushed me right under the girth of a horse coming behind us. And at that point, either timing and fortune are on your side or, if they're not, your right ankle sits up in the only few inches of space in all of Merseyside that you desperately need it to avoid, just at the moment a half-tonne of muscle and bone comes crashing through on its hind legs.

After the fall and after the tumble dryer – that short, sharp, involuntary spin cycle that bustles you away from the back of the fence and to a stop – instinct kicks in and your brain starts into the checklist, from head to toe: where does it hurt? Each box brings its own brief relief as it's ticked off while your mind keeps fast forwarding through the list until it finds the pain, wherever that is. The full force of it never registers immediately, but I don't need an X-ray to know that this one is bad.

I've been remarkably lucky with injury throughout my career. I was 14 when I broke my knee for the first time, out the side of a slippery saddle on a miserable wet day in Loughrea. Since then I've broken my collarbone, once on each side. I've torn the AC joint in my shoulder in one fall, and then finished the job a few weeks later by falling on it again and breaking my shoulder blade as well. I've sat in hospital waiting rooms and told doctors that I could only identify a single point of pain in my back, only to be told that I'd actually broken eight ribs and punctured a lung.

I've broken both arms, and both legs on more than one occasion; cracked my fibula and fractured my tibia, the shinbone, which has to be one of the sorest bones in your body to break. I've had concussions so serious that I didn't know which racecourse I was at and, at a guess, somewhere in the region of 70 stitches in my face over the years: my lip, my chin, and my eyebrow.

I've broken my wrist and a rib in a fall and gone out in the very next race, less than half an hour later, and ridden the winner.

I've had X-rays to assess a suspected fractured vertebra in one part of my back, only for them to discover a completely different fracture that happened God knows when and had been sitting there for God knows how long.

I've shown up on the doorstep in a neck brace, bang on time at eight o'clock and ready to pick Paula up for dinner as promised, not bothered by the fall I'd had a couple of hours earlier or the fact that I'd just been discharged from Naas Hospital with a cracked vertebra. When we got married and went on honeymoon, only to discover afterwards that the ball of my shoulder had been broken the whole time, it was hardly a surprise.

Still, I mean it when I say it: on the whole, over the course of my career, I've been remarkably lucky with injury. When you're racing four or five days a week for more than 20 years, with maybe three or four rides each day, that's a lot of opportunities for something to go wrong, even if you never acknowledge them. The mind – my mind, anyway – tends to forget the minor ones. A fractured thumb causes me as much discomfort as anyone else, but an injury only really becomes important if it's going to stop me going out and doing my job for a significant length of time. If you put all of the other bits to one side in a pile marked scratches and scrapes, I can pick out long stretches of years at a time when I've been very fortunate and injury-free. That's not something to be taken for granted; it's something to be celebrated.

But now, out in the countryside, far from the sound of the hooves and the crowd and the commentator, there's only the silence and the thoughts in my head. The pain is there but the thoughts are worse. There was a time when my first concern would have been missing the ride on Champ in the next race – Mark Walsh picks up that spare and wins easily – or having to sit out the Grand National tomorrow on Anibale Fly – another nice spin for Mark, and they finish fifth. But any immediate worries like that are pushed aside by something darker, more existential:

Is this how it was always destined to end, half a mile from the winning line with only a badly buckled leg for company? Is this it for me? Will I even be allowed to make that decision for myself or will someone else, reading the stark facts from a page on a clipboard, come to that single inescapable conclusion on my behalf? It's over.

Long before any expert arrives to put words on the trouble I'm in – two single fractures, one of the fibula and one of the tibia, both snapped clean a couple of inches above the ankle – I know the sacrifices it will take if I ever want to get back in the saddle again. What I don't know is: will I be able for it this time?

I've been lucky with injury in general, that's true, but the last few years have been brutal and those are the scars that are leading me towards this darkness, mercifully rare and mercifully brief. In 2015, I was appointed to the biggest job in jump racing – first jockey to JP McManus, the biggest and most successful owner in the sport. I was recovering from a broken leg when I accepted the job, and in the four years since then, I've broken my leg, I've broken my arm, I've broken eight ribs and punctured a lung, I've broken my other arm, and I've fractured my shoulder. And now this.

Every jockey understands that they won't be able to run from injuries for ever. That risk is part of the terms and conditions.

They catch up with everyone eventually; all you want is to be able to walk away at the end of it all when your racing days are done with no lasting or life-changing damage. A part of me thinks you could find a way to make your peace with the pain; it's the rehab that's the killer.

Send me out to run the roads for hours. I'll do it. Send me to the gym to lift for days. No problem. Just don't ask me to stand barefoot in the kitchen and arch the sole of my foot, a movement so small that you'd barely even notice it; hold it for five seconds; release; repeat 20 times; and when I'm finished with that, do the exact same thing all over again. And then again. And then when those three sets of tedium are done, move on to the next imperceptible exercise and start all over. Day after day after day until you go for a check-up so that the physio can reassure you that it's working and send you back home with the encouragement that if you trust the programme, you'll see the benefits in a few weeks' time.

Fifty weeks – that's how long I've already spent out injured in the last four years, and who knows how many more months now with this latest one. I think about the long, slow days ahead, filled with the same boring repetitions, how quickly the muscle can waste away to nothing. It's not just the lack of exercise. You could sit at home for a week and do nothing without seeing any dramatic consequences, but with a fracture, that part of the body shuts down and it doesn't move at all. Stirring a cup of tea doesn't even generate any movement. Strength and power vanishes into thin air overnight. Like a duster running across a blackboard, everything erased with a single swipe.

You find a way to get through it, of course you do, and you get out the other side of it, but just as soon as you do, something new happens and you're back to square one. And when they come on you like that in quick succession, it's too bad to cry.

My leg sits broken on the Aintree turf in front of me. I can tell that it's a bad one. There's a part of me that's already afraid that it might be the worst one yet. I want to get through this. I just don't know that I can.

The medics are here now and I ask for the morphine quickly. It's not for the pain; the pain I can handle. I just need to get these thoughts out of my head.

'We need to take your boot off,' the paramedic says to me.

Aintree University Hospital is only down the road from the racecourse, a 10-minute drive at most, even less when you're in the back of an ambulance.

'Before your leg starts to swell,' she says to me again. 'We need to get the boot off.'

She moves to lift my leg to get at the zip of my boot, but as soon as she does, the pain rips through my body and I roar, through gritted teeth, 'Stop! The strap! The strap!'

She hears me. I'm strapped in to the bed on the ambulance trolley, scrambling for the catch on the belt that's securing my leg above the knee before there are any more attempts to get the boot off. The morphine has started to work, but it never works quickly enough.

Paula will be here soon, I know. She has had a bad run of it too these last few years. Whether it's verbalised or not, we both know that there's every chance that one day I'll go off to work and a few hours later, she'll get one of those phone calls she dreads. There are days when the racing won't be on TV, or when she won't be watching, and her phone will ring. One of the racecourse doctors, or maybe a friend at the course who's seen it, and can find out what's happened and how I am, will call or text. There are other days, like today, when she'll be watching with the kids and see it all unfold as it happens. On those days, the TV camera doesn't wait for the wife or husband or mother or father with a sick feeling in the pit of their stomach. It pans away from the only shot that matters to follow something as trivial as a race between some horses. At home they can only wait for the commentator to take a look back up the track and announce that both horse and jockey are on their feet, but sometimes they don't say that.

Paula was watching the race at home with our three children, Síofra, Órla and Rían. They were all watching it together and it was Síofra, our eldest, who spotted what had happened.

'Oh, it's his leg,' she says.

In the absence of any news from the track, that little detail brings its own bit of reassurance for a moment, but when the doctors get to me out on the course, the first thing I do is give them Paula's number.

'I don't know if she was watching. Can you ring her please and let her know that I'm okay? Just let her know it's not my neck.'

I know she'll be here in a couple of hours anyway. She's due to go to the races tomorrow with her sister Liz and Liz's husband Seán, so she already has a flight booked to come to Liverpool later this evening.

When we get to the hospital and I'm wheeled into my room, Fish and Johnny Burke are the first two people allowed in to see me. The gloom lifts once the painkillers do their job and I'm delighted to see the two boys, laughing, joking and having the craic as if this is nothing worse than a sprained ankle and we'll all be back to business as usual in the morning. It's great to see Fish in particular, fit and firing with the green light to ride in the National tomorrow. I could hear the messages coming in over the racecourse radio while I was lying on the ground at the back of the fence and the medics were inflating the air splints to secure my leg:

'Mark Enright down at the Canal Turn with a broken arm.'

11

It was Fish we ran over, I thought to myself; I'm the one who broke his arm. I didn't need that hanging over me along with everything else, so when Fish sticks his head into the room to say hello and let me know that he's been given the all-clear by the doctors, it's the first bounce of the ball to go my way today. Sophie, Nicky Henderson's wife, comes in shortly afterwards to see how I'm getting on, and then Liz and Seán arrive, all happy to sit and keep me company until Paula gets here later.

I'm wheeled off for an X-ray and then into another room when four or five doctors follow me in with their sleeves rolled up. I'm stuck to the bed in my numbed state and they're trying to explain to me what needs to happen now. It's too risky to leave my leg the way it is, stable but still bent in a way that legs aren't supposed to bend, and if we do, there's a higher risk of internal bleeding, which could cause all sorts of complications. That's why they're here, to straighten it out – which explains the rolled-up sleeves.

'This is going to hurt,' one of the doctors explains. 'We can't give you a full anaesthetic in case we need to operate on you this evening, but we'll get you some more pain relief before we do anything.'

If these people are about to wrestle my leg back into shape, I don't want to feel even a second of it.

'Give me everything,' I tell them. 'Fucking give me everything.'

So they give me ketamine, and as the fog descends, taking me to some sort of semi-drunken no man's land, I feel all those sets of hands get a good, firm grip on my leg. And they pull.

Ten thousand volts of pain scream through me and I know that this is not how it's supposed to be because I can feel the agony of each twist and turn and I can hear myself roar, my only release. I'm lying there, still rooted to my trolley as it suddenly takes off backwards out through the door, driven by hands I cannot see towards this blindingly bright corridor, bouncing in vivid colour, that doesn't look like any hospital corridor I've ever seen before in my life. There are no people, only nightmarish emojis, leering and sneering at me with their exaggerated features and their wide, unblinking eyes. I can't move. I can't fight them off. I panic. I need to get out of here but all I can do is cling on for dear life as my trolley takes off like a rollercoaster, backwards, ripping through double doors and whipping around corners at 50 miles an hour. My heart is thumping, pressing on the underside of my rib cage, ready to burst out through my chest if only it could find a way through. I need to breathe, and then I realise that that short, sharp panting is my breath, that I'm already breathing faster than I ever thought the human body could. I don't know where I am. When this will end. Maybe this is the end. Maybe when your clock stops ticking, those final moments of life just dissolve into one last manic blur and then –

My heart slows and my breathing slows and the colours fade back to their usual mix of sterile whites, and I realise that I'm still in the same room where the doctors left me. If that was 10 minutes, it felt like a lifetime, but I can feel the ketamine gradually loosening its grip and releasing me back into reality and a hospital bed that's reassuringly stationary. I'm lying there like a lad after a late one when I hear a voice calling my name.

'Barry, JP and Frank are here to see you.'

'Lovely, lovely, lovely,' I say as JP McManus and Frank Berry, his racing manager, arrive into my room. It's very good of them to call in and see how I am; after all, I wasn't riding for them when I fell. They stopped off on their way to the hospital to pick up a few of the essentials that they know I'll need: pyjamas and some fruit. JP's incredible generosity is no secret to anyone who knows him, but most people never see the little things that he's always thinking of.

'How are you doing, Barry?'

'Lovely, lovely, lovely.'

I don't know what I'm saying but it's all I can say, as if the ketamine trip has wiped every word from my vocabulary except for one. My grasp of the English language slowly returns to me but I'd nearly rather it didn't, because now I have enough words to start rabbiting on and force JP and Frank to put up with me talking absolute rubbish. At least as I gain more and more control of my senses I have the presence of mind to apologise for the nonsense I'm subjecting them to.

'I'm sorry, I'm drunk as a lord here.'

They stay for a while and I try to tell them about what happened, and when they leave, Sophie comes and sits with me again until Paula arrives. X-rays come back and doctors update us and as the bits of the jigsaw start to fit together, we try to figure out what we're going to do. We're familiar enough with the rhythms of hospital life to know that you don't want to be dealing with one surgeon for your operation, and then another surgeon in a different country for your reviews and follow-up consultations, or, worse again, if something goes wrong. If the doctors say I'm okay to travel to Ireland with my leg the way it is and get the surgery there, I want to go home.

We consider the ferry, and then rule it out again just as quickly. Too slow, too long, too much time with the leg in an unstable position. Better to book a row of seats on a plane, I'm told; 40 minutes in the air, and no more than a couple of hours door to door. But we don't need to put ourselves through the hassle of check-in queues on crutches and a wheelchair to the gate. JP kindly offers us to bring us home on his helicopter. It's waiting on standby, ready to come and pick us up whenever we need it. All we need to do is let him know when we're ready to go and where we want to go. A few calls later, we're halfway across the Irish Sea, on the way to Luttrellstown Castle and then – a short crutch hobble later – into the car JP has waiting there for us. The clock comes up on half past five and, in a parallel universe, I'd be riding Anibale Fly in the Grand National. Instead, as Tiger Roll crosses the finish line, I'm watching from the waiting room of Tallaght Hospital's X-ray department.

Jockeys are a tight-knit group in general, never more so than when one of us has suffered a bad injury. As soon as the Grand National is over and he's finished racing for the day, Ruby Walsh rings Paula to see how I'm doing and what the options are for surgery.

'They haven't decided yet,' she tells him. 'They're talking plate or frame.'

Ruby's advice carries the stamp of a man who has been through it all himself on plenty of occasions in the past. His memories are fresh, too; it's only been a little more than a year since his most recent broken leg.

'Frame,' Ruby says. 'Tell him to get the frame.'

Paula relays the advice, but it's not what I want to hear. I know exactly what the surgery to get the frame on entails and I hate the thought of it. A maze of wires threaded through the skin. Screws drilled into the bone. I don't hate it for me, I hate it for the kids. I hate the thought of Síofra and Órla and Rían having to look at me, miserable, hulking this horrible lump of metal around for the next four months. They don't need that to be the lasting memory of their summer. I get a laugh when I try to explain that. I know it sounds like a bit of a cop-out.

The surgery to put the frame on is scheduled for the next day, then pushed back another 24 hours, but before they put me to sleep and wake me up with a leg like Frankenstein's monster, Kevin Tuite, a very good friend of mine, rings to put me on to one other important job. I can hear the noise in the background wherever he is. Saturday night in the pub in Trim, it turns out. He asks how I'm getting on, so I give him the latest.

'What's the plan now?' he asks me. 'Do you think you'll keep going or is that the end of it?'

'What do you mean?'

'There's a bit of chat in here tonight that this is it for you. A good few lads saying that you've decided to retire.'

'What? Tell them no, no chance. I'm not retiring. No.'

I get a similar phone call from Fish the following morning.

'I'm just letting you know that they've retired you again.'

'Who has? Where did you hear this?'

'In Liverpool Airport coming home last night, sure everyone was saying the same thing: that's it, Geraghty's done now, he's retiring. And I was telling them, no, I'd been in to see you yesterday and I didn't think so, that you'd be back riding in a few months. But then I said I'd better ring you and see what you're thinking.'

'No, Jesus, I'm definitely not retiring. Where are they getting that from?'

'I don't know, but they've written you off anyway,' Fish says. 'You're retired.'

Once I'm off the phone to Fish, I know the next call that I have to make. I work out the sums in my head: I was out for the best part of four months with the last broken leg, which means I'll be able to go back racing again in around four months' time. A fracture's a fracture, so surely it will just be the same again. The Galway Races start on the last Monday in July, and I don't need a calendar to know that that's not quite four months away, but close enough not to make a difference.

I pick up the phone again. I need to get a statement out this morning. Set the Galway date for my comeback. Kill the rumour. Because I know the hell that's waiting for me in the next few months, but I'm also certain that I'm not ready to retire. I'm not done yet.

We've always been horse people, our family. The old stone-walled stable that's still there in the corner of the yard of our family farm is a monument to that. My grandfather Laurence must have foaled dozens of horses in his lifetime out of that inconspicuous little shed, but it carries the name of only one of them. We grew up with the book, the pictures, the stories about Golden Miller, this once-in-a-lifetime horse whose achievements are still unmatched many lifetimes later – winner of five successive Cheltenham Gold Cups, including something that no horse before or since has ever managed, winning the Cheltenham Gold Cup and Aintree Grand National in the same year, 1934. That isn't yesterday or today, but the pride is passed down through the generations like an heirloom; years later, when we have children of our own, we make a point of bringing them to visit the Golden Miller bar in Cheltenham so that they can see the black-and-white photos of the horse that their great-grandfather bred and feel the history for themselves.

We cram into the living room and watch Garrison Savannah jump the final fence in the Grand National. Tradition is as much a part of Grand National day as the race itself, with the routine of the day mapped out to match whatever was done the year before and the year before that. It's my earliest memory, not even four years old in 1983, feeling the excitement in this room full of adults shouting for Ireland, shouting for Colin Magnier, the local lad in the saddle, as Greasepaint tries desperately to get his nose in front of Corbiere. But when Garrison Savannah lands three lengths clear in 1991, nobody's shouting. It's three weeks since he won the Gold Cup and he has our family's pride and joy at his mercy. Nobody dares take their eyes off the TV. A disappointed silence is starting to fall until my grandmother breaks it:

'Go, Seagram! Go on!'

To our delight, the TV camera pulls back to show us the history that's quickly slipping away from Garrison Savannah. Seagram, the marginally less tired of two tired horses, chews up what's left of the distance between them and gallops clear to the line. My grandfather's proud legacy lives to fight another year.

It was Dad's dream to be a jockey too, once upon a time. He was an amateur with Georgie Wells, one of the legends of the sport, down in Georgie's yard in Clonee. Georgie was a gentleman and he had the CV – he won the Irish Derby and both Irish Guineas as a flat jockey in the 1940s, and when he moved into training, trained the winner of the Irish Grand National twice. Dad was there for a year but it was his misfortune to be coming of age in the late 1960s, at the same time as Georgie's godson, a young lad by the name of Arthur Moore. Once Arthur arrived in the yard, Dad's chance to get a couple of opportunities dried up. Arthur went on to share the champion amateur title in 1968 and then to win the Irish Grand National for Georgie a few years later; Dad's dream was left on the shelf, and before long, he was back helping his own dad on the farm.

Those 100 acres in the little village of Drumree, County Meath, are our home and our playground. We turn the hay barn into our own private obstacle course, climbing the bales like a ladder and then launching ourselves from the top into the safety of a nicely cushioned crash landing. We build a swing, build a treehouse. The Clarkes and the Geraghtys, our cousins from down the road, come up to play with us and now we have the manpower and the imagination for more ambitious projects, more elaborate designs. It's always a good day when the hay gets sold; with every bale that's lifted out, we have more space to play in, and more space means more room for a bigger swing. Summertime is harvest time and, on a lucky day, we get permission to sit in the back of the trailer as Dad goes out in the combine to cut the wheat or the barley. I sit right up underneath the spout and listen to the grain hammer down over my head until I'm swallowed up in a sea of gold. One day, I discover that I'm only wearing one shoe as I climb out of the trailer. I say nothing, trusting that nobody will ever find out, until a report comes back from the mill that they've just discovered a child's shoe as they poured out one of their sacks.

We all get our first taste of work from a young age. You can nearly set your watch by the big days. Noel Farrell, the man who comes once a year to shear the sheep, is practically a celebrity to us. Dipping day, when we've to help corral our 120 sheep down the road to the dip tank on a neighbour's farm, is another landmark of the year. We don't need anyone to remind us about the importance of mart day or the pressure to get a good price for the lambs. The hay can make or break a summer too. We see the furrowed brows all those evenings when Jimmy O'Rourke – the Garney, everyone calls him – is in the house, nights on end as the good weather and the summer stretch comes in, trying to read the weather forecast like tealeaves. Cutting for hay is an art, bordering on a science, and there's no margin for error. Get it right and you'll have bales and bales of hay of quality good enough to be sold to a stud farm, which will go some way towards lifting the siege for the next few months. Anything less is a bad result.

In the 1980s Ireland is on its knees. Whole families are disappearing overnight. They don't know where to go but the promise of something better drags them nonetheless, while the ones who stay are trying to work out how to survive on half a wage or worse. Our life is a very simple one, by necessity; farming is hit worse than most. We appreciate that there's sacrifice even in little things, the 10p bar at the weekend and the trip to McDonald's once a month. What we never had, we don't miss. Holidays are a few days down in Rosslare, pitched up in a tent borrowed from Uncle Larry, Dad's eldest brother. The first time I set foot on a plane comes about by sheer good fortune. Paddy Toole, one of our neighbours, calls into the house one day and sits down with Mam so that the two of them can write a limerick to send into a competition. Before I know it, I'm being bundled up in the warmest clothes we can find and packed off on a plane with 50 other kids and Ian Dempsey and Zig and Zag to meet Santa Claus himself at the North Pole. As I get a little bit older and things slowly start to get a little bit better, for us and for everyone, we're able to venture a bit further afield.

There are times when farming simply isn't enough to sustain a family of eight: my mam Bea, my dad Tucker – Thomas is his real name – and their six children. I have two older brothers, Ross and Norman, and three younger sisters, Sascha, Jill and Holly. Dad is never afraid to try his hand at anything. There are days when he leaves early in the morning and comes back that night, his hands still crusted with cement after a day laying blocks for the shop that my uncle is building down in Kinnegad.

Things get so bad that we think about leaving. We're told one night that Dad has to go away for a little while, that he's going to America with his cousin Bill so that the two of them can look for a job. He's gone for a couple of months. He gets a house and a car and does whatever work he can find, a building job here, painting there, and then phones home one day to tell us that he has been offered a job managing a stud outside Boston. We wait to hear if he's going to take it or not, if we'll lock up the house and the farm and say goodbye to our friends and our school and follow him out there to start our new life in America. When he comes home a few weeks later and announces that we're going to turn the farm into a riding school instead, everything changes for me.

I'm always the small child in a room full of bigger ones, whether that's in school or at home. I'm still a baby when I'm dropped off for my first day of school. It's the day of my fourth birthday, 16 September 1983. As I get older I ask why I had to start school so early; could they not have waited another year before sending me? The answer I get is always the same: there was no stopping you, all you wanted was school.

Every year I'm always one of the youngest, one of the smallest, in my class. There are other children who are a year, a year and a half, maybe two years older than me. I'm a naturally skinny little child too, timid and weak, and when we go out to play, I don't have the strength to stop myself being pushed around. It puts a quick end to any thoughts of me playing Gaelic football; I'm no good with the ball and I'm worse again without it. We go to Croke Park and Dad throws us over the turnstile to go up to our usual spot behind the posts on the Canal End terrace, up above the entrance tunnel where we'll have a good clear view of everything with nobody standing in our way. We can't take our eyes off Meath and Dublin who tear strips off each other in four ferocious Leinster Championship battles in 1991 until Kevin Foley and David Beggy settle things once and for all and send us home with a smile on our faces. I watch these warriors, Mick Lyons, Colm O'Rourke, and hear how people talk about them. Meath are strong. Meath are tough. Those Meath boys, they never duck a challenge.

That mentality, that fight, never backing down, it stays with me. I'm the opposite. I'm small. I'm easily bullied. I cry. Ross and I fight a lot. He knows better than to pick on Norman because every time he does, it ends quickly, and it's never Ross that comes out on top. I'm easy prey by comparison. I lash back one day, when we're all over at Norman's friend's house. I pick up a stick and fire it 10 or 15 yards as he's running away and clock him in the head. When he lifts his hand off his head, he's bleeding, and all hell breaks loose as apologies are made and we're bundled into the car and brought home. I could make my excuses and say I didn't mean to hit him, but I did; I just didn't think I would. There's another lad who comes over to our house and he picks on me too, and again, there's always tears.

The tears are toughened out of me. When you fall: don't cry, get up, you're a big boy — that's the way in our house and, I suspect, in a lot of houses in the 1980s. With six children, there's a lot of pressure on my parents and it doesn't leave much time for emotions. Problems aren't generally discussed. Mam tries to keep everything calm and simple and day-to-day; if anyone asks, everything is always grand, even though there are days when that couldn't be further from the truth. Dad's the same. No son of his is going to be going around whinging and crying like a little girl. When I get upset, he teases me about it, his way of toughening me up.

The ponies bring me out of my shell. For as long as I can remember, there's always a pony or two around the place. We have an old mare called Vanity and later we have Bluey, one of her foals, and I've been sitting up on her since before I could walk. There are a few years then when we don't have any ponies, when life is all about the farm, but as soon as we open the riding school, there's an endless number of them and I'm in the thick of it. There are ponies to be cared for, and lessons to be led, and I'm out there riding for hours and hours and hours at a time, and without even noticing it, my confidence grows. A lot of kids who come down for lessons are beginners and they need to be led, so I jog alongside these groups for three or four hours, helping them to get started. As they get better and progress to the cross-country course, it's up to Ross and Norman and me to lead the way on horseback, setting the pace and telling everyone else where they should go and where to avoid, and what they need to do and how to do it. I realise that not everybody is good at riding ponies, but I am. It's my thing.

It's work but we love it, and Mam and Dad make sure that we have a brilliant childhood full of great fun and adventures. When you're 12 years old and live in a riding school, you never have to look too far for the next fence to jump. Saturday afternoons are for watching the racing on the BBC, but once the final credits start to roll there's a race out the door to get the ponies tacked up, Ross and Norman leading the way, and me hanging on to their coattails. There's a scramble for saddles and bridles, or even a headcollar if that's all that's left. Just as important, there's a scramble to claim the right name for yourself.

'I'm Adrian Maguire.'

'I'm Peter Scudamore.'

'I'm Richard Dunwoody.'

Our friends – Paddy Burke, the Morrins, the Flynns – come and join us, and with the commentary running through our heads we tear off around the farm, jumping anything and everything in sight until the light starts to fade or the call comes for dinner. When you're learning, you learn to respect your fences, but in nearly 40 years of riding horses, I've never feared a jump like the one that Dad built beside our house. It springs up out of nowhere, built in a couple of hours, and just like that, an otherwise nondescript hill suddenly becomes my nemesis.

I take one look at it and I know straight away that I'll never be able to jump it. The height of it alone isn't intimidating but it's positioned right in the middle of the downslope. I stand at the top and watch the others trot down and clear it without a care, and I can see the ponies' legs quicken into a blur underneath them as they land, freewheeling away down the other side like a runaway train.

I let everyone else go on ahead of me and then realise that was a mistake. Waiting until last has done nothing to quieten the worries in my head. If someone else had hung back, equally wary, you'd find some sort of strength in numbers, but when you're on your own, there's nowhere to hide. Now there's an audience at the bottom of the hill as well and they're quickly losing patience with me. I don't want to jump it. Even if I did, I don't think I can.

Before the tears come, I'm seized by a moment of bravery, a rush of blood, and I go for it. The first taste of that speed, the buzz, the rush as the pony lands and accelerates, it's irresistible. Once that fear of the unknown is banished, all that's left is the thrill. The only way to quench that thirst is to race back to the top of the hill to do it again. The confidence that it brings changes my life. It's like flicking a switch in terms of self-belief. When I fall, I bounce back up and brush it off like a Meath footballer. There's no more crying.

The riding school opens doors for Dad too. Important people come down to see him. Big builders and businessmen bring their children down to learn how to ride ponies and maybe, if Dad says the right things, he convinces them to send down a horse that he can train for them. When he gave up riding and went back to farming, he still kept up his interest in training. We go over to John Fowler's in Summerhill one day and Merrywell, owned by my grandfather and trained by my dad, wins the local point-to-point; I'm only four years old but the memory of this day, such a big occasion for our family, sticks. We go to Fairyhouse and shout home Lovely Run, the horse he trains for my uncle Kevin, as she wins both her bumper – a flat race for inexperienced horses – and

24

her maiden hurdle there. All six of the children in our family are destined to stay involved with horses in some way as we grow up. Ross is the first to become an amateur jockey and has some huge days in the saddle, going on to win both the Irish Grand National and the American Grand National as a professional; Norman rides as an amateur as well as taking up a trade as a farrier; Sascha is a journalist and later goes on to be an editor at the *Irish Field*; and both Jill and Holly ride winners as amateur jockeys. Five of us ride winners for Dad at different stages over the years: Ross, Norman, me, Jill and Holly.

Before long, we all want more than just riding ponies around the farm and leading lessons in the riding school. We start off in pony club, do a bit of showjumping and progress on to mounted games; the relay races and challenges are fun, but all I want is that buzz of tearing around the place and jumping fences at speed. Mam convinces the school principal in Trim that me and my brothers would make a good equestrian team, and he agrees to let us have a half-day once a week during the winter months so that we can go and ride in the local hunt. The intercom goes like clockwork, half eleven every Tuesday morning, and our names are read out:

'Ross, Norman and Barry Geraghty to the office with their bags please.'

There's no need to pack away my books, I know not to even bother taking them out of my bag for that class, and I'm up out of my desk and away out the door with a smile on my face.

If anyone is ever trying to find us during a hunt, the first place to look is up at the front. The three of us have no interest in following around down the back with some of the other young kids. It's the same when we go out to ride in hunter trials, which are time trials run on cross-country courses with fences. Whether it's Ross or Norman or me, it's generally the same; we blitz off from the start as quick as our pony can carry us. Speed is our thrill. People look at us ripping around these tracks in the same way that Paul Carberry did before he went on to be a jockey. We're the new kids on the block now. More often than not, we're the ones to beat.

Dad and Mam travel the country for us. They make sure we're at every hunt, every pony show, every hunter trial with a lorry load of ponies to ride. Everyone knows us, Tucker Geraghty's boys. When we're winning, it's good for business too, the best free advertising that the riding school could ask for. Dad takes in a lot of ponies that have been spoiled or become a bit troublesome. They come to us and it's up to us to straighten them out again and retrain them so that we can either use them in the riding school or Dad can sell them on. It's good training for us too; these ponies are a handful, bucking and rearing and liable to do anything, and we have to learn quickly how to get them under control.

One day I take out one particularly wild pony, Zola, to ride in a hunt and she really loses the head on me. To anyone watching it must look like I'm struggling because, next thing, a woman spots me and rides off to find Dad and let him know that I'm in trouble.

'Tucker Geraghty, there's a boy of yours down there having difficulty with a pony,' she tells Dad.

I can only imagine the blank stare that this woman must have been met with in response. She quickly realises that Dad has no intention of coming back to check on me.

'Well, I wouldn't let one of mine ride it,' she adds, but Dad ends this particular conversation as quickly as it started.

'They wouldn't be fit to,' he tells her, and that's the end of that.

All I want is to be a jockey; by 14, I already have the first scars and screws. I get picked for the Irish team competing in the mounted games at the Royal Windsor Horse Show, which is a huge honour, but before I make it that far, I fracture my leg in four places. We're training down in Loughrea, rain sheeting down on top of us, and we're practising the bottle race – galloping down one at a time with a bottle in our hand, leaning off the side of the pony to place it upright on top of a bucket, and then turning around to gallop back and lean down to pick up a different bottle from another bucket on the way. And then the next person goes, working in a team in a relay race until everyone is finished. At least, that's how it's supposed to go. Except on a miserable west of Ireland day, saddles get wet. I slip as I reach over to grab the bottle and at that speed and distance, I don't have time to right myself before my pony gallops in and slams my protruding knee into the pony that's standing there waiting to go next. The impact fractures my leg in two places above the knee and in two places below it. I get rushed to hospital but whatever pain I'm in is diluted in a few days by the excitement of finding out that my leg will be fixed up by Fred Kenny, the surgeon who takes care of all the jockeys. Hobbling around on crutches with four screws in my leg, I really feel like a jockey now.

A broken leg hardly slows me down. I'm still getting over the surgery when myself and Dad bump into Mickey Maguire over on the all-weather gallops in Kilcock. The Maguires are a great racing family and I know Mickey's son, Jason. He's around the same age as me and already starting to follow in the footsteps of his uncle Adrian, a legend of the sport.

'We have one called The Weed,' Mickey says. 'Sure does Barry want to come down the next day and ride him?'

He doesn't need to ask either of us twice.

'Yeah, he'd love to,' Dad tells him.

It's only three months since the leg break, but that never even crosses our minds. When the chance is there, you take it, so we drive out to Clarinbridge and I limp around the track before the race, trying not to think about it. When I get up on The Weed, it turns out that he has a mind of his own, can't be steered at all. He takes off down the back straight with me on his back and then, before I can suggest otherwise, runs right off the track over on the far side. Thankfully, I convince him to get back onto the track and finish his race.

I get two more rides that day for my trouble, as well as a bit of an introduction to the harsh reality of pony racing. One of the rides is for a man from Galway, and before we leave, he asks will I come down to Ballina the following weekend and ride his one again for him. It's the other side of the country, and it's the only ride I'm going to get that day, but I'm keen to go so Dad brings me down. We're both so excited driving down in the car but when we get there and meet this fella, he tells us that he's sorry, there's been a change of plan and Jason Maguire is available so he's putting him up instead of me. There's nothing we can do except get back in the car and drive the three hours home again, trying not to think about the day we've just wasted.

There's nothing glamorous about pony racing. I spend four hours sitting on a five-gallon drum in the back of a Jeep to get to Derry, only to realise that Gerry Duff, the man I'm riding for, has got his dates wrong and we're there a week early. The tracks themselves can be anything. There's a river running down one side of the track outside Letterkenny. If you're going to take that bend at speed, you either need to be sure that you're on a horse that wants to be steered, or else have your swimming togs ready. All of the tracks use wooden paling posts with rope to mark out the course. A girl falls and hits one of them head on up in Derry and breaks a vertebra in her neck. She makes a full recovery, luckily, but it doesn't take much imagination to know it could easily have been much, much worse.

It might be rough and ready, and dangerous too at times, but at 15, I don't see any of that. I love it. Johnny McGovern and his brother Paddy put me up on a mare outside Galway and I win my very first pony race. I walk back into school on a Monday morning after a weekend's pony racing and I could have £200 in my pocket – five rides at £20 a ride, and £100 bonus if one of them wins. With every ride, I grow into it more and more. Before long, I'm getting offered rides on better ponies, sometimes two or three of them in the same race. Up and down the country, I hear the stories about Norman Williamson and Charlie Swan and Adrian Maguire and their time riding ponies. Only a few years earlier, I stood with Ross and Norman at the final fence in Fairyhouse for the 1991 Irish Grand National, transfixed as they jumped the last and battled up the straight, Adrian on Omerta and Charlie chasing him on Cahervillahow. Now I'm following in their footsteps.

The pony circuit is a great educator, too, a better fit for me than the secondary school in Trim. I enjoy school – like a lot of things in life, I do just enough to stay on the right side of wrong – but when it comes to homework and studying, I'm never really that bothered. Whatever little interest I have fades away to nothing and at the end of fifth year, even though I'm still only 15 and I've only one year left, I decide that's it for me, I'm done. There's no great debate or angst about it. Another year of school isn't going to take me to where I want to go, and it's agreed at home that I'll do a course to qualify as a riding instructor instead. Plenty of lads leave school to do apprenticeships in their mid-teens, and while it's not sparks or plumbing or bricklaying, this is mine. At the very least, it'll be better than a bad Leaving Cert.

Taking out my jockey's licence is the only thing on my mind. I look at different yards, try to pick out the best place to learn, the best place to get a few opportunities. I'm not even 16 yet and I've only had one full season in pony racing and probably half a dozen winners. My riding technique still needs a huge amount of work. If it's a close race and my pony is in a fight to the finish,

I'm still lacking strength, lacking style. I'm nowhere near ready to become a professional jockey, but I don't want to hear that. There's a dream dangling in front of me and that's all I can see. All the advice I get – from Dad, from Norman, and from other people we know in racing – is to wait another year. I come around to accepting that there's no rush, that another year on the ponies will really benefit me. As well as that, Norman has a plan. If I need to work on my strength and my balance for riding a finish, I'm going to need a bit of help. He gets to work building me a wooden horse that I can use to train and practise on.

It's a dangerous time to be a loose bit of wood. We go around the yard like kids at Hallowe'en, gathering up whatever pallets and planks we can get our hands on. We pile it all up in one of the stables out the back and Norman gets to work. He picks out the best bits and saws and chops and hammers and nails until he has one leg made, and then four. He adds on a wooden neck, hammers a few wooden planks in on either side to give it a bit of a body. Woodwork has always been his thing, anything to do with his hands. It doesn't take long, maybe a couple of hours, before it starts to take shape, to look like a horse. When everything's in place, we dig out an old saddle that was given to us by Georgie Wells and some stirrups and strap it all up, and then stand back to admire Norman's creation.

'It needs a name. What will we call it?'

'Let's call it the Iliad.'

2

The Iliad – the wooden one – is named after the first good racehorse I ever sit up on. The real Iliad was owned by Noel Furlong, the Dublin businessman, the carpet king, and only Noel really knows how much he took out of the bookies' pockets when the horse won the Ladbroke Hurdle at Leopardstown in 1991. The Iliad arrives down to our yard when his racing days are as good as done, but from the moment I sit up on him I can tell that he's different. I feel it straight away. I ride ponies and ordinary horses and when I get down to give them a push, there's no reaction, no response. But the Iliad is a different machine. He's ready to shift gears at the slightest nudge and take you off up the gallops with him. I could get used to riding good horses.

I spend the winter on his wooden namesake in the stable out the back. This is no time for cutting corners. Riding weak finishes won't be much use to me when I'm a professional jockey. It's getting late, but I jump up on the wooden horse again and put everything into it one last time for today, driving for the imaginary line as if this moment has been my whole life's ambition. There's nothing sophisticated about how Norman has built it – there aren't even any moving parts, so I have to do all the work. I grab hold of the reins and pump my arms, drive my legs, and go for it. It helps me to work on my strength, my balance, to build up the power and endurance I'll need for the last 100 yards of a race, the sprint to the finish. I use it for two or three minutes, two or three times a day, and I'm exhausted. It's a better cardio workout than any gym session. I go running every day as well until I'm fitter than I've ever been. And when I go up to Derry for the first day of the new pony racing season, I ride a double.

The winners start rolling in every week. In the pony world, all roads lead to the Dingle Races in August. That's our Cheltenham, and the Dingle Derby is our Gold Cup. I finish the weekend as top jockey with three winners – the Ritz Club Champion, I tell people, awarding myself the same title as the top jockey in Cheltenham. The only regret is that one of them isn't the Dingle Derby; winning that is one of the few things missing from my racing CV.

I get my picture in the papers for the first time. My name starts cropping up in conversation. John Fowler lets it be known that he'll have a job for me when I take out my licence if I'm interested. His is a smaller yard in terms of numbers, but fewer horses means fewer jockeys battling for the same rides, and it's likely that I won't have to wait as long to get a few opportunities. It's a very good option, and I like the sound of it, until Mam comes in to me one morning and tells me that Noel Meade is interested in taking me on full-time too.

Noel has been around for as long as I can remember, since I was knee high. The family connection goes way back; Dad and Noel have been close friends for years. There'd be nights when Mam and Dad would go out for a few hours, and I'd wake up the following morning in either Ross's or Norman's bed. Someone would have moved me from one bed to another in the middle of the night, and now there's some auld lad in my bed snoring. I'd try to see who it was without making any noise or waking anyone up, hoping that it was Noel because Noel would always have a green pound note in his pocket for you when everyone came down for breakfast later. And now he wants to give me a job as a jockey.

'Noel was interested in bringing you down', Mam says, 'but Dad told him that you're not going.'

She fills me in on what had happened the night before, how Noel had been asking about my plans but how Dad was reluctant to commit to anything. Ross had been down with Noel a bit before and had done a few summers, but he never got any rides out of it, and Dad's worried that the same thing will happen again.

'No, you gave Ross nothing,' Dad told Noel. 'I'm not sending Barry down too.'

Mam tells me this story and I can't believe what I'm hearing.

'Mam, you get on the phone,' I tell her. 'Tell Noel I'll be down.'

Noel's yard, Tu Va Stables, is no more than a half an hour away. Seven o'clock on a summer's morning and we're up and out the door and into Norman's little Volkswagen Golf. He's doing his apprenticeship as a farrier in Liam McAteer's yard, only down the road from Noel's, so he drops me off on my first morning while he's on the way to work himself. A twenty-something Aidan O'Brien is setting the standard that everyone else in Irish racing is trying to live up to, but after him, Noel is one of the biggest names at the table. He wins his first Champion Trainer title in 1998/99, a couple of years after I start, and then goes on to win it again in seven of the next eight years. I've been in his yard plenty of times before, but this time, as I set foot inside the gate, I'm well aware that this is going to be life in the big pond. Then again, there's only one way to find out if you're going to sink or swim.

I fail the first test – the look test. I've a pair of cherry Doc Martens that I always wear when I'm working at home in the yard. If I need to jump up on a pony, rather than taking off the Docs and putting on my riding boots, I just grab a pair of half chaps with a bit of Velcro and stick them on to my lower legs instead. They're lovely and comfortable and I think nothing of doing the same thing in Noel's until he spots the Doc Martens and calls me out.

'If you want to be a jockey, look like a jockey,' he says. 'If you want to be a mucker-out, look like a mucker-out.'

'Them boots aren't for jockeys,' he adds, just to make sure that there's no misunderstanding.

That's the end of the Docs but, footwear choices aside, it doesn't take me long to realise that I'm out in the real world now and I've a lot to learn. I go into the tack room in the morning and have a look up at the board to see the four or five lots of horses that are scheduled for that day, and who I'm down to ride in each lot. I pick up the routine: tack up your first lot, ride him out, come back in, wash him, scrape him down, put him in the walker, and then off to tack up your second lot. Breakfast after the second lot. Back out and do the same again for the last two or three lots of the day, take an hour for lunch, and then a few more hours in the afternoon brushing the horses down, feeding them, getting them water and sweeping up the yard before finishing up for the day at around five o'clock.

The pieces of work themselves, or the actual schooling of a horse over hurdles or fences, take a bit of getting used to. Graduating from ponies and hunters to racehorses is like getting out of a slow car and into a fast one. Your track might stay the same, but it feels different and you've to think differently. In a slow car, you're always in control, but take a bend in a fast car and you might quickly realise that the car is leading you for a split second, not the other way around. The more you drive it, the more you learn to trust the car. It's the same with a racehorse.

There's a competitive edge to every morning. Racing down two abreast to jump a line of hurdles, the horses spark off each other and start to get competitive, and if they decide they're taking each other on, they're taking you with them. I learn to trust the horse I'm on; I've no fear of going at speed.

Every yard is different and some trainers like to work their horses harder than others, so I look to the senior lads in the yard, Peter Kavanagh and Greg Harford, to get a sense of the pace. I get to know them, watch how they do things, and feed off them. We gallop over a mile, setting a nice steady pace over the first six furlongs, quickening up from six to seven, and then letting the horse extend from seven to eight. All you want is for them to get a bit of exercise, stretch them out, get their blow.

A yard is a business and this job, the morning piece of work, is research. It's valuable information. At the end of a gallop, Noel asks, 'How does he feel? Is he fit?' And if you haven't been concentrating, you're not going be able to give him any real feedback. I figure out a little checklist in my head and make a point to myself to check three things in every piece of work. First, how strong was the work – did we go a good gallop? And how much potential do I think he has? Second, was he moving well? How was his action, which often gives you a clue as to whether he'd prefer running on harder or softer ground? And third, his wind: is he blowing hard, which will tell you that he's unfit, or is he making a noise, which might be a sign of a problem with his wind. That's the information that Noel needs from me, so that's what I focus on in every piece of work. Without even realising it, that concentration and awareness, constantly reassessing where you are and what you're doing so that you can tweak here and fine-tune there every couple of seconds, becomes one of the most important skills I ever learn in racing.

All these little chats with Noel, reporting back to him, a quick word here and a couple of lines there, bring me out of myself again. He asks me for my thoughts and I give it to him the way I see it. Back my opinion and put my head on the block. And I can see that he's taking note of what I have to say and respects it, and my confidence takes another leap forward. He's been keeping tabs on how I've done with the ponies, so he knows I've a bit of a CV behind me, and now he can see that I'm progressing well in my work, getting my horses to settle well, getting them jumping well. He's not making any promises but the understanding has always been there – keep your head down, work hard and you'll get your shot. The only thing is, I'm not the only lad looking for a shot. Not everyone wants to be a jockey – the racing world needs plenty of people doing plenty of jobs to keep it ticking along every day. There's a great team spirit among everyone in the yard but for me and any of the lads with a bit of ambition to make it, there's only so much work and so many rides to go around.

I don't have to wait long for my first ride. Two weeks after my seventeenth birthday, Noel finds me a mare called In The Evening that he has entered for a race on the flat. It's four o'clock on an October Wednesday in Navan – hardly Cheltenham on Gold Cup day – but it's a surreal feeling, walking into the weighroom for the first time. Every aspect of my preparation, stuff that will become so routine and so mundane over the next 24 years, is a novelty of special significance. A milestone. I only have one ride so I watch the clock, wondering what time Noel will come to weigh me out. Dave Fox comes to introduce himself. Dave is the jockeys' valet, one of the people who make the weighroom tick, and someone who becomes a father figure to me and a lot of jockeys over the course of our careers. He gives me my silks, checks my weight and makes sure I have the right saddle, and then I sit and I wait. In The Evening is a 9/1 shot in the bookies – not the favourite, but in their eyes not without her chance either. Noel comes back in after the previous race and I meet him out by the clerk on the scales. The clerk asks me the horse's number, checks my colours, checks my weight. I hand the saddle over to

Noel and go back inside to the rest of my gear: put on my hat and tie it up, a wristband for my silks to keep them in good and tight, goggles clean, ready and on, gloves on, whip in hand, and then out to the parade ring to go over the instructions with Noel one last time.

This is everything I've been working towards. It's no longer a dream.

In The Evening travels really well for me across the top, moves up into third and, for a moment, we're right there in the thick of it.

And then she goes out like a light. I push and I push, and it's like pushing water up a hill, going nowhere as fresher horses pass us by in the final couple of hundred yards.

We finish seventh.

3

've never been afraid of losing. If you're going to have a race, someone has to lose. It doesn't have to be a reflection on your performance – you can give your best ride and finish second, and on another day, give your worst ride and win. I see others wrapped up in a fear of failure. It's paralysing. I was never tortured that way.

I sit in front of the TV on St Stephen's Day 1994, and I watch Adrian Maguire from just down the road in Kilmessan come to the final fence in the King George VI Chase eight lengths clear on Barton Bank, close enough to taste the win. The memory doesn't stay with me because of the mistake that ends Barton Bank's race or because of the camera that lingers on a distraught Adrian afterwards, head bowed, leading his horse back to the enclosure. It's the image of his trainer, the legendary David Nicholson – the Duke – coming up to Adrian afterwards and putting his arm around his shoulder, patting him on the cheek, telling him to keep his chin up.

Someone has to lose.

When I start racing myself, I find myself saying it. Jason Maguire, Adrian's nephew, comes back in after giving a horse a gem of a ride and finishing second, beating himself up, knowing that the grand inquisition is coming.

'Jesus, Jason, you gave that one a brilliant ride,' I reassure him. 'There wasn't much more you could have done there. Someone has to come second. Someone has to lose.'

Withdrawn from Stock
Dublin City Public Libraries

I ride 17 losers before I ride my first winner, a mare called Stagalier, in January 1997. She's not showing a massive amount in her work at home but I ride her in a maiden hurdle in Navan at the start of the month and she runs a cracker and finishes second. Noel enters her into another maiden in Down Royal a few weeks later, and when I wake up that morning, I see that she's going to start the race as the odds-on favourite, an 8/11 shot. I've never been into betting but I still see the prices and take note; if nothing else, they're a reflection of your chance in the race. There's no pressure, though. Give me a fancied runner any day of the week. The shorter the price, the easier it's likely to be for us to win.

It all goes perfectly to plan until we come to the third last and she gallops through it. She does the same again at the second last. It's a little bit of immaturity on her part, but there's never an anxious moment. I keep a hold of her and keep it simple and, after she jumps the last nicely, I give her a bit of a kick and a smack and she runs away to win by a length.

'You did well there,' Noel tells me when he comes to congratulate me afterwards. 'You kept your head well.'

I'm very fortunate that, in the years to come, that winning feeling becomes a very familiar one. Some wins are forgotten as soon as I cross the finishing line – it's on to the next one – but some will live with me for ever, and the first taste of that buzz is something I'll never forget. The handshakes and congratulations, the photographers trying to get my attention for a quick shot, the press gathering around with their notebooks for a couple of quotes. I go home that night to my parents and my grandfather, and I'm floating.

Things start to happen very quickly. Noel gives me plenty of opportunities and, more than that, he encourages me and fills me full of confidence. 'If you can win on everything that you should win on, and a few that you shouldn't, that's when you are riding well,' he often reminds me. Even when I get beaten, he recognises a good ride and praises me for all of the things I did right. When we go to Navan at the start of March, he pulls me aside the day before to talk me through the entries.

'Oh, you're nearly a real jockey tomorrow, you've got five rides in Navan.'

It's the Saturday before Cheltenham and a lot of the top jockeys are over in Sandown and Chepstow for Britain's last big day of racing before the festival. Noel's first-choice jockey, Paul Carberry, has a retainer to ride for the big British owner Robert Ogden. Charlie Swan is there too to ride one for Aidan O'Brien. It opens the door for me to fill my book, and the first ride of the day is a horse that I've been waiting to get my chance on, a horse called Saving Bond.

Saving Bond's form is nothing to get excited about. The horse is a conundrum but solving the puzzle becomes a project for me and one of the head lads in Noel's, Damien McGillick – Les, as everybody knows him, after Lester Piggott. Saving Bond has had six runs so far that season and keeps hitting the crossbar: third, third, second, second, second, third. He's running good races, getting himself into good positions, but when it comes to the final furlong, he can't get the job done. He's not seeing out his races. He's a weak finisher.

When he runs and loses, I inevitably end up chatting to Les about him in the yard.

'He only has one run so,' Les suggests – one short, sharp, burst of acceleration and then his race is run.

Noel puts me up on him in Navan, hoping to make it seventh time lucky. In a conditions race, like this one, the horses don't all carry the same weight. A horse might have to carry more weight depending on a number of factors – sex, age, previous wins – while other horses carry less weight. In a handicap race, the weights are

41

assigned based on a horse's official rating, which is a reflection of their ability. In theory, it levels out the playing field and gives every horse a reasonably equal chance of winning. That's why weight is so crucial to a jockey, why we have to be so careful when it comes to our diet, why we spend so long in the sauna – we have to stay light. If a horse is supposed to carry a heavier weight in a race, you can always use a heavier saddle to make up the difference, but if a horse is supposed to carry a lighter weight than his jockey comes in at on the scales, the only option is to find a lighter jockey. Saving Bond is up towards the top of the weights in this race. He's listed to carry 11st 12lb but because I've only won a handful of races so far, I'm entitled to claim seven pounds off his weight and bring it down to 11st 5lb, which, with a bit of luck, could make the difference between a horse that's starting to tire and a horse that's already beaten when it comes to those last few strides.

I plot out the race from start to finish with Les and, later, Noel too; where I need to be at every stage, and when to make my move.

'He has one run,' Noel reminds me. 'You need to just switch him off, hunt away and see if you can creep into it then. If you're still there with a chance at the end, you have to attack in one go. One burst of speed, two hundred yards, that's all you're going get out of him, remember.'

I go out with Noel and Les's instructions hammered into my head: get Saving Bond into position, and save him up for one squeeze after we jump the last. I get my timing just right. We win by a length. There are dozens of ways to win a race, but the tactical ride – meticulously plotted out, executed with precision – is my favourite. Anyone can bully a horse to the line but it takes a horseman and a jockey to read the subtleties of a race that's changing around him every second, to know what he's got left under him, to make the little adjustments, and to get to the line first, whether it's by the tip of a nose or 10 lengths. I keep the ride on Saving Bond after that. We win again in Leopardstown a few weeks later, and then again in Roscommon. The Galway Festival quickly comes into focus. He'll have every chance if he runs in the Galway Hurdle, and if that's the case, I'll be the 17-year-old riding a top contender in one of the biggest Irish races of the summer.

If only it was that simple. Three weeks before Galway, I have a bad fall and need surgery to repair a fractured collarbone.

'When will I be okay to go back riding?' I ask Fred Kenny, the surgeon, after he's put in a steel plate to help the bone fuse back together. All I'm thinking about is whether or not I'll be fit to ride in the Galway Hurdle, but he's not going to make any promises.

'Sure we'll see how it is, we'll see how it is.'

I do what I'm told and go home to rest up. For the most part. But two weeks later, I'm out on the farm, helping Dad a bit, moving bales of hay into the barn. I feel fine. I toss one bale up on top of another to stack them and I think, fuck this – if I'm fit enough to do a morning's work on the farm, I'm fit enough to ride Saving Bond next week.

There's racing on in Naas that evening. I can jump in the car, be there in three-quarters of an hour, see the racecourse doctor, and get passed fit to go back riding again. I ring Noel to tell him that I'm on my way down to the course, but he's not happy.

'No, no, give it more time,' he tells me. 'Take your time. Don't be rushing.'

Later that evening, he rings the house and leaves a message for my parents on the answering machine. When they ring him back, they get the same talk that I got that afternoon.

'No, don't be rushing, tell him to take his time, take his time.'

Maybe Noel's right, maybe I do need another couple of weeks, but there's more to it than that. He won't come straight out and say it, but the reason he doesn't want me rushing back is that he wants Paul Carberry to ride Saving Bond. I've no interest in waiting around. I get passed fit and Noel lets me ride in another race on the same day as the Galway Hurdle. I'm so determined to prove myself, to prove that I'm the one in the right here, that I put myself under huge pressure and completely overthink it – something I've rarely done before, and nearly never again since. I give the horse a desperate ride, get involved way too early, and she goes out like a light. When I come back in, Noel reads me the riot act. When I look back in later years with a bit more maturity, I know that he was dead right; it was a desperate ride, and I only had myself to blame.

In the end, Paul finishes fourth on Saving Bond, but there's a bit of tension between me and Noel after Galway. It probably only lasts a few weeks but it feels like a lifetime. I'm worried that I might fall out of favour, but I only asked the question because I was fit and ready to go. I wasn't going to sit on the sidelines because it suited Noel or Paul. A dumb priest doesn't get a parish.

Two months later, In The Evening comes down to the last in Clonmel, falls, and slams me onto my back. I get checked out on the course, but sitting in the back of Noel's car on the way home, there's darts of pain stabbing into my back. In the middle of the night, I wake up in agony, my back in spasms. I know something's not right but if I don't show up for work in the morning, I'm going to land myself in even more trouble. I get up and go down to Tu Va to ride out, but every time the horse I'm schooling nips up and over his jump, another jolt of pain fires up through my spine to the base of my skull.

'Jesus, my back is in a bad way,' I tell Noel. 'I'm going to have to get it checked or X-rayed or something.'

I can tell he's not impressed. He's probably fed up with lads skiving off and pulling sickies when it's a busy morning.

'If you want to get it X-rayed, get it X-rayed,' he says – which might as well translate as, if you want to go arsing around for the morning with doctors and hospitals when we're flat out with work here, do what you want.

I don't need a doctor to tell me that something's not right. I get into the car and drive myself to Our Lady's Hospital in Navan to see the orthopaedic surgeon there, Imran Sharif.

'It's not good news,' he tells me, reading my scan. 'You've broken a vertebra.'

No matter how lightly you can brush off injuries, nobody wants to be sitting in a doctor's room and be told that they have a broken back. I know I'm still able to do everything that I could do yesterday before the fall – I was on a horse only a few hours ago – but it doesn't take much for teenage thoughts to start jumping to some extreme conclusions.

'What does that mean?' I ask him, a bit panicked.

But as soon as he starts to explain, it puts my mind a bit more at ease. He tells me that I'll be okay to go back riding in six or seven weeks, and then I'm zipped into a body cast and sent off home to recover. By the time I ring Noel, I'm over whatever little bit of shock I got and I'm nearly half-happy to be telling him that I've broken a vertebra, that I wasn't just swinging the lead.

By the time I'm fit, I'm straining to get going again. When you're learning how to ride, your way is your way. It comes down to your make, your shape, your centre of gravity, your balance. It falls into place subconsciously as you learn to work from your instinct, and any little adjustment takes you out of sync. No two jockeys are the same. It's very hard to replicate someone else's style. It might work for them, and be very successful, but it's not your way.

Noel brings me into the tack room and locks the door behind us. He pulls down a saddle from the rack on the wall and throws it up on the saddle horse, starts fiddling around with the stirrups and tells me to jump up on top.

'Do you see the way you are there?' he says, breaking down my riding position. 'I want your arse here and your shoulder and your hands here. Try and see if you can do that.'

Noel adores Paul and loves his style of riding. He never says 'I want you to study Paul and try to ride like him,' but that's exactly what he's encouraging me to do. It doesn't feel natural to me, but I'm here to learn, and if Noel wants to teach me, if he feels that this will help to make me a better jockey, I'm happy to do what I'm told.

But when I get back from injury, as soon as I start trying to ride the way he wants me to, I fall off everything over fences. Neither of us could ever have thought that it would have such an effect on my riding; the time I've spent out injured doesn't help either. My technique is gone completely. I can't stay on a horse. Between all the Fs for 'fell' and Us for 'unseated rider', my form over fences is starting to look like a bold child who knows they're not allowed to curse. I keep going out and I keep trying. I'll ride anything. But I know in my heart and soul that this is the textbook definition of insanity because the same thing keeps happening over and over again. It gets to the point where it's an achievement to get around a course. I've no problem over a hurdle, but put me over a chase fence, and any little bit of belief vanishes. I start to obsess over it, in the hope that obsessing will lead me to an answer. I drop my leathers right down as long as they will go and start riding horses like John Wayne just to try and stay on. I talk to Dad and Norman and explain exactly what I think is happening, but neither of them can put their finger on the answer. I don't really want to make a big deal out of it with Noel either, or start asking too many questions in the yard. It's embarrassing. I'm nearly afraid going out to ride over fences – not afraid of getting hurt, but afraid of looking like a fool.

I'm out at Noel's walker in the yard one morning after riding out and Noel arrives out to me with the phone in his hand and a smirk on his face.

'Barry, Jim Dreaper's on the phone,' he says. 'He wants to know if you'll ride Merry Gale tomorrow.'

I can see Noel smiling to himself as he waits for my answer, and I nearly would too if I weren't so devastated by all of this. Knowing Jim, he's trying to do me a favour, but is he not watching me ride or seeing the results? Merry Gale has been one of the stars of my teenage years, the great white hope, the horse we all thought would be the one to follow in Dawn Run's footsteps and win the Cheltenham Gold Cup for Ireland. Getting the call to ride this superstar should be a dream booking, one to tell the grandkids about – the day I rode Merry Gale. Instead, it seems like a cruel joke.

'Yeah, I'll ride him,' I tell Noel. 'Tell Jim I said thanks.'

I have to keep trying. At 10, Merry Gale's not the new kid on the block that I fell in love with, but he's still got class and we go down to Naas as the favourites in a five-horse race. Noel is there and he tries to reassure me that it will be okay.

'This fella knows more about the job than you do,' he says. 'Just lie up his neck and enjoy it.'

We jump the first fence well and as we head towards the second, I think about Noel's words. I lie up his neck and enjoy it, and as we come to the fence, I give him a squeeze to go and take it on with a big one. He puts in an extra stride, hits the fence, shoots me forward up over his head, and I'm left sitting on the ground with his bridle in my hand having taken the whole lot clean off his head with me in the fall. As I walk back up the straight in Naas, the bridle in my hand, I can see a few thousand people standing right there before me, and yet I'm in the loneliest place on earth.

The tradition after racing in Naas or in Punchestown is for everyone to go back to Hayden's Bar in Naas to watch the replays. I go, even though I'd rather be anywhere else. John Shortt sees me coming. He's one of the senior jockeys in the weighroom, a great friend and sounding board, but a wicked messer. He doesn't spare me.

'Here's Slippery Arse himself now,' he announces to the room.

I hang around for long enough to watch my fall and then I make a quick, quiet exit. I go home and I can finally allow myself to cry. This was Merry Gale, and I fucked it up.

I'm crippled by these falls for the best part of a year before I finally figure out what's going on. Like John Shortt, Terry Mitchell is another of the senior lads in the weighroom who takes me under his wing early on. He advises me to get a mobile phone; I have to put it in my mam's name because I'm not eighteen yet. He advises me to get an accountant. And one day, he casually drops a couple of sentences into a chat and unlocks the problem in an instant.

'I've been watching what you're doing with all of these falls,' Terry says. 'You're galloping down and you're not taking your horse back. You're not getting them on their hocks.'

I can instantly visualise what Terry is saying to me. It's the same principle as running to kick a ball. You don't just sprint at it full tilt with your head down over it and leather the ball mid-stride. Three or four steps before you make contact, you start to adjust the length of your stride, you get all your body's power behind you, and you measure it.

'You've no contact,' Terry says. 'You've no hold of their head going to the fence. You're not helping them. Just go down to the fence, sit up, and take a little contact.' As soon as he gives me that little bit of advice, everything clicks and the change is instant. I say goodbye to John Wayne, pull my leathers back up, and away we go.

The only saving grace for my own sanity is that when it comes to riding over hurdles, things are flying for me. A couple of weeks after I come back from the broken vertebra, Noel throws me in at the deep end for one of the first big showdowns of the Irish winter. I'm to ride last season's Irish Champion Hurdle winner, Cockney Lad, in the big Grade 2 race at Navan, the Lismullen Hurdle. In the other corner, my main rival is Aidan O'Brien's Theatreworld, runner-up in last year's Champion Hurdle at Cheltenham, a feat he'll go on to repeat this year and again next year when there's only one horse better than him on each occasion: the legendary Istabraq. It's no surprise that he's the odds-on favourite and, what's more, he'll be ridden by Charlie Swan, Irish Champion Jockey for each of the last eight seasons and already on his way to nine in a row. When I was growing up, Charlie was a god to me, but there's no deference, no fear factor here. Let him ride his race and I'll ride mine.

Noel gives me very clear instructions sending me out. He knows they're going to go a good gallop, that Charlie's going to go hard, and all we want to do is get a bit of cover in behind the leaders.

'Don't make a move until after the second last. Don't commit until after the last. They're your goalposts.'

I have to believe in my horse, believe in the instructions and believe in myself, and I do. If we're going to get beaten, we're going to get beaten the way that he's supposed to be ridden. Noel gives me all the confidence I need. Do it this way, and if you do get beaten, there's nothing more we can do about it.

Noel's read of the race is right on the money. Coming across the top after the fourth last, Charlie decides that it's time to put the race to bed. He ups the pace again to make it a real test of stamina, and kicks and sends Theatreworld for home. And while everybody watches me to see what we've got in reply, I sit and I wait.

I know I haven't played my hand yet. I know the plan. My lad has a massive fifth gear, but we're still motoring along in fourth. I chew up the distance between me and Charlie, and as he goes to jump the last, I close up on him. That's as close as he gets to me in the home straight. Cockney Lad is first past the post, winner by nine lengths.

And ridden, as Noel would later say when asked about me in interviews, by a cocky little fucker.

4

You can feel a horse change underneath you in the final strides before a jump. It all happens in the blink of an eye – his stride adjusts, gets a fraction shorter or a fraction longer depending on what we both see, the power builds through his hindquarters, and then, hopefully, lift-off.

There's a constant communication, a conversation, between a jockey and a horse. It's in the hands. The best jockeys have a lightness of touch, the subtleties of their message changing with the smallest variation in the tension of the reins.

This is the gospel according to the great Tommy Carberry: when you go down to a fence, you go for a long stride or you go for a short stride; if you're on your arse at the back of it, you were wrong. There's a lot of truth in Tommy's theory. It makes falls easy to analyse because there's only one party who can be held accountable and it's not the horse. But horse racing is not an exact science. Sometimes you can do all the right things and still get the wrong result. I learn to see things with that perspective when I'm riding for Noel, and it's a similar situation when I start to ride for Jessica Harrington.

Although I'm based in Noel's, he's happy for me to move around and get experience of working with different trainers on the days he doesn't need me. Jessie and I meet for the first time in November 1997 in Naas, a few minutes before she gives me a leg up for my first ride for her. I've never been down in Commonstown, but it's hard to miss the success stories coming out of her yard in Moone, County Kildare, with the promise of more to follow: Oh So Grumpy's success in the Galway Hurdle, Dance Beat winning the Ladbroke Hurdle and, only earlier that year, Space Trucker's third in the Champion Hurdle. I don't know what puts me on her radar, I don't ask, but there's a family connection there from my days riding ponies for Lady Jennifer Fowler – Chich, as she's known – who is married to Jessie's brother, John. If my name was mentioned over dinner some night, any recommendation from John and Chich would surely have helped to open the door. I finish third for her that day on a mare called Market Lass, enough to reassure her that I could come in handy again some day. Three weeks later I get the call to ride Market Lass again and this time we win.

Like Noel, Jessie understands racing, how it ebbs and flows, the good days and the bad, how things can turn in a heartbeat for better or for worse. She knows what it's like to compete at the very top because she did it herself. Jessie was one of Ireland's best three-day event riders – a mix of dressage, cross-country riding and showjumping – and was all set to make her Olympic debut in 1980 until Cold War politics got in the way. The Soviet Union invaded Afghanistan, Jimmy Carter's America responded with a boycott of the Moscow Games, and although Ireland did send a team to compete that summer, the country's equestrian team refused to travel. Four years later Jessie qualified for the Olympics again and walked in the opening ceremony in Los Angeles only to discover that her horse had gone lame before the competition started. So Jessie needs no reminder that sport is as cruel as it is unpredictable.

Respect. Loyalty. Decency. That's Jessie's way of doing business. That's Jessie full stop. She gives me a chance on her Irish Grand National hope, Miss Orchestra, in the trial at Fairyhouse in February 1998. It's a huge opportunity for me, and the RTÉ TV cameras are there and rolling as we jump the last in front, a nose ahead of Richard Dunwoody on Tell The Nipper. The only problem is, Miss Orchestra's nose is on the floor. She catches her front legs awkwardly as she lands and sprawls – she genuflects, Ted Walsh says in his post-race analysis. The result is the same, however you describe it. She gives me no chance of staying on.

Jessie owes me nothing. If she's looking for a scapegoat, the kid who fell at the last with the race at his mercy would be a good one. But that has never been Jessie's way. Instead of hanging me out to dry, or even discreetly deciding not to use me again, she offers me a second chance, a shot at redemption, when she sends Miss Orchestra to Uttoxeter for the Midlands Grand National the following month. There's surely a queue of English jockeys lining up to take the ride in my place but Jessie is not for budging. The race is a marathon, four miles and two furlongs, 24 fences, and my five-pound allowance will take even more weight off Miss Orchestra's back. The press ask why she's rolling the dice again on the unproven teenager rather than bringing in someone with a bit more experience. 'The divil you know is better than the divil you don't,' she tells them.

The stamina test has already bitten and lots of the others have faded away or given up on their chances when I hit the front with six or seven fences left to jump. Kamikaze, the joint favourite, and Norman Williamson are our only company. I let Miss Orchestra roll on, see if Kamikaze can come with us, and he does, briefly. By the time we come to jump the second last, only a mistake can stop us, but there's no danger of a repeat this time round. She pops them both with a bit of spring still in her step and we coast to a seven-length win.

And so four weeks later, I go down to the start sitting on the second favourite for the Irish Grand National. You wouldn't quite throw a stone from here back to the farm in Drumree, but you wouldn't miss by too much either. We jump the last fence, just like Omerta and Cahervillahow did seven years earlier. This year's race is every bit as thrilling as the one that I fell in love with as an 11-year-old, but by the time we jump the last, the finish has already happened without us. Bobbyjo beats Papillon by a half-length; Miss Orchestra and I finish eighth. Not every fairytale can come true.

The Midlands Grand National is my first win in England. The phone doesn't suddenly start ringing off the hook but, even if it's only for a few minutes, it puts my name in front of a new audience and, all going well, some future employers too. But when the summer of 1998 comes round it is Australia, not England, that I'm most keen to make my mark on.

The stories from the annual Australia trip are the stuff of legend in the weighroom. Officially it's billed as the Australia vs Ireland Jockey Challenge; every year since the late 1980s, a team of four Irish jockeys have been invited out for a series of races against the Australians. And every year, the Chinese whispers come back across the world at the speed of light and it's safe to say that exactly none of the stories involves racing of any sort. You wouldn't know what to believe, but even if half the tales are true, its reputation as brilliant craic – and the most unmerciful piss-up – is deserved.

Four pasty Irish young fellas in their late teens or early twenties don't need much more reason than that. Myself, Jason Maguire, Paul Hourigan and Kieran Kelly have our bags packed and we're ready to go before they've even finished asking us. The four of us are thick as thieves. We're together at the racecourse. We're together on a night out. You'd be hard pushed to find one of us without at least one of the others around. Kieran's peg is next to mine in a lot of the weighrooms when we're both starting out, and when you're sitting beside someone practically every day, you get to know them quite well. There can be a lot of emotions in the room in the few minutes before a race or after it, but Kieran is like me – he doesn't take himself too seriously – so we've always been on the same wavelength.

Four imaginations are running wild in the weeks before we go to Australia and we're bouncing off each other with promises of what it will be like once we get out there. We're due to fly out after the Galway Festival and it's all systems go until, two days before we leave, I get a bad fall from a horse called Verywell. Instead of triple-checking that I know where my passport is and that it's still in date, I'm lying on a hospital bed in Galway, waiting for someone to come and tell me exactly how bad the damage is, and if it's the kind of thing that would make a 24-hour flight to the other side of the world inadvisable. They take an X-ray but if there is a problem, it's not an obvious one. None of the doctors can see it.

Saturday night turns into Sunday morning and I'm still stuck on this bed, none the wiser as to what's going on. Every time I look at the clock, it's another minute closer to departure time. Finally the frustration gets the better of me and I take matters into my own hands. I ring Dad and a few hours later he arrives at the hospital to pick me up with a body cast tucked under his arm, the same one I used for my first broken vertebra. Ten months later it fits a little bit more snugly, but I zip myself into it – most of the way, anyway – and tell the doctors that I'm signing myself out.

Australia has never seemed so far away. I'm resigned to the fact that, at best, I might be able to follow the lads out a day or two late and tag along as a spectator, which doesn't sound like the greatest hardship ever suffered. That's what I want Fred Kenny to tell me when I go in to see him in Navan the next morning for a second opinion, but that little bit of hope disappears with one look at the X-ray. I've broken a vertebra and the only small mercy is that it's a different one this time, slightly higher up in my back than the one I broke a few months ago. Fred gets me a new body cast, one that fits properly, and I go home to feel sorry for myself and wait for all the stories of late nights and early mornings to make their way back from the other side of the world.

Dreams are fragile things and it's only after the fact that I appreciate how close I was to having them all taken away from me right there and then in the summer of 1998. I find out that if the surgeon in Galway had spotted a broken vertebra on the initial X-ray, he would have recommended putting a rod in my spine. My career as jockey could very easily have been over right there and then, 18 years old with only a couple of winners to my name. Sitting around for the next few months won't be fun, but I'll be back racing by October, just as the new season is getting going, with plenty of time to get on some good horses and maybe give myself a shot at winning the Conditional Jockeys Championship. I'll have to put up with the stories from Jason, Paul and Kieran for ever and a day, but there'll be another trip to Australia next summer. I'll happily pay that price. It could be so much worse.

5

Octber 1999. Jessie rings me and asks if I'll come down and ride one of hers in a schooling hurdle in Punchestown. It's a very simple request, but it utterly changes the course of my career.

A schooling hurdle is like a challenge match or a behind-closed-doors friendly for young horses that are starting out. There's a full card of races, one every half an hour, but there's nothing at stake. It's the next step up from working out on the gallops at home, a chance for them to get a bit of experience of travelling to the track and running against horses they don't know. Everything there is pretty untested, unproven. You don't really know anything about them. This lad of Jessie's is a bay horse. Five-year-old. Ran in a couple of bumpers earlier in the year, but no wins yet. Even if she had told me his name – Moscow Flyer – it wouldn't have meant a thing to me.

Every racehorse has a background. Every racehorse has a hopeful owner. But when you're going out to ride in a schooling race, you're not invested in learning their life stories. They come and they go. There are a lot of horses there to be schooled, and a lot of money already spent just to get them that far. By the law of averages, some of them will go on to be good enough to win races on big days, but equally, a lot will turn out to be little more than a hobby.

And then once in a generation – again, by the law of averages – one will come along and prove himself to be one of the greatest of all time.

A few minutes later, when this Moscow Flyer fella runs out through a track marker and turfs me off his back, I'm not expecting the latter.

I know Jessie quite likes him, thinks he has a bit more potential than the bare form of his bumpers would suggest, but I don't know the story: how Jessie and her husband Johnny had been given an order for a horse by a prospective new owner, a man who had never owned a racehorse in his life; how they went to the Derby Sale the previous summer and were convinced by Jim Mernagh to take a look at this gelding, sired by Moscow Society, with a big white star and a pretty unremarkable pedigree; and how they set their heart on him that day, and then watched as the auctioneer's asking price ticked ever closer to the limit of their budget before stopping on 17,000 guineas. Their successful bid.

What I do know is that he's quirky. I can tell as soon I get up on him and we make our way down to the start with the other horses. There's nothing straightforward about him, even before we start racing. He's not settled and he's ducking and diving, generally making life a bit more difficult than it needs to be. It's enough that he's inexperienced when it comes to running over hurdles; I don't need to be battling with him as well. But when we jump off, he's happy enough to get out and get on with it.

We jump the first two hurdles without any difficulty. The schooling track at Punchestown is left-handed, and as we get ready to make our turn into the back straight, I pick out the line of plastic poles that will guide us round the bend. There's no running rail today, so we just need to keep outside the poles and follow them around. We gallop down but just as we get to the bend, Moscow decides that he knows a quicker way and ducks left without any warning. As he tries to dive one side of the pole, I grab hold and try to correct him. We cancel each other out and end up in no man's land. Moscow gallops straight over the plastic pole and turns over, taking me with him. He picks himself up, dusts himself off and gallops away; no harm done, thankfully, to either of us. When Jessie calls the next time to tell me that Moscow has been entered for his racing debut over hurdles and to ask me if I'll ride him, at least I know that I have to expect the unexpected with this fella.

It doesn't take Moscow long to show me why Jessie and his owner, Brian Kearney, have such high hopes for him. He wins his first two races over hurdles impressively, beating two good horses of Noel Meade's that I know well from riding out in his yard. I give Moscow a similar ride in both: nice and steady until we get to the second last and then I give him the nudge to quicken off the front. He responds in a way that I never would have expected – it's electric. He wins his first race by three lengths and his second, against more experienced horses, by fifteen. You can't let yourself get too carried away with a young novice but, by any metric, it's a huge performance. This horse who didn't have the flat speed to win a bumper is transformed when he's jumping. It's raw. It's exhilarating. And for anyone who tries to take him on, it's impossible to live with.

But it doesn't take much for a promising young horse to be found out by a step-up in class, so we still have it all to prove when we go for the Royal Bond Novice Hurdle in Fairyhouse at the end of November. The best races in the National Hunt calendar are graded as Grade 1, Grade 2 or Grade 3. Grade 1 status is reserved for the most prestigious races, contested by the top horses, with the biggest prize money up for grabs. For any jockey, the Grade 1 races are the ones you want to win. The Royal Bond is Moscow's first time in a Grade 1 race, and even though only three other runners are entered, we have our work cut out for us. Dermot Weld's Stage Affair has been making light work of his races all summer, winning four in a row and going for his fifth today. It's his first time stepping up to Grade 1 level too but he's the horse that arrives with the fanfare and reputation – coming out of the star yard, with AP McCoy booked to ride him. He gets a bit more respect from the bookies and the punters. They don't make much of a fuss about our chances against him or the way we won the last day. Stage Affair is the 4/11 favourite; we go off a 7/2 shot in a four-horse race.

They don't know what we know – or what we have good reason to believe, at the very least. There's no reason for us to change our plan. I let Moscow out into an early lead, the same as before, and we take them round at a nice even pace. Three, maybe four, lengths cover us from front to back when we jump the third last, but I'm exactly where I want to be. When it gets to the endgame, and a jockey's about to make a move from the front, you expect him to look over his shoulder and check for the danger. It's an obvious tell, as blatant as they come, but there's only one way to find out what's coming behind you. It's a necessary evil. This time, I don't need to know. I sit tight and don't give any indication of what I'm about to do until we reach the turn for the home straight and I let Moscow rip.

The others have to react, have to come after me. There's no other option. Moscow flies over the second last and lands without breaking stride, but we get in a bit close to the last and it leaves the door open for Stage Affair to come and challenge us. As soon as he draws up alongside us, Moscow finds a burst of acceleration. It's a rare feeling, to have two good horses with seemingly little to separate them only for one to reveal such a conclusive gulf in class with one quick turn of foot. Moscow's move is devastating, and it ends the race right there and then. A hundred yards later we pass the post, Moscow first and then, three lengths later, Stage Affair.

It's the second Grade 1 win of my career – my second Grade 1 win in the space of an hour, coming hot on the heels of a lovely spin on Alexander Banquet in the race beforehand, the Drinmore Novice Chase. I hope that this is just the beginning, and with Moscow on my side, the sky's the limit.

6

When you want to be the champion, the summer is where you start. There's no time for holidays, no days off. One season's scores are tallied up and settled, and the next time you set foot in the weighroom, everyone starts again on zero, whether you're the eight-time champion or the teenager still looking to ride out his claim. Summer racing takes you up and down the country, the sun hanging on to its last beat of heat as you get a leg up in Bellewstown, Killarney, Galway, Tramore, Listowel, tracks that wait all year for the stretch in the evenings and then come to life. The big yards put their stars away to rest up for the serious business of the winter, but for the smaller trainer, the smaller owner, the summer is showtime.

Despite the broken vertebra, I ride 41 winners in the 1998/99 season and finish as Champion Conditional Jockey, and as the calendar flips from one campaign to the next, I know that the opportunity is there for me to hit the ground running that summer.

Every champion needs a good agent, someone who can spot the horse that you should be riding and phone you to tell you that you're booked to ride it before you're even aware that the horse has been entered to run. Ciaran O'Toole, my agent in Ireland, and Dave Roberts, who looks after me in England, are the best in the business. Ciaran approached me in my first summer after turning professional, and when he couldn't convince me of the necessity of a good agent, he decided that he'd show me instead.

Up until my decision to turn freelance in the summer of 2000, I'm based with Noel and I'm getting the nod to ride a lot of his good horses. But my broken collarbone that summer happened on a spare ride for another trainer, and I didn't want to upset Noel by getting another injury on someone else's horse. It seemed like an unnecessary risk, especially when the last one had ended in tears.

'You'll regret that,' Ciaran told me when I explained why I didn't want an agent, and he was right. At different stages, when things weren't going well for me, Ciaran was pushing Richard Dunwoody, Norman Williamson or one of his other jockeys and getting them on some of Noel's ahead of me. No matter how quick I was, I wasn't quicker than Ciaran. He'd proved his point and now he's scouring every small summer card for me, picking up any rides where he thinks I'll have a chance.

There's a certain equality to the jockeys' championship. Every winner counts the same, whether it comes in a Grade 1 race or a donkey derby in front of two men and a dog. I'm not going to be riding the favourite for the Hatton's Grace or the Hennessy Gold Cup this season, but there's nothing in the rules to say I can't work hard and clock up the miles and the numbers. I'm fired up for the summer. I drive the length and breadth of Ireland to get on anything I think will have a chance, raring to get scores on the board whatever way they come. It's relentless, but it's the only way to get your name out there, show people what you can do, and put yourself in position to ride a better horse the next day. When it comes to jockeys, trainers and owners like to buy high. If you're on a hot streak, they want you on their side before you go cold. Jockeys go in and out of fashion and the only way to make sure you stay in the shop window is to keep riding winners. It all works in a cycle: the more I ride, the more chances I'll have to win; the more I win, the more Ciaran's phone will ring; the more Ciaran's phone rings, the more good horses I'll have to choose between. And if I'm getting on fancied horses, I'll keep winning and the phone will keep ringing.

By mid-July the season is still only really getting going, but I'm the first to hit the front in the championship, a nose ahead of Ruby Walsh and Charlie Swan. Ruby is the defending champion, having won his first title the previous season, and Charlie is Charlie, having monopolised it throughout the rest of the 1990s. As well as a good agent and good spares, you need to be in favour with a yard in form so that you can build a good base. I have that too. Noel is the reigning Champion Trainer and has all the ammo for another big season, and when Paul Carberry suffers a really nasty injury – a ruptured spleen – I become Noel's de facto first rider for the five or six months until Paul is fit again.

Just as I'm starting to string together a few wins, the Australia trip comes around again. After missing out on it last summer, I've been waiting a year for another chance to go, but now that it's here, I know that it would be a mistake: I'll miss rides; I'll miss winners; the momentum that I've built up will be gone. There's any number of reasons. Take your pick. I don't need years of bitter experience to know that opportunities like this – the possibility of building and sustaining a season good enough to challenge for the title – won't come around every year. I pull out of the trip to stay at home and it teaches me another lesson: there are no guarantees in this game. I don't ride a single winner for the whole time the lads are away.

Cockiness and confidence are often confused; Ruby tells me that one day when we're both a lot older and wiser and starting to reflect on the lessons learned from a life in racing. I'm confident, and I'm not fazed by the big occasions, but sometimes people can misinterpret that as cockiness. If there's an opportunity to nick a race, or to take the others out of their comfort zone and maybe force a mistake, I'll take it. I get beaten on a lot of average horses by riding them too aggressively, but I win a lot of races that way too.

There's no point in pretending otherwise – one of the reasons why I'll win this year's championship is because good fortune has been on my side, as well as good form. I'm the only one who stays injury-free for the season. When Paul comes back from his injury in September, he starts hoovering up Noel's rides and racking up winners, but he's already given me too much of a head start to even consider chasing me. Just as the door closes for me in Noel's, it opens for me in Willie Mullins' yard. Ruby goes out to the Czech Republic at the start of October to ride in the famous Velká Pardubická, their equivalent of the Grand National, and suffers a really nasty leg break that rules him out until Cheltenham. I pick up a lot of rides that he would have had for Willie and there's a steady stream of good horses, including their good novice Alexander Banquet, that helps to carry me through the winter months.

By the end of November I've already ridden 41 winners, matching my total from the previous year with half the season still to go. By the third week in January, I bring up a half-century. The only injury I get is a comparatively minor one – a sore wrist and a few stitches – that rules me out for the last few days when the championship is good as over. I finish the season with 84 winners, 15 clear of Paul in second place. It's as good as it gets for a 20-year-old, particularly one who is still learning his trade. The only thing that it's missing is a win at Cheltenham.

Cheltenham is often a feast or famine in terms of rides; that's life as a freelance jockey. Entire seasons are carefully planned around this one week in the Cotswolds in March, and no trainer is going to take a risk on an untested partnership unless it's absolutely unavoidable. The big names – jockeys who are committed to either one yard or one owner – ride the vast majority of the big horses. A freelancer who wants to get an invite to the big dance needs to put in the groundwork. Get their foot in the door early in the winter, get a few 'off Broadway' rides, and build up that relationship with the horse and with the trainer. Of course there's a chance that someone might go down injured in the first race or you'll pick up a last-minute spare but if you're relying on that, you have to be prepared to come home empty-handed.

I might be riding winners for fun in Ireland, but with Paul and Ruby both back in action, I don't have any rides booked for Cheltenham in 2000. Moscow Flyer and Sackville, another good novice hurdler that I've been riding for Frances Crowley, were all set to be my two big hopes but neither of them make it: Moscow fractures his pelvis, which rules him out until Punchestown, and Sackville is given a break ahead of the Aintree Festival where, thankfully, I ride him and we win. Still, I'm determined to go to Cheltenham and to show up in the best nick possible. The buzz from my first ride at the festival is still ringing in my ears. Fishin Joella gave me a lovely run round, doors opened when we needed them to, and everything just happened for me. We were bang in the heat of it coming down the hill, still there with a chance jumping the third last, the second last, and just getting a taste of it was pure fantasy. We finished fifth, five and a half lengths behind Fran Berry on the winner, Khayrawani, and I'm hooked.

When March comes around again, I go on a diet. I don't particularly need to lose much weight, but the lower I can get it, the more spares I'll be eligible for in any of the big handicap races. I hear about this programme called the Nutron Diet and I go to a clinic to get tested for it. They take a sample of my blood and then give me a list of the foods that I have to avoid. The theory is that if I've an intolerance to a certain food, it will cause me to retain water and put on weight. I stick to the diet sheet religiously for three weeks – I'm baking my own bread, I don't touch a drop of alcohol, I do all the right things.

When I get to Cheltenham, my book of rides is still as bare as my fridge. I ride out on the course on the Monday morning, waiting for Tuesday's declarations to come through to see if anything crops up for me, but I have nothing. After three weeks of living like a monk, I break. I head off out into Cheltenham town and spend the evening making up for lost time. I'm still making up for lost time the following morning when I head down to the stable lads' canteen with last night's head on me and have a breakfast and a half, just because I can. The appetite disappears when I answer the phone to Ciaran O'Toole.

'I've got you something for tomorrow,' Ciaran tells me. 'Nicky Henderson needs someone to ride one of his in the Coral Cup.'

Before I can thank him, Ciaran slips in the kicker.

'You'll have to do 10 stone for it.'

It would be a lot easier if the breakfast just came back up on me there and then while I'm on the phone to Ciaran and saved me all the trouble. There's every chance it will be the only offer I get this week, so I can't turn it down, but equally, there's no way I can make 10 stone by tomorrow when I've barely left the tomato ketchup on the plate in front of me. I go to find Paul to ask him for his help.

'How do you flip?' I ask him.

'Just stick your fingers down your throat and that'll do it,' he tells me.

I go upstairs to the bedroom and try, but I can't make myself sick. My eyes feel like they're about to burst out of their sockets with every heave but there's nothing coming up. In the end, there's only one thing to do: I go back to bed.

I wake up in time to watch the first race of the week, the Supreme Novices' Hurdle. Paul rides Sausalito Bay for Noel, but they're up against the Irish banker of the meeting, a horse called Youlneverwalkalone that Conor O'Dwyer rides for Christy Roche and JP McManus, as well as a young English horse trained by Henrietta Knight that has a bright future ahead of him: Best Mate. Going to Cheltenham is déjà vu for Noel. Every year, the press latch on to whatever his best chance is and fire up the hype machine and ask if this will be the year – will Noel Meade finally get his first winner at the festival? And every time he has a good one, fate seems to find a new cruel and unusual way to say not this time, maybe next year. One year, Batista gets beaten by a short head in the Triumph Hurdle. Another year, the stewards take the best part of 20 minutes to read the photo finish of the Arkle; when they finally split them, Hill Society is beaten, again by a short head. And then there are the beaten favourites and late falls, a disappointment for all seasons.

So when Paul drives Sausalito Bay up the hill, Best Mate and Youlneverwalkalone snapping away but staying at heel's length, it's a win that Noel has been waiting more than 20 years for. While he's dropping to his knees and kissing the Cheltenham turf in celebration, I'm on my way down to the racecourse from the stable lads' canteen. When I get there, I meet Paul coming back in and go to congratulate him.

'You're on,' he says. I've no idea what he's talking about.

'How'd you mean, I'm on?'

'I'm not riding any more. You're riding.'

It's his back. He's been carrying an injury for the last few weeks – not that it would keep him from Cheltenham – and as Sausalito Bay landed after jumping the last, he aggravated the same problem again. He's finished for the day, and maybe for the week. I don't need my watch to know that his next ride, which is now my first ride, is due off in about 20 minutes.

I spend the evening in the sauna only taking sips of water as I try to wring myself out to get down to do 10 stone. Paul's still not fit to go back racing, which means that his ride in the Coral Cup for Noel, Native Dara, is now a spare. I go to Nicky and ask would he mind if I get off his horse to ride Native Dara. Nicky's okay with me switching. His horse is a 100/1 outsider while Native Dara is a 25/1 shot and, even better, I'll only have to get my weight down to do 10st 4lb now to ride Native Dara.

That's the funny thing about opportunities. Sometimes they only come about after years of graft and planning and preparation; other times, there's a chain of events that unfold to put you in the right place at the right time. Take any one link out – Paul doesn't hurt his back a few weeks before the festival, or I don't travel over because I don't have a ride – and the whole chain collapses and disappears without you ever even knowing about it. But it's when all the links come together, that's how I end up turning into the straight with one hurdle left to jump, a double handful of horse beneath me, and my first festival win just a couple of hundred yards away. I see my chance and we kick for home going down to the last. I couldn't ask for a better jump. Native Dara wings it and we set sail together up the hill to the finish line.

Cheltenham's hill is not particularly steep, but it is as long as it is famous and it is littered with broken dreams and regrets about what should have, would have, could have been. I take a quick look around after the last and see a cavalry chase of half a dozen lined up behind me but already beaten, no matter how hard they tried. The line is there, waiting for us, but each stride is just taking a little bit more energy, a little bit more effort. I feel Native Dara start to tie up. The course commentator's voice goes up a few decibels of excitement, rising to reflect a race that's not over yet. All I can do is keep my head down and drive and pray that the line comes first. And when the line does come, even though I don't know who he is or where he's come from, I know that he's got there ahead of me.

When I took that quick check around to assess the danger, this ghost that's after robbing me of my first Cheltenham win wasn't even in the picture. What's Up Boys and Paul Flynn jumped the last hurdle in 13th place, with nearly half of the field still in front of him, but then the tape of his race switched to fast-forward while the rest of us were stuck in normal speed at best. He comes flying, carving up the straight, and does me by a neck on the line. If only I had waited 50 yards – if only I hadn't been so aggressive, hadn't kicked on so soon on the run to the last – I'd have got home. Now I will be sick. Sick for Noel too. His book is already full of festival hard-luck stories without me adding another cruel chapter, but even in his disappointment, he doesn't say much or hold it against me; thank God for Paul and for Sausalito Bay.

It's the school of harsh reality and I get taught a lesson about Cheltenham that I'll only need to learn once: the moment you start to dream, you'll get put in your place in a flash. Don't dare.

7

T o truly know how good you are, you have to test yourself against the best, but we never really get to find out just how good Moscow Flyer is over hurdles. He doesn't just run in to the best two-mile hurdler of his time – he runs in to arguably the best two-mile hurdler of all time. Istabraq has already won three straight Champion Hurdles, his place in the horse racing hall of fame secure by the time our trilogy unfolds over the winter and spring of 2000/2001. Moscow wins two of their races and Istabraq wins one, but we never get to see them in a head-to-head fight to the finish; either Istabraq falls, or Moscow does, and foot and mouth disease forces Cheltenham to be abandoned in 2001 and denies us a Champion Hurdle showdown between the two of them. When it's all over, there's little argument that Moscow is good enough to stand toe-to-toe with any horse in training in Ireland or in Britain. He won't be back hurdling again next season. It's time to take him over fences.

The best two-mile chasers need to live on the edge. When they're in full stride, they're moving at nearly forty miles an hour. To go at that speed, and take on those fences without blinking, they need to be a little bit mad. Otherwise they'd never do it. Every time they jump, they take a chance. A measured horse will always show enough self-preservation to make sure he gets round safely, but then you have the horses that like to take a risk and throw caution to the wind. And when they get it right, they're very hard to catch. That's Moscow, always wanting to go forward, always wanting to roll on and attack his fence at speed rather than sitting off it. He's not worried about hurting himself. He just wants to go. And if that's the way he wants to race, he's got the right man on his back.

We could tell that he would excel over fences by the way he jumped a hurdle. He jumped big and bold, but you don't get the full benefit of it over hurdles, where you're better off getting down low and zipping across the top of them. When you come to fences, which are much bigger obstacles, his style becomes an asset. It's partly what he gains: carrying that momentum and springing past other horses in the air with big, fluent leaps. And it's partly what he saves: he finds it easy, so while a rival might be giving his all to jump a fence, constantly dipping into that tank that he'll need to fight a finish, Moscow is filling up. I'd often look at a horse running over hurdles and be able to tell from their style that they'd be ten pounds better over a fence. If they're at a decent level over hurdles, they'll step up another couple of levels once they go chasing. And if they're so good over hurdles that they're the biggest threat to Istabraq, well …

But Moscow walks a fine line between carefree and careless. He's so good that he could jump most of these fences in his sleep; I just wish he wouldn't try to do it so often. He gets so comfortable and confident that he strays the wrong side of the line and becomes a little bit blasé, so he's prone to mistakes. And the laws of physics aren't on the side of a horse cruising at high speed when they make a mistake at a fence. Crash.

His first time out over fences, he falls, but it doesn't take long for him to show what happens when he does get around safely. He gets back up, dusts himself off, and wins three on the spin before the end of the year. The last of the three, the Grade 1 at Leopardstown on St Stephen's Day, is usually a good yardstick to get a sense of who's who among the best of that year's Irish novices. And Moscow, it seems, might be top of the class not just in Ireland, but potentially in England too. He wins by two lengths and the bookies immediately make him favourite for his biggest race of the year, the date that's been circled on his calendar since the start of the season: the Arkle Chase in Cheltenham.

We have one more race before Cheltenham, back to Leopardstown for the Baileys Arkle at the end of January. It's a real chance for Moscow to put a peg in the ground, to set himself up as the one they all have to beat. But if he's going to do that, he'll have to do it without me. A week before the race, I get an awkward fall at Fairyhouse and I break my elbow. It rules me out for three weeks, so Paul Moloney steps in and takes over the ride on Moscow for the day. Six weeks before Cheltenham is not the time to be blotting your copybook with an F, but unfortunately for Paul, that's exactly what happens; Moscow clips the top of a fence and loses his footing.

One fall can be explained away as a blip, but two starts to resemble a pattern if you care enough to go looking for one – and there are enough critics out there that are happy to poke holes in Moscow's potential. They can't trust his jumping. They're entitled to their opinion – Moscow's happy to give them enough evidence to build a case anyway – but they're on the outside and they're only guessing. For anyone on the inside – me, Jessie, Jessie's head lad Eamonn Leigh, Brian Kearney – he's never given us a reason to doubt him.

Most trainers won't send a horse to Cheltenham on the back of a fall. They'll try to find one more prep race somewhere, just in case the horse's confidence is a bit shaken and they're a little more hesitant than usual. Jessie has plenty of options but she's not too concerned – Moscow doesn't know the meaning of the word timid. Instead, she brings him out for one last racecourse school in Leopardstown.

We have company for the run. Ted Walsh is there with Commanche Court, his Gold Cup horse, looking to get one more good piece of work in before they travel over. We line up in the back straight, me on Moscow, Ruby on Commanche, with Jessie and Ted keeping a watchful eye. The opening day of the festival is eight days away, but this is no mid-morning matinée – these are two good horses and we let it rip. Coming down to the second last we're at full tilt, Moscow leading Commanche, and all I can hear from behind me is the clatter of hooves and the *tssh-tssh-tssh* of Ruby's stick as he gives Commanche a few smacks of encouragement on the neck. The second last at Leopardstown is a bogey fence, one where you can very easily find yourself upside down if you're not careful. There's absolutely no need for me to encourage Moscow to have a go at it. Some risks you can justify, but if this goes wrong in a two-horse school a week before Cheltenham, I'll be explaining myself for ever and a day. I know that, and I kick him at the fence anyway; he flies it. When we pull up and I jump down off him, he has confirmed one thing anyway. Twelve horses will line up at the start of the Arkle next week, and I have no doubt in my mind who the best is.

But when the day comes, we're not the horse that people are talking about. The hype of Christmas has died away and Moscow's no longer favourite. The press and the punters are drawn towards the big English yards and the big reputations. Champion Trainer Martin Pipe has AP McCoy on Seebald, looking to make it eight wins out of eight over fences; his owners, former Liverpool footballers Steve McManaman and Robbie Fowler, add a little bit of celebrity to the occasion. Nicky Henderson, who is bidding for back-to-back wins in the race, trains Fondmort with Mick Fitzgerald up top. Barton, another one of the top English hopes, already has a festival win over hurdles on his CV. They're the three horses to beat in the race, according to the markets, with Moscow the next best.

The only expectation is the expectation that we have ourselves. It's only the second race of the festival but I know I won't have a better chance all week of riding a Cheltenham winner. I walk the track before racing and take a phone call while I'm out there. A friend of mine, a lad that we all know as The Horsebox, rings to see how I'm feeling and wish me good luck. When it comes to Moscow's chances, I tell him straight, no holding back, no bullshit – 'Clear round, he wins.'

I wouldn't even call it confidence. It's something more than that. It's belief. I have no problem telling anyone that he's head and shoulders above anything else in the field, despite what the press, the bookies and the punters might think. A lot of people won't speak their mind, either because they don't want to come across as arrogant, don't want people to get ahead of themselves, or they don't want to make a rod for their own backs and invite the pressure. If they go out on a limb at all, it comes with a caveat, a reminder that there are a lot of good horses, that anything can happen on the day, the language of 'Ah I don't know', and 'we'll see', and 'hopefully'. There's always a risk that if you say something, if you write the cheque and then you can't cash it, you'll look like a fool. But if something happens and Moscow doesn't win, me looking like a fool is going to be the least of my problems. So I call it – 'Clear round, he wins.'

It's as black and white as Moscow's silks, but that's the way it is. To us, the other horses are no danger. The only danger is the fences.

Once the white flag is raised and we jump off, I let him drop in at the back, with only one or two of our 11 rivals behind us. When you drop in like this, it might look like you're giving up an easy lead to anything that wants to press on and make the running, but I'm happy here. If you start overthinking at this stage, sizing up chess pieces and trying to read the next 12 moves on the board, you won't be relaxed or concentrating on your own job. I'm not worried about Seebald or Fondmort or Barton or how they're trying to plot their way to victory. My only thought is how I can get Moscow settled and into a nice jumping rhythm, concentrating and taking on his fences with confidence.

It takes him a couple of fences to warm up – nothing that you could call a mistake, just not as fluent as you might like. We're a long way off the leaders, but when you have a good horse, and he's jumping in a nice rhythm, it's easy for him to make up ground without using up any of his energy. We float through the back half of the field, passing horses in ones and twos without even thinking about it, just letting this nice easy canter and the running of the race carry us into position. There's a plain fence in the back straight, five from the finish, and when we land running on the far side of it, there are only three others in front of us and one blanket would be enough to keep us all warm. Barton is right there beside me with Fondmort on the rail and Seebald tucked in behind us as we come down to the open ditch. I can see from a long way off that Moscow's coming to it on a long stride and I give him a squeeze, letting him know that it's time for a big one, and then I do something that I shouldn't do. I change my mind. It's too long. I sit so that he'll back off. But Moscow has made up his mind and he's already committed, so I need to be too. On his final stride, I give him a squeeze again. We're in this together. Let's go.

He takes off a mile from the ditch and dives at the fence. Of all the things that could go horribly wrong, none of them happen. We pass out a couple of horses in the air and we touch down in second, running away with only Armaturk, the leader, out in front of us. Now you start to size things up, figure out where you are, who's around you and what they all have left. Now the race is ready to begin. We race down the hill towards the third last, but the last place we want to be is in the lead when we're still so far from home. If you hit the front too soon, there's very little to gain and a lot to lose. You're a sitting duck, inviting the rest to size you up and take their shot when they feel the moment is right. Instead of taking on Armaturk, we sit tight and wait for the company to come and join us. Fondmort is still there on the rail, Fitzy doing what he can to save ground with every stride. I can't see AP and Seebald, but they can't be too far away, keeping an eye on every move we make.

We jump the third last side by side with Armaturk, only we jump it better. Just as he starts to struggle on one side of us, the all-white silks arrive on the other and jump the second last a breath behind us. AP and Seebald. We've been listening to all the talk about Seebald for the last few weeks, but the time for talking is over. I don't even need to give Moscow a smack to remind him that we still have one fence to jump, that now is no time to let the mind wander. He knows there's a job to do and he is fully dialled in. I sit tight and he races down as if it's a Wednesday morning back in Commonstown and he's popping fences with a few of his pals. He measures it. A clear round. Now the rest, as I'd been telling anyone who would listen, is a formality.

Seebald chases us up the home straight, making sure we know that we haven't passed the winning post just yet, but Moscow is still full of running. I take one last look over my shoulder. There'll be no repeat of Native Dara this time. Six or seven strides from the line, I stand up in my irons and salute the crowd, invite them to show their appreciation for the best two-mile novice chaser in training. It's undisputed now.

Timmy Murphy comes to congratulate me. Ruby pulls his horse up alongside me and leans over to grab me on the shoulder and give me a squeeze. He has a smile on his face as broad as if he'd just won the race himself. He knows exactly what this moment means to me. There'll be good days and bad days until the world stops turning, but there'll only ever be one day when I ride my first winner at Cheltenham. I give Moscow a kiss and a couple of pats on the neck. We did it.

8

The weighroom is built on respect. This is a competitive sport, it's a fight to the finish, and all jockeys have that gene that drives them, but there's honour to it. You get what you give. You look out for each other. These are big animals travelling into obstacles at high speed. Nobody needs to be reminded of the risks. It's dangerous enough without the jockeys on their backs trying to cut each other's throats as well. If I get a shout from someone behind me looking for a bit of a room, I'll give it to them. If I close the door, I'm putting them in a tight spot and increasing the risk of a fall. And if I do it to them today, they're doing it to me tomorrow. You play nice until the business end, a good clean fight until the last half-mile or so. And then the gloves can come off.

I'm straight but I'm fair – I'll treat someone the way they treat me. I'm not as cynical as some of the others but I won't suffer fools either. You learn to read the room, to know which jockeys will only ask you for a bit of room on a rare occasion that they really need it, and the ones that are asking all the time because they're panicking, worrying, their bottle's gone a bit shaky. Some lads are wired differently, though. They'll cross the track in a flash to do you and put you into the rail. You don't even ask them the question. If you see the gap, say nothing and grab it before it's gone.

The old saying about taking your job seriously but not yourself – that sums me up. And those are the type of people I'm drawn to. When you go into the weighroom, the pegs are split between two sides. Conor O'Dwyer, Paul Carberry, Terry Mitchell, Liam Cusack and Kevin O'Brien are the senior men on my side starting out. They set the tone – nice and laid-back but always with room for a bit of divilment as well. Anthony Powell is another one who's always looking for a bit of craic, but he shows me very early on that he's looking out for me as well. I'm only fresh in the weighroom and he's over giving me a bit of advice on the horse I'm about to ride, Appellate Court. The horse is near the end of its career, but I'm only starting out, so any ride at all is a big ride for me, and I appreciate him coming over for a word.

The lads I become friends with over the years are all the same: good jockeys, sound men, who never take themselves too seriously. That goes for Kieran Kelly, John Cullen, Tommy Treacy, Frannie Woods, Shay Barry, Ken Whelan and lots of others. In later years, I do a lot of travelling with Davy Condon, Paul Carberry and Robert Power – the Wolfpack, as Davy christens us. Paul is so laid-back when he's going racing that as soon as he gets into the car, he's fast asleep. This is the lad who was coming in to win the Lexus on Beef Or Salmon and turned around in the saddle to wave at Best Mate, who was chasing him; the lad who got beaten by a neck on Harchibald in the Champion Hurdle and shrugged it off.

When it comes to Cheltenham or Aintree or any of the bigger meetings, he sits over beside me and Ruby Walsh. He calms our corner of the room, and I feed off his light approach to the day. When you're sitting beside Paul, there's no room for getting caught up in the occasion or for getting tense. There's no time to overthink things because you're too busy listening to another story or breaking yourself laughing. There's a good bond between the three of us. We have good days and bad days at those big meetings, but even when we can't find a winner between us, there's never a 'poor me' in that corner.

The three of us are all competing against each other. We're all fighting for the same things. It's a rivalry but there's nothing negative in it. It's fast-paced and feelings run high but if you're beaten, you're the first one there to congratulate the other. There's a huge mutual respect. There always has been – respect for your judgement, respect for your tactics, and respect for how you conduct yourself.

We're not out to knife each other. If it was that kind of relationship, the two lads certainly have an opportunity to screw me over one Wednesday in 2002. It's the day before the Aintree Festival starts and we're racing in Fairyhouse, the last meeting before we fly out to Liverpool. I'm booked for a big ride on Florida Pearl the next day, but I get a bad fall at the ditch over on the far side of Fairyhouse and I'm knocked out as I hit the ground. I don't know how severe my concussion is but it's somewhere on the spectrum. When I come back into the weighroom, I sit down beside Paul and Ruby and start talking more shit than usual. It wouldn't take a doctor long to cop that I haven't a clue where I am, and I'd be stood down and wouldn't be allowed to go and ride in Aintree. Before I talk myself into trouble, the two lads grab hold of me.

'Sit down, shut up, and stop talking shit.'

Both of them have ridden Florida Pearl plenty of times in the past, both of them were flying out to Aintree themselves anyway, and neither of them had a ride booked for that particular race. It would have been the easiest thing in the world to sit back and let me talk my way into trouble and when I was stood down, make the phone call and pick up the easiest spare ride in the world. I go out the following day and win by 11 lengths on Florida Pearl, and a few weeks later, I keep the ride on him and win the Punchestown Gold Cup as well.

There can be a different atmosphere in the English weighroom, a different approach. The lads who are riding over there full time, they live it. It's day after day. One end of the country to the other. There's an intensity to it that's just not there as much in Ireland. It's not as laid-back, not as carefree. It doesn't matter if it's a mickey-mouse Monday in Plumpton or a big card on Saturday at Sandown – if their horse gets beaten, they feel the pressure.

I see it when I fly over to ride two for Martin Pipe at Cheltenham's November meeting in 2002. AP McCoy is the first jockey at Pipe's, but he's picked two others in the two big races of the day so David Johnson, who owns Stormez and Cyfor Malta, flies me over to ride his two. I breeze in, win on both, and breeze back out again. I'm delighted, but at the same time I know it's a sickener of a day for AP – it always is when a horse you could have ridden wins without you, and it's just happened to him twice in the space of 45 minutes; to make matters worse, he had to do 10st 10lb to ride one of the ones he picked as well. But the atmosphere in the weighroom turns faster than milk. There's no laughing or joking or brushing it off like there would be in Ireland. It's as if someone has stuck a pin in the room. Everyone is walking on eggshells.

Mick Fitzgerald is another lad who's over there seven days a week, riding as first jockey for Nicky Henderson. I've always admired him, but when we're out there on the track, he's in the zone more than anyone I've ever met. I get a reminder of that in the Galway Plate in 2002. Fitzy is riding one of the fancied horses, but he's already beaten by the time we get to the last fence. He jumps it a few lengths in front of me but at that stage, he's going backwards and I'm going forwards. Somewhere along the way, I dropped my stick or it was knocked out of my hand,

and as I'm coming up alongside Fitzy to pass him, I give him a shout.

'Fitzy, can I have your stick?'

He's probably the worst person I could have asked. I put my hand out for it as I'm going past him but it's only grabbing fresh air and he roars at me.

'FUCK OFF!'

If a lad ever asked me for my stick and my chance was gone, I'd hand it over straight away, but that's Fitzy – unapologetically dialled in until the finish line, and then great company afterwards when it's all over.

There's a different style as well between the jockeys riding in Ireland and jockeys riding in England. It's much more aggressive in England. They get better ground in the winter on a lot of the tracks and so the races are run at a stronger pace. The English press love the ride from the front. If a jockey goes for it early in England and gets caught, it's a heroic defeat, horse and jockey carried out on their shield, whereas in Ireland, it's the quickest way to a surefire bollocking. The Irish way is much more opportunistic: there's only one winning post, so take your time, box clever, deliver him late, rob your race, out the door, job done. Nicking, as Paddy Brennan calls it in the weighroom – 'That was some bit of nicking by your man, wasn't it?' You expect it when you're racing in Ireland but some of the lads riding in England have a gift for it too. Paul Moloney is a great man for nicking, same with Leighton Aspell and Andrew Thornton too.

There are plenty of jockeys who would be out racing eight days a week if they could. That's never been my way. I love racing, love the thrill of riding the big winner on the big day, but there's always been more than that to life for me. It's a three- or four-day week when you're riding in Ireland and that's plenty for me. I buy a piece of land close to home and set it up as a livestock farm. It's a great outlet for me, and I really enjoy having another interest that's completely separate to racing. We start off with 450 sheep but I quickly realise that I'm in over my head and Kevin Tuite, a good friend of mine, comes in to help me and soon takes over the running of the farm on my behalf. Kevin advises me on what stock to buy and sell, but he's a great sounding board in every respect and someone whose opinion I would often seek when making a decision.

I get involved in a pub as well with another good friend of mine, Barry Callaghan. Barry played Gaelic football for Meath and won All-Irelands in 1996 and 1999. His dad, Gerry, owns Stagalier, the horse I rode my first ever winner on, and we became very close friends off the back of that. Barry asks me if I'm interested in buying into a pub, Arches in Kells, with him, as an investment. I love going down on a Saturday night, learning the ropes, chatting with customers and pulling a few pints. We have plans to open up a nightclub as well, but I'm away so often with racing that I don't really have enough time to commit to it. I stay involved for two years or so, and in the end, I'm happy to sell my share to Barry rather than run the risk of us falling out.

Sitting down on a Tuesday afternoon to watch racing from wherever in England has never interested me. I'll watch a race that I want to watch, I enjoy it, but I don't need to have it on all the time. It doesn't consume my life like that. Over the years, different people see that attitude and they misinterpret it as being complacent or not bothered or not interested, but that's not it. I wouldn't love it in the same way if I was out there racing every day. I know how much is enough. It's one of the main reasons why I turn down Paul Nicholls when he approaches me to offer me the job as his first jockey.

It's a huge offer to get. Nicholls is one of the biggest trainers in England, second only to Martin Pipe in terms of winners, and hammering away at Martin's stranglehold on the Champion Trainer title. He has an army of top-class horses and, with so many big owners in the yard, the promise of lots more to come. When Nicholls wants to hire a first jockey in April 2002, Ruby and myself are the two names on the top of his list. It's no surprise that he's interested in Ruby – Nicholls first offered him the job 12 months earlier and Ruby turned it down – but it's a huge compliment to know that I'm at the top table too. He asks the two of us to come over to the Scottish National meeting at Ayr to ride a couple for him and it goes well. I win the Grade 2 novice chase on Valley Henry and then ride Shotgun Willy, his runner in the National; Ruby rides Take Control for Martin Pipe instead and beats me by half a length.

It must be enough to convince Nicholls that I'm the man he wants. I fly into Bristol Airport and he picks me up and brings me down for the grand tour of his yard in Ditcheat. He brings me out to show me the gallops, introduces me to Paul Barber, his landlord and one of his biggest owners. It's all very impressive. Any advice that I get from lads who are already riding in England is positive: it's a huge job, it will be great for your profile, it will open the door to so many opportunities. In short: take it.

There's a bit more to consider than that. I've worked my way into such a strong position in Ireland. Between Jessie, Edward O'Grady, and a few for Tom Taaffe, I've built up a really nice book of rides while keeping all the freedom of a freelancer. I'm the first man up if there's a good spare ride for Noel Meade or Willie Mullins. That would all be gone if I moved over to live in England and join the Nicholls team. I'd still be able to ride Moscow – part of the offer is that I can pick two horses that I'm allowed to ride ahead of any of Nicholls's – but even at that, it's a lot to give up.

And then, like anyone who changes jobs, there's always a chance that it won't work out. If I'm going to trade away everything I've built up, I need to know that I'm moving to a job with some bit of security and, to be honest, I don't see it. I speak my mind and I stand my ground, and I don't know if that's the kind of jockey that Nicholls really wants. There's been a lot of chopping and changing in the yard over the last few years, from Timmy Murphy to Joe Tizzard and back to Timmy again. Timmy is one of the most naturally talented horsemen I've ever seen, and Nicholls had sacked him before back in 1998. If Timmy's riding isn't good enough, then what is?

I know that this isn't the right job for me, for all of those reasons. Nicholls lets it be known afterwards that things fell apart because we couldn't come to a financial agreement, and that's true in a sense. When I weigh it all up, I put a figure on the table that I feel I would be forced to consider, in spite of all my concerns and reservations: €100,000 a year for three years. I never expect Nicholls to make me that kind of offer, but if he wants me that badly and he finds the money, then I'll have a decision to make. It doesn't make for much of a negotiation.

Within a few days, Nicholls and Ruby have come to their own agreement. They have years of success together, unforgettable days with some incredible horses, but not once do I look at Ruby from the fence and think, fuck it, that could have been me. I know it wasn't the job for me. It never feels like one that got away.

9

I t starts out as a joke.

'You'll be feeling the pressure now,' Eamonn Leigh, Jessie's head lad, tells me down in the yard one morning. The 2003 Champion Chase is just around the corner, and Moscow's the favourite.

'Sure, pressure's for tyres,' Eamonn reassures me.

That word keeps cropping up in interviews and previews: pressure. Have I noticed it more this year? How does it feel? How do I handle it? And every time it does come up, I give the same answer.

'Pressure's for tyres.'

I can't help but think how much things have changed in the space of 12 months. Moscow's the champion in waiting, the Irish banker. He's not just ours any more. He belongs to the public now.

There's a lot of expectation, but a lot to prove as well. Only a mistake can stop him, that's true, but he's nowhere near as bulletproof as that makes him seem. He makes mistakes regularly. That's why people keep second-guessing him; I get it. I have to tune out all of that noise, isolate myself from newspaper talk and public opinion. The weight of my own expectation is enough. Or Jessie's expectation. Or Brian Kearney's. They're the people that I really have to deliver for. They're the people who will be there to share in the moment if everything goes to plan. And they're the people who will still be standing by me if it all goes wrong.

It's easy not to feel pressure when Jessie is the one you're riding for. She's not one for sitting on the fence. She'll speak her mind, tell you straight up how she feels. But she's never found fault or held me responsible for any fall.

Sitting in the taxi, leaving Sandown after the Tingle Creek Chase a few months earlier, she never said a word. We'd gone there with a real chance but the race was only getting going when we came down. It all happened before we could do anything. Moscow jumped the fifth fence perfectly, but it wasn't our jump that we needed to worry about. Flagship Uberalles, the favourite, the reigning champion, jumped it in front of us and made a mistake. He caught it on the way down and sprawled as he landed. He pumped the brakes and, two strides later, we crashed straight into the back of him. The impact of the collision stopped Moscow dead in his tracks but I kept going, my body weight and momentum launching me over his shoulder. I was on the ground before I had time to say boo. Game over.

Heading home that evening, I was beating myself up. There must have been something I could have done differently to stay on him. It's one thing when a horse falls, it's a little bit easier to take, but Moscow never fell. It's officially recorded as a UR – unseated rider – the two letters that every jockey hates. Dress it up however you like and make whatever excuses you need, but UR means fell off. Carberry, Dunwoody, O'Dwyer, they rarely get URs, they're brilliant at just sticking to their horses like glue no matter what happens. It's like scoring an own goal; it doesn't matter if you were trying to do the right thing, it's embarrassing.

I should have anticipated it before it happened. I should have been strong enough to hold myself in place. When all your weight and your centre of gravity lurches forward suddenly like that, you'll never stay on unless you have the core strength to pull yourself back before you go beyond the point of recovery. In later years, as I get a bit more experience, I'm more alert and aware. I'm stronger too; the muscle tone that runs from my foot through my legs up to my chest, its reaction time is better.

An incident like that is always open to interpretation. It would be easy for a trainer or an owner to find fault if they wanted to. Did you not see the other horse? You fell off him – Jesus Christ, would you fall out of bed? But Jessie never even asks a question. Years later, I remind her about that taxi journey home from the racecourse.

'That Tingle Creek with Flagship Uberalles, I wouldn't have fallen off Moscow if it was tomorrow. But you know, you never said a word.'

She looks at me.

'No, I didn't need to,' she says. 'These things happen.'

When I look at the field for the 2003 Champion Chase, I don't see anything that can trouble Moscow. Tiutchev is the horse that's being talked up as our main danger. He's an Arkle winner too, from 2000, when he was at Nicky Henderson's. He has already had a go at the Champion Chase, ran in the race 12 months ago, but he did nothing. He's been switched to Martin Pipe's yard since then, and that explains the hype around his chances as much as anything else. The English press love to latch on to the big yard and the big trainer. But I just don't see the threat. As a hurdler, the closest Tiutchev ever got to Istabraq was 10½ lengths. He's not a concern.

By the time we jump the fifth, I don't have to worry about him anyway. He crumbles on landing and goes down in slow motion, placing AP McCoy on the ground beside him. Moscow is tucked in behind the leaders as we come around the top bend and race down towards the fourth last. He dived at this ditch in the Arkle, the only really hairy moment in the whole run around, and he's come down to it on the exact same long stride again. We're still a mile away from the fence when he takes off. It's a big leap, but his trajectory is just off. We come down a fraction too early and his hind legs brush through the top of the fence. My right arm shoots out to call a cab as I try to keep my balance, but we're over it safely and running away on the other side. I breathe a huge sigh of relief.

Swinging down to the third last, we're doing a hack. I know I'm on the best horse. I knew it coming out. The only danger now is in front of us, and I don't mean Seebald and Latalomne, the two horses that we're still taking a lead off. If Moscow jumps the fences, he'll win. Instinctively, I leave the rail and pull him out wide. I don't need to be on the inside saving ground. I don't need to be running up another horse's tail. It's a luxury. If we weren't going as easy as we are, I'd never give up the inside like that. But when you're cruising, you've plenty of time to focus on the risks, the things that could go wrong and cost you the race rather than having to worry about what you need to do to win. That bit is taking care of itself.

As we jump the second last, my decision to move Moscow to the outside looks like a moment of pure inspiration. Seebald and Latalomne jump it together and come crashing down together. They don't collide. One doesn't bring the other down. Just two simultaneous falls by the only two horses that could cause us any trouble, leaving us out in front on our own with the race at our mercy.

Native Upmanship swerves the two horses and gives chase but he wouldn't beat us even from a standing start on level terms, never mind giving us a five-length head start. I don't even need to do much to put the race to bed. We swing off the bend and I kick Moscow along for a bit. He pricks his ears and starts looking up at the stand, at his public. All I need to do is keep him concentrating. He's got so much left in the tank that even if something comes at us, he's still got gears to burn. The Champion Chase at your mercy, all of Ireland willing you on, and you're going through the motions. It's an incredibly comfortable feeling.

He's perfect jumping the last, and as we run up the hill into a wall of noise, the gap between us and Native Upmanship in second is getting bigger rather than smaller. Stop the talking. Forget the question marks. Moscow Flyer is the champion.

The emotional release of the post-race interview, the brief but beautiful walk back down to the winners' enclosure, it's all becoming a very familiar feeling for me. It's the middle of the second day of the festival and I've been through it all twice already. I had my first winner of the week yesterday on Youlneverwalkalone for JP McManus in the William Hill Handicap Chase. I got my timing spot on. The only other time I'd ridden him was in Leopardstown in January and he just barely got home for me on soft ground. I needed the line that day, and I got it, but it's not a good feeling when you're hanging on. I made sure I gave him a more balanced ride this time around. I sat quieter, didn't get involved as early, and when I challenged, I challenged with more horse. Youlneverwalkalone hit the line running and won by three-quarters of a length.

I was still high as a kite an hour later when I went out to ride Inching Closer in the Pertemps Final. At least I had ridden Youlneverwalkalone once before Cheltenham; I had never even sat up on this horse before and only got the call from Jonjo O'Neill, his trainer, because I'd been riding a few of JP's horses for him over the winter. Inching Closer was the 6/1 favourite, not that I'd have known it from talking to Jonjo beforehand. He never talks up his horses' chances, it's just not his way. He's always a pleasure to meet and ride for. He never complicates things with a list of instructions. Instead, he tells you what you need to know and lets you figure out the best way to win. The instructions he gave me going out on Inching Closer were the bare minimum in terms of expectation: if you're there at the last with a chance, that would be great, but you wouldn't want to be there any sooner. They were typical Jonjo instructions. The chance came and I did exactly as I was told. I went, and we got there just in time; Inching Closer won the Pertemps by a short head.

Travelling over this week, I knew I had a good book of rides but Moscow was easily the standout, my best chance of a winner. Now I've had three and all I can do is pinch myself.

I'm not expecting much when I go out the next day in the Triumph Hurdle. I'm riding for Jonjo again, a horse called Spectroscope. I've won on him before but it was a fairly ordinary race and he's an outsider for the Triumph; it's a big field, 27 runners, and he's a 20/1 shot. AP rides Well Chief, the hotshot in the race, a real strong travelling horse. He runs keen, pulling hard to get to the front, and then leads us the whole way around. My fella's a lazy one by comparison. While Well Chief is at the front, running with the choke out, I just sit Spectroscope in behind him, a few horses deep, and nurse away at him over the hurdles.

You have to respect Cheltenham. You have to respect the hill. The ghost of Native Dara is sitting on my shoulder reminding me of what happens when you don't. When you get to the bottom and start that climb up the home straight, you have to hit it with so much in the tank. You can sit with your foot on the accelerator, poised, but if you let the lights go green too early, you'll pay the price. Cheltenham doesn't play favourites and it doesn't forgive. It's cruel.

I'm in a good spot to watch Well Chief, to keep tabs on what he's doing, but the horse isn't making life easy for AP. I wait for him to take a pull when we come to the top of the hill, to slow things down a bit and get a quick breather and fill up to go again, but Well Chief is still rolling along, going forward at the same pace. I jump up into second place at the second last, but I'm still conserving. It's too soon for us to challenge, I don't want to get sucked into a scrap too soon, but AP doesn't wait for us anyway. He kicks off the turn in, but by the time we jump the last, the two horses are side by side. The margins are so fine but they're in our favour. We just have that fraction more left in the tank. With 50 yards to go, Spectroscope sticks his head out in front. A head. That's all that separates us at the line, but it's as good as 10 lengths.

I'm walking on air. I wish this week could last for ever, but that's about the only thing I can't make happen at the moment. I jump up on Spirit Leader for the last race of the festival, the County Hurdle, and promise myself that I'll enjoy it. Jessie has had her in flying form all season. She's already won two of the big English handicaps, the William Hill in Sandown and the Tote Gold Trophy in Newbury, with Norman Williamson able to do the 10 stone weight to ride her in both. The Tote Gold Trophy was a bit like this race, nearly 30 runners, every hint of form scrutinised by the handicapper, super-competitive.

But that's the problem with handicaps – once you have your day in the sun, you're exposed. You shoot up in the weights and it's a big ask to win from the top end. In the County Hurdle, they always go flat to the boards. It's going to be sharp, two miles one furlong, and Spirit Leader has got 11st 7lb to carry. That's more than enough to kill a chance; only two horses in the race have more, and you can bank on something running on at the end from the bottom of the weights with a feather on their back by comparison.

I don't really fancy her chances with the weight so I just drop her in and let her float along and see what happens. If you try that on a slow horse, you'll end up badly out of position, but Spirit

Leader has enough natural speed to come from off a fast pace. I just ride away and see what happens and then it happens. We're bunched up in a full house of contenders jumping the third last but by the time we jump the second last, they're dying all around us. Spirit Leader weaves her way through all these fallen soldiers and we jump the last hurdle in second place. And because we haven't done a tap of work up to now, she's hitting the hill with a bucketful of energy and ready to go.

We drive into the lead. Graham Lee and Through The Rye are right there with me but Spirit Leader won't give up on me. She's still full of running and loving it. I know I've got them covered as we race towards the line. It's happening again. Three full strides from the line, Through The Rye is straining, doing everything she can to get past us on the outside. The excitement gets the better of me and I stand straight up in my irons and give the crowd a mighty salute. Don't let anyone be fooled into thinking we're fighting out a race to the finish. You can stick a fork in this one. It's done.

I feel the horse on my inside flash by before I see him. There was a third horse in our two-horse race to the line. Balapour and Martin Mooney have come from the bottom of the weights and finished like a steam train. While I was celebrating, they were right there, closing with every stride, ready to sneak it away from us. Balapour was only a neck behind Spirit Leader when we hit the line; another few strides and who knows what might have happened. I get away with it and I know how lucky I am. A scar like that would haunt you for ever. I'll salute again, but never when I'm riding a finish like that. Let this one be my great escape. Only a fool would tempt fate twice.

I leave Cheltenham feeling like the king of the world – 23 years old, five winners and the leading rider of the week. Nobody has ever won more than five at one festival. Before I walk out the gate, I catch a hold of myself. This has been my fairytale, but for every happy ending in this place, there are dozens more hard-luck stories. There's no code to crack in Cheltenham. You don't solve the puzzle and keep the solution locked away for the next time you need it. I need to fully appreciate how special this week has been, because I'll be back here in 12 months' time and I know that it won't be like this. It won't be this easy.

The party starts in Cheltenham town that night and it's still going strong a couple of days later, with a little bit of racing sprinkled in between. By the time I arrive back to Drumree, I'm only fit for sleep, but as we turn towards the crossroads close to home, the blaze of the bonfire tells me that everyone else has other plans. It's Saturday night and everyone is out to welcome me home – Mam, Dad, all the family, our cousins, and most of the neighbours too. We go back down to the house first, and then on to Lawless's pub. The Lawless family are cousins, and there's a big racing community in Dunshaughlin where they have their pub. We fill the place, elbow to elbow, and make sure that this incredible week gets the celebration it deserves. By the time we finally make it home, it's nearly morning again.

10

n all my idle moments, the third last fence of the Grand National is never the one that I dream of.

You grow up with the history of this race hardwired into you. It paints your imagination. But it's never this picture, it's always somewhere else. It's the first few yards after the final fence, 30 obstacles safely behind you and nothing left to trip you up; add an asterisk for Devon Loch, who still found a way to lose. Or it's the run to the line, the chaser or the chased, coming from behind to snatch it in the final strides like a young Red Rum, or drinking it all in like Tommy Carberry on L'Escargot, with a pat on the horse's neck and a job well done. It's the roar of the crowd, caps and newspapers thrown in the air, and bookies' dockets shredded and bookies' dockets clutched.

Not now. Out here, three from home, it's just eerie silence and a race unfolding in slow motion. I'm going as easy as I could be. I look at the only horse in front of me, and I look down at Monty's Pass beneath me, and it's at this very moment that I realise: this is happening. It's 5 April 2003. Today is the day I win the Grand National:

You're always the main character in your own dreams, but while I'm waiting for my day to come, there's a thrill just in being adjacent to the magic. Ruby and I watch the 1999 Grand National together on a small TV in the press room in Wexford racecourse. We haven't graduated to Aintree yet; we're riding on a card that will be lucky if it even makes it into the footnotes of the day's news. At least someone had the good sense to schedule races at 3.15 p.m. and 4.15 p.m. with a long break in the middle. When Bobbyjo passes the winning post, the little Meath town of Ratoath suddenly becomes the centre of the sporting universe.

Aintree was always something you watched on TV, its heroes and heartbreak were always far away, but now it feels closer than ever before. As a child you'd spot Tommy Carberry down in Ratoath village, and you know he's the jockey who won the Grand National. You'd give Ross or Norman a nudge – over there, look who it is – or feel it in your ribs if they spotted him first. Now he has done it again, playing the part of winning trainer and proud father all at once as he welcomes Paul and Bobbyjo back into the winners' enclosure.

My first thought is 'Holy shit, he's just won the Grand National'; my second is 'This is going to be one hell of a party.' I've come to know Paul so well over the last few years, both through working in Noel's and through nights out. Everyone will be there – the whole Carberry family, all of Paul's friends who have since become my friends too: Niall Lord, Niall's brother Adam, Mike Foley. Norman, my brother, shod the horse. I'm still sitting in the press room, my jaw on the floor, when Ruby comes back in, ready to race.

'Have you weighed out yet?'

'Fuck, no.'

I race back down to grab my saddle and get weighed, and because I'm late weighing out, I'm late getting organised and I'm late out into the parade ring. I'm riding a horse called Clifdon Fog for Paddy Mullins, a man who is known for saying very little even when he has all the time in the world. Before I even have a chance to ask him what he'd like me to do or how he thinks the race might shake out, I'm legged up and on the way down to the start.

I'm on autopilot, barely aware of the fact that I'm about to ride in a race. My body is in Wexford but my mind is still lost in Aintree. I steer Clifdon Fog over to have a look at the first fence, and Jason Maguire is there on his fella. Jason looks at me.

'Jesus, what's wrong with you? You're white as a ghost.'

'I haven't a clue. I don't know. I don't know what I'm at.'

The only thing I know about this horse is that I've lost to him before. It was more than two years earlier, one of my first races when I was just getting going as a professional, and something about that day in Gowran has obviously stuck with me – Clifdon Fog came from off the pace, breezed past me on the run down to the last, and ran on to win by seven lengths. In the absence of any better ideas, that's what I do when the tape goes up. I drop him in halfway, wait until the last, and just get up in the nick of time to win by a neck. I ride the winner in the next, throw my gear back into my bag, and race out the door straight to Dublin Airport to jump on the first flight to Liverpool to join in the celebrations.

In 2000, I'm sitting beside Ruby in the Aintree weighroom, this unfamiliar place that we had only ever been in a handful of times before and never on Grand National day. I couldn't care less that I'm on a 50/1 outsider. What I'm riding is irrelevant; the fact that I have a ride is enough in itself. A jockey without a ride in the National is like the 17-year-old standing outside the nightclub, watching on jealously as all his older friends get waved through. These fences are part of racing folklore and just to take them on, to survive, is a celebration. Call It A Day never has a chance of winning, but I'm buzzing the whole way round as he runs on to finish sixth. Up ahead of us, the other 20-year-old making his debut in the race is surrounded by cameras and photographers; Ruby and Papillon are living my dream and I couldn't be happier for them. Maybe it's closer than I think.

A year to the day. That's how long Jimmy Mangan has been planning this.

We barely have the saddle off Monty's back after the Topham Chase in 2002 and Jimmy has his eye on a much bigger prize. The Topham is a great test of whether or not a horse will handle the Grand National fences, and Monty was loving it out there. He has just run a cracker, finishing second to Ruby on a horse called Its Time For A Win. Maybe he was missing that extra gear at the end to chase him home, but over a longer distance that won't be as decisive. Jimmy plants the seed straight away.

'Back him for the Grand National,' he tells Monty's owners. 'We'll come back and win it.'

The little horse with the heart murmur has turned into an artist over fences. He's been with Jimmy in Conna since he was a four-year-old, running in point-to-points and hunter chases for a local syndicate. It's a hard ask to buy a horse when he can't pass a vet's examination, but there's something about Monty that catches Mike Futter's eye. It's a gamble, but gambles are Mike's bread and butter, and he buys Monty with a group of friends from Donaghadee in County Down – the Dee Racing Syndicate, they call themselves.

The point-to-pointer in Monty shines through any time I ride him over fences. He's gifted, there's no other way to describe his jumping. Everything is measured to a tee, so clinical. The beauty about him is that he can do it at pace too when he has to. I ride him in Tralee one afternoon in one of their big summer handicaps and, even on a sharp track when he's flat to the boards the whole way round, it's second nature to him. I can sit and not move a muscle with complete trust that he'll do it all for me.

After finishing second in the Topham, Jimmy keeps him busy for the summer but it's nothing too strenuous. He takes his chance in the Galway Plate and finishes sixth, but it's at the Kerry National in September that he really comes to life. He's carrying a bucket of weight, 11st 9lb, but when he jumps to the front at the second last, there's no catching him. After that performance, he is laid out with the Grand National in mind. He has one last run in the Munster National a few weeks later and finishes third; then he's given six months off. When he comes back in March, Cheltenham isn't even on the horizon. Jimmy gives him a couple of runs over hurdles to get him sharp and then he's tucked up and put away for the big day.

Mike rings me in February to ask if I'll ride him in the Grand National. He knows that I'll have a few to choose between and that loyalty to a horse can only count for so much. Even though I've been riding Monty for most of the last three years, I'll have to pick the one that I think has the best chance. Before I commit to anything, I check to see what JP McManus has planned for Youlneverwalkalone. But when I chat to Frank Berry, it seems the Grand National is not in the plans, and that makes my mind up for me. I ring Mike and tell him to book me in for Monty, which is fine until I win on Youlneverwalkalone at Cheltenham and it's decided that he is going to the National after all. I don't want to do anything that might damage my relationship with JP and Frank, but I've already committed and I have to stick with it. I'm riding Monty.

And then, as fate would have it, I nearly don't. A horse can be wrapped up in cotton wool until just before the off, but a jockey can't. I have two other rides booked for Grand National day and an hour and a half before the biggest race of my life, Rathgar Beau crashes out at the fourth last. It's a heavy fall, but once I sit up I know there's no major damage done and that I'll be okay to ride on. It's a bust lip and nothing worse, thankfully. The blood is still there on my teeth when I give my interviews after the National.

The unpredictability of the race is as compelling as its history. Not every year turns into chaos and leaves the door wide open for a Foinavon to come and win it at 100/1, but the thrill of the Grand National is in negotiating, surviving and completing. You have to ride your horse like it's having its first run over fences; every one of them is a challenge. The race changes and evolves over the years. The fences are softer, more forgiving, and the drops are shallower, but there's more pace and more traffic, which brings a different set of problems to solve. So the golden rule stays the same: if you get round, you've had a good ride. Anything else is a bonus.

Every dip and turn in the four and a half miles is etched into your mind. Every fence has its spots, where you ideally want to be and, more important, where you don't want to be. You know which will forgive a slight mistake and which won't think twice about punishing you. They nearly have personalities of their own.

If I needed a reminder that there's no guarantee of getting round, I get it in my second National, 2001, when Hanakham gallops into the second fence and turns straight over. A year later, Alexander Banquet makes a mistake the first time we jump Becher's and he dumps me out the back door.

When I come out to the parade ring for my pre-race instructions on Monty's Pass, Jimmy Mangan is dealing with a 23-year-old jockey whose record in the race is sixth–fell–unseated. It's Jimmy's first ever runner in the National, but he knows he has to manage the jockey as well as the horse.

'I was talking to Paddy Kiely', Jimmy says, 'and the only thing Paddy said was don't be asking any questions.'

Whether the instructions are for my benefit or for the horse's, I don't know, but they're crystal clear. Paddy Kiely is no stranger to Aintree and if a jockey of his standing and experience is giving me advice, they're words to heed. But that's how I ride races – if I see a big one that I think we can go for, I'll ask the horse to go. If I were naturally risk-averse, I'd weigh it up and look at how it costs you a race when it goes wrong. The thing is, it will win you one too, and that's what catches my eye.

As the years pass, I learn to choose my moments and to know when to pull back; put it down to maturity, maybe. But this is the Grand National, and I'm getting a good ride, and my blood is up. Coming towards the end of our first circuit, I see this lovely stride at the second ditch – juicy, just tempting you to have a go. We've still three more to jump on this circuit, and another full circuit to go, so I can't even claim that it's tactical; there's no race being won with a jump here. But all my instincts override Paddy's wisdom. I give Monty a squeeze to go for it.

When I ask, I'm expecting take-off. He can't tell me that he doesn't fancy the long one, that it's a bad idea – did nobody say that to you? – and that he's going to stick in a short stride just before to give himself a better chance to get up and get over it. He just does it, and the first you know about it is when it happens. He gets in close to the board of the ditch and jumps it perfectly. As we land at the back, I remember what Jimmy said. Right, I tell myself, this horse knows more about this than I do. No more questions. No more big ones. I give him a squeeze as he's going to a couple on a nice forward stride, just to let him know that he's good to go, but other than that, I don't move a muscle. Lesson learned.

We come down past the stands, jump The Chair and the water jump, and head out on our final circuit. We're sitting third and everything is going much easier than I expected. It's too soon to get excited. There's a long way to go and I need him to conserve as much energy as possible. He's jumping really well and travelling really well and the danger is that he'll start to enjoy it too much, that he'll try to jump out to the front. If he goes, the horses in front will probably go too, and then they'll take each other on and burn themselves out. Monty's not an out-and-out stayer. I got my proof of that in the Galway Plate last summer when he couldn't shift gears at the end. That race is nearly a mile and three quarters shorter than the National; if we don't keep a bit in the tank for a final push, we've no chance.

Barry Fenton hits the front on Gunner Welburn. When he ups the pace, tries to stretch it out a bit, I do just enough to keep him within reach but nothing more. On the run down to the third last, I start to take stock. You couldn't script a better run to this point. Monty is relaxed and jumping for fun, he hasn't made a mistake and we're still sitting on what feels like a full tank. We're going as easy as you ever could be. I'm on the verge of winning the biggest race in the world, and I could hear a pin drop. I've been waiting for this moment. It feels like I should be sussing out my rivals, plotting my way to the finish, but it's much, much easier than that. I can sit and savour it because this might never happen again. We've done the hard work. All I have to do is do nothing.

We jump past Gunner Welburn at the second last, and then pop the last. Whatever it is I decide to do, it feels like I have all the time in the world to do it. I don't want to kick for home or start driving him to the finish. We don't need that. I just want to let him extend, use the full length of his stride, without going into top gear. We're five, six lengths clear and that will be more than enough to beat these tired horses. We pass the elbow, and halfway up the run-in I raise my right hand and start to salute the crowd. I do it, but I know it's too premature for celebrations, and put it away again. I savour those final few seconds and when Monty passes the winning post, the celebrations start again and this time there's no stopping. I'll be celebrating this one for the rest of my days.

I've watched this moment so many times, but now it's me in the centre of it. Andrew Duff and Donie Fahy, two local lads from back home, are the first two people I see. We're led back into the old winners' enclosure, living, breathing racing history. The BBC want interviews. Sue Barker has Jimmy, and he's promising renditions of 'The Banks of My Own Lovely Lee' until the sun comes up in the morning. Sue asks me how it feels and I try to find the words to tell her how easy Monty made it. He's a cat. A bird. A stag.

Clare Balding grabs me for another quick word when I'm back in the weighroom watching the replay. I forget that we're live on TV when I tell her about how I gave him a kick for a long one at the second ditch. 'He stuck in a short one and I just said to myself, you fucking eejit.' The words are out of my mouth and in millions of living rooms around the world before I even know I've said them.

There's a press conference, and a photo shoot, and a party, and somewhere in the middle of all the madness I go to weigh in to make sure that the result is official: Monty's Pass, trained by Jimmy Mangan and ridden by Barry Geraghty, is the winner of the 2003 Grand National.

I want to savour every second because you might have spent your entire life waiting for this moment, but once it happens it's gone in a flash and you only get one chance to enjoy it. Tonight will turn into tomorrow morning, and life goes on again as normal – I've a ride in the first at Tramore at 2.30 p.m. – and while we're celebrating, everyone else is loading up and leaving and heading for the boat and the airport and home.

We take the party into the city centre: my family, Noel Meade, Paul Carberry. Mike Futter is there too. Buying a horse with a heart murmur and sending it out to win the Grand National is one hell of a gamble, but one gamble wasn't enough for Mike on this occasion; he has taken the bookies to the cleaners as well. He started backing Monty's Pass at 66/1 before the weights for the race were even published. As Monty's price started to tumble – 50/1, 40/1, 33/1, 25/1, 20/1, all the way down to his starting price of 16/1 – Mike kept backing him. He's been tipping it up in his bingo halls up and down the country. He's after taking about £800,000 from the bookies, as well as his share of the £350,000 prize for winning the race.

The night's over before we know it, the best kind of blur, but we've to do it all again the next day in Conna. We fly home on Sunday morning. My brother Ross has a couple of rides in Tramore as well, so he drives me down. I give my first horse a shocker of a ride and get beaten by a neck, I get a fall off my last horse, and the one in between isn't much more successful. We go to Portlaw to see Shay Barry for a drink – we meet him for one and stay for the others – until we realise that Conna's not around the corner and we better get going before it's too late.

This little village in east Cork is bursting when we get there. They've been waiting all day. The party in Liverpool went on a bit the night before and by the time Monty's horse box got down to the port, the 3 a.m. ferry crossing had already set sail. No harm, the 9 a.m. was just as good, and then it was off to the Curragh to parade the hero in front of the stands and then, finally, the road home.

Jimmy is Conna born and bred and his success is everyone's; in a few months' time, they'll have signs up when you enter the village: Welcome to Conna, home of Monty's Pass. For tonight, the pubs are packed. There isn't a seat free in the Winners'

Enclosure on one side of the road or in the Fisherman's Rest on the other, but that doesn't matter because the party is spilling out into the middle between them. It's parents and children, old people and young, and no matter what age, everyone knows that this day, in this place, might never come again.

11

t all happens so quickly. Life takes off, and not even my wildest dreams can keep pace with it.

I'm the 23-year-old who has just strolled into the biggest week of the National Hunt season with a smile on his face, and strolled back out with five winners, a shrug of the shoulders, and the same cheeky grin. Great jockeys have come and gone and never enjoyed a week like that. To go and win the Grand National a few weeks later takes it out of this world and into the realm of pure fantasy. I'm nominated for the RTÉ Sports Personality of the Year Award at the end of the year, and I'm up against some of the giants of Irish sport – Mick O'Dwyer, Peter Canavan, DJ Carey, Roy Keane – in a public vote. I win that too – no jockey has ever won it before. By the time I collect my prize in the Burlington Hotel, I'm already well on my way to being crowned Champion Jockey again for the 2003/2004 season.

The good horses, the big days, they all come so easily. I take it for granted, think that this is the way that it will always be for me. I'm spoiled by the success. The confidence and self-assuredness that has served me so well veers towards arrogance. The sensitive child of my early years is scrubbed, replaced by what I think it means to be a winner: self-centred and driven. There's a hardness that spills over from racing into life: when the gap opens up, you have to take it. If someone challenges me or rubs me up the wrong way, I speak without thinking and don't hold back. It's not particularly likeable but that's who I've become. I'm not worried about what people think of me. I just do what I need to do.

I'm walking on water. As long as I keep winning, I feel I can say anything, do anything, and there won't be any consequences. It's the same when I'm drinking.

There's a part of me that's wired for speed. There's a constant 'Go' in me, no matter what I'm doing. Everything is done at 100 miles an hour. Driving cars fast. Skiing black slopes. Riding good horses over big fences. And I'm always in control. Until I'm not.

I race to the races. Race back from the races. Race to the pub. Race until the night ends, whenever that is. Everything about the build-up to a race is so calm and then as soon as the flag falls, the adrenaline surges. It doesn't always stop at the finish line. I don't want it to. I want to bring that same buzz with me, so the rest of my life carries on at the same pace – off the horse, into the weighroom, shower, change, out to the car, off to the party, and before I know it, I've two drinks in me and a third in my hand. Crash, burn, bed. Repeat.

It's part of the lifestyle, and I embrace it. Drinking stories are a badge of honour and the sauna is the confession box. The smell of stale alcohol hits you before the heat does. The conversation is often about the craic that was had the night before, who was still standing when everyone else wilted and faded, who made it home under their own steam and who had to be carried out the door. As a teenager in Tralee, Listowel, Galway, I was mesmerised as the very same lads who were spinning the most outrageous stories headed out the door to ride their next winner. That's the culture that I grew up in, and now I'm slow to give it up.

I can go out and fill up and it never causes any problems with my weight. I go to the pub with Jason Maguire, knowing that I have to do 9st 10lb the following day, and the pair of us sit there and drink Bacardi and Diet Coke all night long. Jason adds a couple of pounds over the course of the evening but I wake up the following morning five pounds lighter. I don't even have to go to the sauna to do my 9st 10lb. The weight just falls off me.

If there's any saving grace, it's that I can't drink as much as I think I can. Instead of having a small glass or two of wine and going quietly, I try hard and floor myself easily. The only upside is that I usually end up at home in bed early, and because I'm home early, I save myself from myself and wake up reasonably okay the following morning. And if it's not affecting me or getting me in trouble when I get up to go racing the following day, I don't see the problem.

There was the morning when I opened my eyes in the back seat of the car, still parked in the car park of the Royal College of Surgeons in Dublin; there weren't any closer alternatives when I stumbled out of Lillie's Bordello nightclub at who knows what time. One look at the clock was enough to snap me fully awake. It was twenty to twelve and I needed to be in Ballinrobe to ride at a quarter past three – the other side of the country, the bones of a three and a half-hour drive away.

Before I knew what I was up to, I was on the road and on the way. I drove for about an hour until I came to a filling station on the far side of Mullingar. I pulled in, filled the car and went inside to pay. I picked up a bottle of 7-Up and some crisps for my breakfast, and when I got to the till, the woman at the desk handed me a packet of chewing gum.

'You might want this as well,' she told me.

I made it to Ballinrobe in time and Gerry Keane met me at the scales to weigh me out. I've known Gerry since I was knee high and it was one of his horses, Victor Boy, that I was riding. All Gerry could do was laugh at the cut of me as I handed him the saddle. He didn't say anything. He didn't need to. I had a nice little cruise around on Victor Boy, singing Robbie Williams's

'Rock DJ' to myself as we floated around and enjoyed ourselves. With two to jump, I let him go and Victor Boy took care of the rest for me.

Then there was the Christmas festival at Leopardstown in 2000. We got two days of racing before the snow came and everything was called off for a few days. Right around the time that I should have been going down to the start on Moscow Flyer and sizing up Istabraq, I was in Dublin city centre instead, drink in hand in Bruxelles pub. If you were looking for a jockey, this was where you'd find them. The entire weighroom was there, ready to go since the moment the doors opened. Before long, we were looking out the window singing 'Let It Snow, Let It Snow, Let It Snow'.

The snow kept falling and we kept drinking. My brother Norman was with me and the two of us stayed in Dublin for the night. The next morning, word came through that racing had been called off again, and the two of us got in the car and started to make our way home. We got as far as the pub in Dunshaughlin before we pulled in for a pint, which turned into another day of them. By around eight o'clock in the evening, the day was starting to take its toll on me and the only thing for it was to go for a bit of a kip. I told Norman that I'd be back in a few minutes and I went out to the car park, climbed into the car, curled up and closed my eyes.

I was only asleep for about 20 minutes but when I woke up, I was ready to go again. As I was peeling myself out of the car and heading back inside, there was a flash of headlights and a Jeep swung into the car park in front of me. It was Dad and he wasn't coming to join us for a pint.

'Do you not realise there's racing tomorrow? What are you playing at? Get in the car now.'

I couldn't understand how Leopardstown had passed an inspection – there was still four or five inches of snow on the ground in Dunshaughlin, which is only 40 minutes away – but I was in no fit state to argue. He loaded me up, drove me home, and sent me off to bed. I woke up the following morning with a bit of a head but not much worse. Moscow Flyer's race against Istabraq had been rescheduled as the first race on the card, going to post at twenty past twelve, so I needed to get going. Mam and Dad drove me back down to the pub in Dunshaughlin so that I could pick up my car from the car park.

'Your mother is going to drive you,' Dad told me.

Quick as a whip, I had the smart answer on the tip of my tongue.

'Is she going to ride the horse for me as well?'

I won that argument and drove myself to the course. There wasn't a mark on me from the last two days as Istabraq fell and Moscow won the first race, and then I hosed up to win the second race by 12 lengths. I went up for the presentations with a quick double already under my belt, I headed for the sauna. I was booked to ride for Noel Meade in a handicap hurdle later on the card, and I was supposed to do 10st 8lb, not my natural riding weight after two days solid on the beer. I had tried to sweat it off earlier, but I was already so dehydrated that there wasn't a bead coming out of me. It just wasn't going to happen. There was only one thing for it. When I got off my next ride, I reported myself lame. I'd broken a metatarsal in the run-up to Christmas and I used that as my excuse to get myself stood down for the rest of the day. And because I'd won the first two races, nobody ever said a word.

I showed up 20 minutes late to school Moscow the week before the Arkle, not because of poor timekeeping but because I didn't know what time to cut my losses the night before. I bounced into my biggest days and got away with murder. Maybe if I'd had a proper dinner instead of a starter in a Chinese restaurant and a couple of glasses of wine, I'd remember going to bed the night before I won the Grand National, but I don't.

No matter how far I push it, I keep getting away with it. I go down to Shay Barry's in Waterford on New Year's Eve to ring in 2004. When we go racing in Tramore the next day, Shay wins the first. I win the third. Shay wins the fourth. I win the fifth. And Shay wins the sixth. By the time we're done, we've won five of the seven races on the card between us, which is probably more wins than we've had hours of sleep.

I never stop to consider if it might be a good idea to slow down a bit. It's not affecting how I'm riding and that's all that really matters. If I get up after a late one and ride a winner the next day, it's twice as good a result. You never know how close you are to trouble until it catches you. Somehow, I always manage to keep myself on just the right side of wrong.

12

AZERTYUIOP.

The letters that make up the top row on a French keyboard.

The horse that has become the pretender to our throne.

The name that seems to follow every time that Moscow is mentioned.

Azertyuiop.

The first shots are fired before we even know we're in a fight. While Moscow has been making the two-mile division his own personal playground, Azertyuiop hasn't been shy about staking his claim as the next big thing. He carves his way through an unbeaten novice season – 30 lengths, 16 lengths, 25 lengths, and then routs them all again in the Arkle for good measure. Now he's got us in his sights.

The racing public is giddy with anticipation of what might happen when we run into each other, and the date is set: 6 December 2003 in one of the great showpieces of the racing calendar, one of my favourite races, the Tingle Creek Chase at Sandown.

There are seven horses in the race but it's billed as a match between two. In my eyes, it's not even close. Nobody laid a glove on Moscow in the Champion Chase, and I'm the only one who knows how much he had left in the tank crossing the line that day, how much of a stroll in the park it was for him. Azertyuiop is a very good horse. But superstars are few and far between and they stand alone.

Familiar faces, new kids on the block – Moscow puts them all to the sword and wins the Tingle Creek by four lengths with Azertyuiop chasing home in second. But I know today is not the day when our rivalry will be settled. That day will come, though. We'll meet again.

Even as it's still being written, as we're living it, their rivalry feels like a classic one. It's easy to appreciate, respect, admire both but when it all comes down to it, there can only be one champion and you have to pick a side.

On St Patrick's Day in Cheltenham, with Moscow's Champion Chase crown on the line, there's no need to ask which side the Irish are on.

Azertyuiop has won plenty of admirers, even if his first senior campaign hasn't fully gone to plan. He didn't manage to jump a single fence in his first race of the season, unseating Mick Fitzgerald at the first in Exeter, and then couldn't trouble Moscow in the Tingle Creek. He just came up short in the Victor Chandler Chase in Ascot, only losing by a neck despite the fact that he was carrying 19lb more than the winner, Isio. But on the basis of his most recent run, a walk in the park when winning the Game Spirit Chase, he's ready for his rematch.

His age is waved in front of us like a trump card. He's the young horse, seven years old, open to all sorts of improvement; at 10 years old, Moscow is coming into his prime, or at it, or past it already – nobody is quite sure. All I know is that he's showing no signs of slowing down. When I got to the front in the Tingle Creek, I had the luxury of taking a pull and slowing things down. I didn't mind if we had company on the run to the finish; I had total faith in Moscow. Most people drew a line through that race afterwards, dismissed it out of hand. Straight away, Paul Nicholls came out and said Azertyuiop wasn't fit. That's fine, but you don't need excuses for a great horse. Great horses overcome a lack of fitness or running a bit keen or a lack of pace in the race. They win on unsuitable ground, they win on unsuitable tracks, and that's what sets them apart – the good and the great.

Azertyuiop is the one with the point to prove, we're the one with the title to defend, and as the roar goes up and we jump off in the 2004 Champion Chase, the betting reflects that – Moscow is the 5/6 favourite and Azertyuiop's at 15/8. We settle in to our usual spot, towards the rear with maybe two horses behind us, but Moscow takes me by surprise with the way he goes for the first couple of fences. He hasn't run since winning at Leopardstown at Christmas; he wasn't fully right early in the new year and, wisely, Jessie didn't take any risks. The bit of extra time off doesn't bother us for a minute. But now he's mad fresh and flying up over his fences like a horse who has been waiting to get back out and racing for the last three months.

We run down to the third, the noise of the crowd in our ears as they send us out away from the stand, and Moscow puts in a big, showy look-at-me of a jump. It's a little bit longer than I'm expecting, but he's enjoying himself and eager to get on with it, and there's no harm done. Ruby and Azertyuiop are tucked up on the inside of us on the rail and, heading away from the stands, we jump the next together, two good jumps side by side in fifth and sixth place.

Ask half a dozen jockeys at what point they're able to see a stride as they come down to jump a fence and you'll likely get half a dozen answers. Everyone's slightly different, everyone has their own feel for what works. I usually start to lock on when we're about a half a dozen strides away, but my theory is that a jockey only truly sees the stride when the horse sees it himself. You have to wait for him to look and start measuring with you. In a two-mile championship race, like the Champion Chase, you need your horse to be concentrating. Whether it's a short stride or a long stride, you need him to be measured. You need him to be accurate. Anything less is a recipe for disaster.

Coming down to the first in the back straight, I can tell that Moscow is not tuned in at all. He's looking left and he's looking right and he's looking anywhere except for the fence that we're about to run straight through if he's not careful. Not for diamonds can I get him to concentrate, to take a look. I take him back to look for a stride, but he's totally zoned out. He gallops in and hits the fence and gallops away on the other side. Only good luck saves him from himself, and still, he's completely unfussed.

He survives the four in the back straight and as we get over each one, I wait for him to snap out of it and get into a nice calculated rhythm before our luck runs out. And each time, I get nothing from him. Ruby and Azertyuiop get a nice jump at the last in the back straight and lengthen out for a few strides. It's a confident move, a warning shot that we're going to have a battle on our hands if we want to leave here as champions again. They move up on the inside and take charge of the race as we come down to the fourth last. The ditch.

Moscow knows what's coming next. He was long at the ditch when he won the Arkle. He was long at it again last year when he won the Champion Chase. And now we're coming down on the same stride again, virtually three abreast with Tiutchev like a guardrail between ourselves and Azertyuiop. I sit and wait for Moscow to take a look at the fence. Four strides out, I'm sitting and he's not looking. It's not a good idea to play poker with a horse. Three strides out, I give him a squeeze. Please take a look before we get in too close. He doesn't respond. One stride out, I make the decision for both of us and give him another squeeze in the hope that, even if he doesn't see the fence, he'll switch into autopilot and take off over it.

It's the sound of him hitting the fence that frightens me the most. A wallop that would make you instantly fear the worst. I barely feel my own fall. No sooner than I've hit the ground, I'm on my knees, looking back towards the spot where he's lying, terrified of what I'm about to find. But when I look, he's not there. I check in the other direction, down the track to where the battle to take our crown is unfolding and I see him, right there in the thick of it, happily galloping away without me. I can't understand how he's on his feet, how he never fell. He stepped at the ditch and completely lost his balance. He got his front legs out from under himself quickly enough to keep himself upright, but with the position he was in and the way he landed, his head hit the ground at the same time as his hooves. That he's up and running free is nothing short of a miracle. It's the only result that really matters.

While I pick myself up and walk back towards the weighroom, Ruby and Azertyuiop win the Champion Chase. I'm angry and I'm upset but, more than anything, I'm relieved that Moscow is okay.

∩

I wind the video back and watch it again. Watch him gallop into every second fence. A 10-year-old running like a novice. Not an ounce of self-preservation. That's how little he cares. That's how little he's concentrating.

I'm trying to figure out the pattern that's developing with him: 17 runs over fences and he's won 12 of them, never been beaten when he's stayed on his feet. It's not my doing – or maybe it's partly my doing. There's a shared responsibility there. I know going out that he's prone to taking a risk and I'm being a bit casual by allowing him to go for it. He has to be a bit more clever with his jumping, and I have to be a bit more clever about helping him. I have to make the right decisions. But it all happens in a split second and Moscow's indecision, or whatever it is, makes my decision harder. It leaves me in a tricky spot. It reminds me of something Norman Williamson said to me back when I was starting out and he saw me beating myself up over a mistake at the second last: 'It felt like the right thing to do', he said, 'and you have to go with what you feel.'

I watch the video to try to put it to bed in my own mind, but nobody is looking to point the finger of blame. 'That silly old fool,' Jessie said when we came back after the fall, and that was it. It's the same with Brian Kearney and his wife, Patricia; if anyone has the right to ask the question, it's the owner, but they don't. Jessie's husband Johnny, Eamonn Leigh – everyone involved with Moscow is on the same page. All it takes is one person to start framing the conversation in a different light and the weight of pressure becomes an avalanche. I'm so grateful that nobody ever does.

The silly old fool shakes it off. He's none the worse for his fall and goes to Aintree two weeks later, winning easily, before finishing the season with a win at Punchestown, two more clear rounds, two more Grade 1s to add to the collection. He's up against a lot of the usual suspects – Flagship Uberalles, Native Upmanship, Cenkos – but there's no Azertyuiop. It's one win apiece and we'll have to wait until Sandown in December, the 2004 Tingle Creek, to make it best out of three.

In any of the meetings between Moscow and Azertyuiop, I never have any doubt that I'm on the best horse. If others want to dismiss Moscow as an old man or a dodgy jumper, that's their opinion. It doesn't carry any weight with us, but that doesn't mean that we don't hear it. The people who shout loudest are generally the least qualified to comment. They're people who like to be heard. For Moscow's sake and nothing else, I want to see him silence the doubters. Put them back in their box. Show them that they shouldn't have come out of their box in the first place.

In the days leading up to the Tingle Creek, I already have the race ridden. It plays out in my mind in crystal-clear definition, exactly where I'll want to be at every point, where the others will be and the moves I'll want to make. I've never heard of visualisation, but that's precisely what it is. I tell Jessie the plan: I'll move to the front on the run down to the third last and then take a long, deliberate look around to call Azertyuiop and the others on. Catch me if you can.

For the first time in two years, Moscow is not the favourite. He's the underdog. Well Chief, last season's Arkle winner, lines up to take his chance as well, another rising star with us in his crosshairs. He's only five, half Moscow's age – how good could he be? Strip away the hype and the anticipation and all that's left are the bare facts: this is the biggest test of Moscow's career, no doubt about it. But I've seen this one on the big screen in my mind. I know how it ends.

Cenkos takes off in front to make the running and I tuck Moscow in behind, with Ruby and Azertyuiop sitting in our slipstream. That's how it stays, 1-2-3 in that order, as we jump the first few in the back straight and come down to the railway fences, three of them in quick succession. Bam. Bam. Bam.

Cenkos chugs along but we're all over him, with Azertyuiop stalking away in the background. I'm ready to take it up and start to call the shots but we don't need to rush or make any sacrifices.

Cenkos is jumping left, so that rules out any move down that side. I'm happy to sit and take a lead and wait for my window. He leaves us a gap at the last of the railway fences, jumping out left again, and we jump up his inside and into the lead.

For as long as we're at the front, we're in control. It's one of the oldest tactics in the book, setting the pace from the front. We're the ones dictating the rules of engagement. I slow the pace right down, take all the sting out of it. Because I know I'm on the best horse, I switch my attention to two things: risk management, and what we can do to inconvenience our rivals in the race. Azertyuiop is a keen going horse. He wants to get on with it. He has a good cruising speed but not the acceleration to beat us in a foot race to the finish. So I stack them up. Slow them down. This is exactly what I've been planning. There's five lengths covering me at the front and Timmy Murphy on Well Chief in fourth and that's perfect. I don't want a big lead. I want them to bunch up behind me. I want them to chase me.

I lead them down to third last, the pond fence, and take a long look back, longer than I need, to see who's where and what they've got. Wherever Jessie is watching from in the stands, she's expecting this. I want them to think that I'm sizing them up. I want them to think that I'm weighing up my options, what I've left in the tank and playing it off against what they've got. I can already answer those questions without a look. None of them can catch me today. I'm willing to bet on it.

Come on, come with me. The last thing I want is to be out in front alone. That's when Moscow's the biggest danger to himself, when he's got nothing on his tail to keep him focused. That's when he's likely to stick a foot straight in the middle of a fence. Azertyuiop sits on our tail, full of running, but Ruby doesn't move a muscle. Not yet.

Moscow is gunning for the third last but he gets in a bit tight. We land over it still a length clear and I look around again, daring Ruby and Timmy to come and have a go. As soon as I take that second look, Ruby comes for us, and Timmy has no choice but to go too. Game on.

Moscow pricks his ears coming down to the second last. He's ready for a race, ready to show them who's boss. We jump it a length ahead of the others and Moscow starts to extend into big, long strides, upping the pressure. Azertyuiop and Well Chief hammer away behind us, but the gap is not getting any smaller. I give Moscow a couple of smacks – one, two, three – coming down to the last, just to make sure he's paying attention.

Nobody wants to come out on the wrong side of a classic, to see it replayed time and again over the years, and every time you're reminded about what might have been.

Moscow pops the last. A clear round. There's no horse in the world that could stop him today. Moscow two, Azertyuiop one. This time, it's decisive.

13

'm lying flat on my back, looking up at the sky above Punchestown, and I'm stuck to the ground. I try to clench my hands, to grab the grass beside me so that I can pull myself upright into a sitting position. For a split second, I'm terrified. I can't move, although I still have feeling in my arms and legs, which is reassuring. I've been left shaken by plenty of falls before but I've never got a fright like this. My first thought is to fear the worst: have I just done some serious damage here?

I'm supposed to be picking Paula up to go for dinner in a few hours' time. Paula is brilliant and beautiful and from the moment I first met her, I've been trying to impress her. We're still very much in the early days of our relationship, though, and a phone call telling her that I've been taken to hospital with a suspected broken neck doesn't seem likely to help my case. Paula's family aren't a racing family but they're from Ballylongford, a little village not far from Listowel in Kerry, which is real racing country. By the time the ambulance crew stabilise me and move me onto the spinal board so that they can take me to Naas Hospital, I've come to my senses a bit. When I'm reunited with my phone, I send Ross a text and ask him to get in touch with Paula: tell her I've had a fall and I'll give her a call later.

But Paula has already heard the news by the time Ross calls. She had an exam earlier that day and when she was driving home from college afterwards, listening to the radio, the sports news came on the radio:

'In horse racing, jockey Barry Geraghty has been taken to hospital to have an X-ray on his neck following a fall at Punchestown earlier today …'

While Paula is sitting in the car wondering what kind of madness she's getting herself into, the doctors in Naas are X-raying me and strapping me into a neck brace. It's nothing more serious than a cracked vertebra, which, given my initial concerns, feels like a very lucky escape. I'm discharged the same evening and when I check the clock, I realise I can still make it out to Clonee, where Paula is living, in time to pick her up for our date at eight o'clock. I do my best to clean myself up but I'm pretty sure I still look like a man who has just broken his neck in a racing fall. The neck brace they've put me into is one of the stiff ones, and it's too big for me as well, which is torture; but I'm a man on a mission. When Paula opens the door, I can tell that she's not expecting to see me. I'm ready to go out for dinner as planned, but thankfully – and not for the last time in our relationship – Paula convinces me to see sense. We stay in and get a takeaway instead as a compromise.

I fall for Paula quickly. She's smart and she's fun and she's the kindest, most compassionate person I know. She's moved to Dublin to study naturopathy, and when she brings me down to Kerry to meet her family I'm made to feel welcome immediately. Kerry football and traditional Irish music are the two big passions in the Heaphy house. It becomes a home away from home for me, the first place I want to go whenever I have a bit of time off from racing, even if it's only for a couple of days. Coming home from Kerry always feels like we've been on our holidays. Paula opens me up to life outside racing and, as I introduce her to my world and show her that it's not all ambulances and neck braces, she helps me to find some much-needed balance and stability in my life. The two of us are opposites in a lot of ways; but luckily, opposites attract.

You can tell when a horse is built to be a three-mile chaser. They have that blend of strength and speed and stamina in perfect harmony. The best ones live on for ever: Golden Miller, Arkle, Mill House, Dawn Run, Desert Orchid, Best Mate.

Kicking King is a big solid horse, close to 17 hands high, and he's built like a tank. From the first moment I sit up on him, it feels like three miles over fences is where he'll really shine, and if that's the case, there's a lot to be excited about. He has the speed and the class to hang tough with the best two-mile novice hurdlers, staying on to finish second behind Back In Front in the 2003 Supreme Novices' Hurdle. When he starts out over fences, he learns his lessons quickly. He falls on his second run, charging to the second last in Leopardstown on a long stride – come back to me, come here – and just gallops straight into it and turns over. He won't make the same mistake twice, won't disrespect his fences again; it's nearly five years before he has another fall. By the end of the season, he has improved into one of the best two-mile novice chasers; finishing second in the 2004 Arkle, chasing Well Chief to the line, rubber-stamps his reputation.

It's hard to keep a lid on his potential. Tom Taaffe, his owner Conor Clarkson, we're all thinking the same thing: if he's been this good as a two-mile hurdler, and this good as a two-mile chaser, how good is he going to be when we step him up to the trip where we think he'll be at his best? The Taaffe family and the Cheltenham Gold Cup are no strangers. Tom's dad, Pat, won three in a row on Arkle and a fourth on Fort Leney in the 1960s, and then trained Captain Christy to win another in the 1970s. If that pedigree is passed down in the Taaffe blood,

Withdrawn from Stock
Dublin City Public Libraries

maybe the hope of another contender isn't as much of a fantasy as it seems.

Kicking King goes to Gowran Park in October 2004 for the two and a half-mile Champion Chase and announces himself as a force to be reckoned with, but when we go for the JN Wine Chase in Down Royal a few weeks later, his first time out over three miles, he's beaten by Beef Or Salmon. Tos, Tom's uncle, sticks a pin in our balloon. 'That horse doesn't stay,' he tells us.

Tos's opinion carries plenty of weight – he was Champion Jockey twice in his time, as well as a very respected trainer. When we drop Kicking King back to two and a half for the John Durkan in Punchestown at the start of December, he eviscerates a very good field. But both Tom and myself are adamant that Tos has got this one wrong. Kicking King is a three-miler, he'll stay every inch of it; we're sure of that. There's one sure-fire way to find out, and that's what Tom decides to do: he enters him in the King George VI Chase.

The little bit of Christmas dinner I was allowed is long forgotten by the time I arrive in Kempton on the morning of St Stephen's Day. I sit down at my peg in the weighroom, open my copy of the *Racing Post*, and start to mark it up. It's something I learned from Tom after he gave me the mother and father of all bollockings one day.

'Is there much pace in the race?' he asked me as I got weighed out for whatever I was riding for him.

'I don't know really,' I said, which wasn't the answer he was looking for.

Tom is meticulous in his preparation, one of the most thorough analysts there is, and he peeled me right there and then in the weighroom. I'm sure there was a less public way to get the message across, but from that day on, I always know which horses will be setting the pace whenever I'm asked. I take the pen and mark it all up in the paper – which horses will make the running, which I want to keep tabs on as we're going round, what way the favourite is likely to run – in case an owner or trainer asks and, more important, to know for myself. If I didn't physically mark it, I'd never remember it, but now all I need to do is throw my eye over it quickly before leaving for the parade ring. The routine stays the same, whether I'm on the favourite for the King George or riding an outsider in a nothing race. If I went out without doing it now, I'd be like a lad going out naked.

Kempton is a quick, sharp track, which suits Kicking King perfectly. A horse with a high cruising speed will really be able to stretch his rivals, and there's one in particular that myself and Tom are wary of – Azertyuiop. It has only been three weeks since he lost in the Tingle Creek against Moscow, but Paul Nicholls and his owner John Hales want to step him up to three miles for the first time and see if he improves for the longer trip.

We run a race that we know will give us the best chance of beating him and hope that it will also be enough to take care of the other 11 runners in the field. We go a good gallop and, as we come down the back straight to the fourth last, I up the tempo again with Azertyuiop following a few lengths behind us in second. It's way too early to be kicking for home, but this is the plan. I want to seal the deal for Azertyuiop now, make sure that he doesn't have anything left for a fight to the finish.

We turn into the straight and Kicking King wings the third last. Wings the second last. Going down to the last, we're ten lengths clear of Azertyuiop. He can't make any ground on us. The plan has worked. I sit to take Kicking King back to jump the last, but he's just gone numb. His head is sticking out and when I try to take a little contact to get him to pick it up, there's no reply. He's legless, out on his feet after going for it so early. He just keeps galloping at the fence and dives at it.

Nine times out of ten, this would be my Barton Bank moment, a disaster at the last with the King George wrapped up and only missing the ribbon on top. He sprawls on landing and the only thing that saves me, the sliver of luck that averts complete catastrophe, is that he stays in a straight line as he gets his back end under him and stays on his feet. I drop a hand on each side of his neck to keep him between my legs as I'm thrown forward, and then wrap my arms around him, hug him, to stay on. It's all instinct. As he rights himself and gallops on, I'm still in the saddle.

I drive him to the line before Azertyuiop or Kingscliff, the only two horses still in the same parish as us, can chase us down. Out of the corner of my left eye, I see a red flash. Santa Claus, or someone who dresses very like him, darts out and runs across the track in front of us. I have my head down and he's already gone by the time I even register him. Kingscliff is finishing the strongest of the three of us but he's still two and a half lengths down as we cross the line. We had to step out of our comfort zone to make sure Azertyuiop was beaten, but we overdid it and very nearly paid the price. We know that we've got out of jail.

It's still nearly three months away but the Gold Cup speculation begins the moment we cross the line. Some bookies have Kicking King as short as 6/1 to win it. Best Mate, the darling of the British horseracing public, the three-time Gold Cup winner bidding for a fourth, is a pretty imposing obstacle in our way, but nobody can tell us that we're not entitled to take our chance. Whatever else is up against us on the day, he's hands down the best horse I've had going in to a Gold Cup, a worthy challenger, which is why Tom's phone call comes as such a blow.

A little over two weeks out from the race, I'm in Dubai with Paula for a short break when I get a message from Tom asking if I can give him a call. When I hear what he wants to tell me, I feel like I've just been punched in the stomach, all the wind gone out of me.

'You won't believe this,' I tell Paula. 'Kicking King's out of the Gold Cup.'

He hadn't worked well that morning, Tom explained, and when the vets checked him out afterwards, he had a dirty scope – an airway infection. There is no way he'll be ready in time for the Gold Cup. They're releasing a statement to declare him a non-runner. With a bit of luck, he might be fit for Punchestown and we'll get one last run before the season finishes. I can't believe it. I hang up the phone; the rest of the day is a write-off.

By the following Thursday, everything has changed again. Kicking King comes back to himself. Whether he's 100% or not, nobody can say for sure, but he's healthy enough to convince Tom that he'd be mad to leave him at home in his stable during Cheltenham week. Before Tom can make an announcement, Henrietta Knight, Best Mate's trainer, releases a statement of her own. Her horse broke a blood vessel on the gallops that morning. We're back in and the Gold Cup favourite, the three-time champion, is out.

Turns out a week is a long time in horse racing too.

Eleven-year-olds don't win Champion Chases.

Or horses don't win a Champion Chase one year, lose it the following year, and then come back again a year later and regain it.

We hear all the reasons why Moscow can't win again at Cheltenham in 2005. Fortunately for us, he was never that much of a history student.

If people knew what we know, if they could see what we see, there wouldn't even be a question. The 2004 Tingle Creek is instantly anointed an all-time classic, a heavyweight showdown that lived up to its billing. The official winning distance we beat Azertyuiop by is a length and a half, and yet I know that Moscow was only playing cat and mouse with them after we jumped the last fence. Just doing the bare minimum, never letting them get any closer to him but at the same time not wanting to be any further away.

His CV stands alone. After the Tingle Creek, he has run in 21 chases, finished 16 of them, and won 16 of them. He hasn't been beaten in a race he's finished in nearly four years, and never over fences. We go to Punchestown in January for the Tied Cottage Chase, his final run before going back to Cheltenham, and he makes it win number 17. The horse that chases him home, Steel Band, is not in Moscow's league. He's over four stone worse than Moscow on the official ratings, and even if Moscow is giving him an 11lb advantage on the day, he should still be beating him by a lot more than two and a half lengths. I have to give him a couple of smacks just to get that much out of him. That's how little he does.

And that sums him up: the same horse that beat Azertyuiop, the reigning champion chaser, by a length and a half only beats Steel Band by two and a half lengths. He's dossing and he doesn't care who knows it.

The frightening thing is that he might even be getting better as he gets older. His jumping in the Tingle Creek was better in 2004 than it was in 2003; he was a much better ride at ten than he was at nine. At 11 years old, he's finally copped on to himself a bit. If dogs eventually start to resemble their owners, maybe the same is true of horses and their jockeys: wouldn't show much at home, only ever do as much as we have to, and late to leave the party and get a bit of sense.

As we're leaving the parade ring to go down to the start, Eamonn grabs me by the leg:

'Don't send him at the ditch.'

And with that final instruction, we canter down to get to work. We know what we have to beat but there's no reason to fear either Azertyuiop or Well Chief. There's never been reason to fear anyone.

Kadarann, one of Paul Nicholls's other runners, takes us down to the first with Central House. Moscow settles immediately, jumping in a nice easy rhythm. He's much more relaxed this year. When we jump the third, he wants to go on after the front two, so I leave him to extend a little bit and stretch his legs. We clear the first fence in the back straight easily; his mind is on the job. Azertyuiop blinks first, makes a mistake at the water jump that knocks the wind out of his sails and costs him a couple of lengths. Moscow, on the other hand, is cruising.

We swing off the bend out of the back straight, and the ditch, our kryptonite, comes into view. It comes up on you quickly – there's only 12 strides from the elbow of the bend to the fence – and Moscow is rolling. He's on the same long stride that has given us grief every year, but this time I sit and let him do his own thing. He's fully focused and I trust him now more than ever. We're long, we're long, we're long – and only at the very last second, when he'd normally be ready for lift-off, he sticks in a short stride for safety and pops up over it. It's not his tidiest jump of the day, but we're over it with no harm done. Now we can start to race.

But it isn't much of a race. Azertyuiop has left his season in the King George. Between that and the Tingle Creek, he had two hard races in the space of three weeks, two hammerings in the space of three weeks, and although he's won at Newbury since, it's very hard for a horse to keep going to the well like that. We jump into the lead as we come over the third last and I take a quick look around to see what's behind me. Well Chief is right there in touch but Azertyuiop is a good six, seven lengths back, still trying to work his way closer after his mistake. I take another look after the second last, just to see if Timmy has made any move yet on Well Chief, and then I let Moscow go. It's a two-horse race, and Well Chief might have five years on us, but he's going to need to be a superstar if he's going to get past us up the hill.

Moscow jumps the last two lengths in front and the cheer explodes from the crowd as he touches down safely. There's a shift in tone as we draw closer to the line – 'Go on Moscow, go on Moscow' is replaced by the sound of celebration. 'Olé olé olé' rolls off the stands as Eamonn comes to meet us at the top of the walkaway and lead us back into the parade ring, to the winners' enclosure, to the number one spot, his rightful place. They love this horse. I love this horse. He's the champion again.

The wind and rain whips in on Moscow's celebrations but when Friday comes, the sun shines on the Cotswolds and the track is drying. It's Gold Cup day and with every bit of moisture that's wrung out of the ground, Kicking King becomes even harder to beat. While he's making the most improbable comeback, the others are falling all round us. Best Mate's withdrawal leaves Kingscliff, the horse who chased us home in the King George, as the presumptive favourite. But a bad piece of work rules him out too and when the bookies' boards go up, one horse stands alone at the top of the market: Kicking King, the 4/1 favourite for the 2005 Cheltenham Gold Cup.

Just a fortnight ago, the thought of sitting up on the Gold Cup favourite seemed like a delusion. The race that Golden Miller, bred by my grandfather in our back garden, won five times. The race that Tom's dad won five times as jockey and trainer. If history is waving us on to come and join them, I look the other way. For now, that's only a distraction. I block it all out, leave the epic stories of heroes and history for someone else to write, or for another time. There'll be nothing worth remembering unless I can keep a clear head and go and ride my race.

We get the run of the race earlier than some of our most obvious rivals. I settle Kicking King in the middle and leave him to jump away in his own time. Celestial Gold, the second favourite, is held up at the back after a couple of early mistakes. Paul Carberry's not having much more joy on Beef Or Salmon, really struggling to get him going. We've travelled like a dream by comparison. We jump the fence in front of the stands in sixth but we're easily in touch as we head out on the final circuit.

My biggest concern is trying to keep him covered up and settled. The way the race is unfolding, he's his own biggest danger. The last thing I need is to set him alight this far from home. I'm quiet as a church mouse on him but he's travelling so strongly that as we jump the fifth last at the top of the hill, he effectively lands in front. We've still got the best part of a mile to race, but he's ready to go. I take a pull to slow him down. It looks like a statement of pure audacity – yes, that's how easy we're going in the Gold Cup – but really, it's what I have to do. Kicking King is a speed horse. He doesn't need a stamina test. If there's any question about him, it's his ability to see out the full Gold Cup distance, not just the first three miles but then the extra two furlongs and 110 yards tacked on to the end that so often find a horse wanting. The Cheltenham hill. If he hasn't fully recovered from his infection, he could be found out late on. But the way we're going, taking a pull at the front as we gallop down the hill, he feels fighting fit to me.

Grey Abbey has led us most of the way around but he's fading as we get to the third last and we jump up outside him into the lead. It's still far too early to kick for touch. I take a look over my right shoulder to see what's coming with me. Take The Stand is there, pushed along by Tony Dobbin, and Sir Rembrandt, last year's runner-up, is going okay too. Kicking King is practically perfect at the second last but Take The Stand is still right there, jumping it side by side with us. The two of us have pulled a few lengths clear of the others but Take The Stand is hard at work and I'm only riding Kicking King with my hands and heels. He's got so much left in the tank if I need it, but I don't think I will. We roll down to the last and he jumps it as well as he's jumped any of the 21 other fences up until now. Take The Stand is over it safely too, two lengths behind us, but as soon as Kicking King's feet touch the ground, he takes off again. Two lengths become four in the blink of an eye and after that, the winning distance is all that's left to be decided.

It's the sweetest thing. Only two Irish-trained horses have won the Gold Cup in my lifetime, and now I've just ridden the third. Someone hands me a tricolour on the way back to the winners' enclosure. I raise it up and I couldn't be more proud. Now we can take our place on the honour roll; we've earned it, and there'll be a party worthy of the occasion. Everywhere I look, people are dabbing at damp eyes, wiping away tears of delight and gratitude and relief and disbelief at this horse who wasn't even supposed to be here. But here he is. Our Gold Cup winner. Long live the King.

I spot Paula as she makes her way over to me through the crowd. It means so much to have her here by my side on a day like today. In a few months' time, the two of us will have even more reason to celebrate. Our first child, our baby daughter, arrives into the world healthy and well in August 2005. Her name is Síofra.

14

aybe the tide has already started to take you out by the time you feel it turning.

I leave Cheltenham in 2005 convinced that I'm riding the two best chasers in training. The proof is there for everyone to see. Moscow's second Champion Chase doesn't feel like one last, defiant stamp of his class on the two-mile division. There's no Azertyuiop or Well Chief to reoppose when we go to Aintree, but the manner of his victory, 16 lengths pulling up, is as impressive as any of his others.

'That's the best ride I've ever got off him,' I tell Jessie when we come back in – not necessarily his best performance, but certainly the most enjoyable run I've had on him. He jumped so well that I never needed to worry; I could just go with the flow and let him do his thing. At 11 years old, it seems the penny has finally dropped with him. He had so much raw ability that he was able to win good races almost in spite of himself at times, but now he looks like a horse that's finally learned how to race. And because he's more relaxed and jumping better, he's conserving more energy. Only a freak of nature would still be improving at his age, which is why I'm so reluctant to rule it out.

I know that Moscow can't go on for ever but there's never a sign that he isn't the same horse until, all of a sudden, he isn't. He goes to Punchestown looking to make it 20 wins out of 20 completed races over fences, and we're beaten by a short head by Rathgar

Beau and Shay Barry in a photo finish, his first time finishing a race but not winning it in more than four years. It has been a long season and it's a big ask for any horse to do the Cheltenham–Aintree–Punchestown treble, particularly an Irish horse, because they have to travel to England twice in quick succession. We hope that he's in need of his summer holidays and nothing more, but when Moscow comes back the next season, he's not right at all. He loses two more races and we're clutching at straws when we go back to the Champion Chase in 2006. We hope that he might spring back to life when he gets there, that Cheltenham might bring out the best in him. He's the two-time champion and we're entitled to hope, nobody can deny us that, but hope never won a Champion Chase. He finishes fifth and Jessie decides there and then that we can ask him for no more. He has been the horse of a lifetime, for all of us, and she announces his retirement on the spot.

Every jockey needs a flagship and mine was the real deal. Moscow brought me to the top table at an early age and once we were there, we got quite used to it. Because I was winning Grade 1 races on him from the age of 20, I never had any fear factor when the time came to go out and ride the big race on the big day; in fact, I relished it.

'You're some jammy bollix,' Paul Carberry told me one day as we were going down to the start, 'steering that fella around in fifty grand races' – and he was right. It was Moscow who gave me my first Cheltenham win at the age of 22. It was Moscow who opened doors for me. I was riding freelance for three good yards, but I never had the big job anywhere. You need to build a profile, you need to stay in demand, and in the early years of my career, it was Moscow who kept my name in the headlines and my face in the sports pages.

But good horses don't last for ever.

Moscow struggles through his last season in 2005/2006. Kicking King makes it back-to-back wins in the King George but injures himself in the process; we don't know it at the time, but it will be two years before he's fit enough to get back racing again. And while my flagships are sinking, Ruby seems to be getting on every good horse in town. I can feel him getting on top of me, just easing a couple of lengths clear and establishing himself at a level above everyone else – there's Ruby, and then there's the rest of us. I can't let that happen. Finishing second in a race might not keep me awake at night, but settling for second best would.

I try to hit the ground running and put everything into winning back the Champion Jockey title in 2005/2006, but by the time we get to the Killarney Festival in the middle of July, Ruby is flying and has already opened up a nice lead at the top. He gets on everything that week in Killarney. He's on the good spare before I even know there is a spare. Ruby rides six winners for six different trainers, and the best I manage all week is a short-head second. I'm fit to burst with the frustration.

Barry Callaghan, who I owned the pub with, is in Killarney that week and he becomes my sounding board. We spend hours talking about it, massive deep discussions as the two of us try to figure out where I'm going wrong, what I can do to try to get some sort of a foothold.

Ciaran O'Toole is a brilliant agent, but he has a lot of jockeys on his books. I'm looking enviously at Ruby, who has Jennifer, his sister, as his agent. He's the only jockey she's looking after, and between them, they seem to have the whole thing sussed out and sewn up. They're talking to trainers, keeping in touch with them to let them know where Ruby is going to be riding on certain days; if a trainer has his horse entered in a few different races, he'll send it to the one where Ruby can ride it. I'm getting the runaround by comparison. There are only scraps left over for me.

This carries on long after we leave Killarney. I start to fixate on this battle between me and Ruby, trying to get on the right horses and get a few winners in my column, and Barry can see how much it means to me. We could talk about it for ever, but when it gets towards the real business of the season, Barry promises me the one bit of concrete help that he can give me: he'll put me up on Dun Doire.

Dun Doire is shaping up to be one of the big Irish bets of the week in Cheltenham, and Barry's the head of the syndicate that owns him. There are eight of them involved – a couple of lads I went to school with and socialised with over the years, like Kevin Brady and Ted Dowd, and then a few others they know through their involvement in Dunderry GAA. The horse is primed for a big win, and it's no secret. He has won five races in a row and gone up more than three stone in the handicap weights over the course of the season, which is like night and day in terms of improvement. There was a huge gamble the day of his most recent win, the Thyestes Chase in Gowran Park, and given the amount of buzz locally about his chances, it sounds like a good chunk of it might be going back on him at Cheltenham. I don't expect to be the lads' first choice as jockey. Paul Carberry won the Thyestes on him – I couldn't have got down to 9st 10lb even if I tried – so he'll be top of the queue, unless he's needed to ride for Noel Meade instead.

'If Paul isn't riding him, you're riding him,' Barry tells me, and Barry's word is good enough for me.

Tony Martin, Dun Doire's trainer, enters him in a couple of races at Cheltenham. All trainers do it to keep their options open until the last minute, but for a freelance jockey it means a few uncertain weeks between entries and declarations. You know what you're in line to ride, but if plans change and horses are declared for the same race, two rides can very quickly become one. You're vulnerable. Everyone is calling in favours and twisting arms and doing everything they can to get the best book of rides for the week, and everything is up for grabs. The last thing you want is to lose a ride you thought you had, so there's a long wait until Monday morning, the day before racing starts, when the first declarations come out.

I head for Dublin Airport with Paula and Síofra, still not knowing for certain what I've got locked in, waiting for Ciaran O'Toole to ring me when he finds out. He calls me before the official declarations are announced. Dun Doire is going in the William Hill Handicap Chase, the race I was hoping he'd run in. But I'm not riding him. Ruby is.

It lands like a body blow and absolutely flattens me. I knew that Noel would have a runner in that race and that he'd need Paul, so I had Dun Doire marked down as a virtual certainty. I trusted Barry.

'Ring Barry,' Paula tells me as we're getting on the plane. 'Ring him yourself and ask him.'

I get through to him straight away.

'Barry, what's going on? I thought I was riding Dun Doire if Paul wasn't on him.'

'No, we spoke to Tony and he wants Ruby to ride him tomorrow.'

'Would you not give Tony a ring and tell him that you want me up?'

'He's decided on Ruby, Barry. That's it.'

'Would you even just talk to the lads and see?'

'I can't, Barry. There's nothing I can do about it.'

And that's it. That's the end of the conversation. They close the aeroplane's doors and taxi away from the gates. No more phone calls. Nothing I can do. It's bad enough that the big local syndicate, fellas I went to school with, don't want me on their horse. That certainly doesn't reflect too well on me. But my best friend, the lad who sat with me for hours discussing how I could close the gap, the lad who is effectively another brother to me, is picking Ruby over me. That's what hurts. Even if Barry had called me the night before and teed me up a bit – this is the way the conversation is going and it's not looking great for you – it might have helped to soften the blow a little. But no. I can't even convince him to make one last call before declarations to try to argue my case. I don't say a word for the entire flight. I sit there, staring out of the window at the clouds, holding seven-month-old Síofra and squeezing her tight. It's all I can manage.

I know Dun Doire will win but that's not what's bothering me. I can make my peace with that. The fact that he will win doesn't really matter. But when the race comes and goes, I'll still be left with the hurt.

Ruby goes out and gives him a brilliant ride, timed to perfection. I walk past the lads as they're piling onto the steps for the presentation to collect their trophy, the moment that every owner dreams of. I give them a nod to acknowledge them and I walk on.

The self-pity has already started to evaporate by then. Once the first race goes off, there's a winner and there are losers and hard-luck stories and fallers. And it's non-stop, one race into the next, every 40 minutes, bang, bang, bang. The tension goes out of the weighroom. There's a lad over there who has just been beaten on the favourite that he's been waiting all year to ride. There's another lad somewhere else who has just ridden his first winner, wanting to just sit there and soak it all in. Someone else is carrying a knock. Someone else is struggling. There are all of these emotions and Dun Doire fades into the background and just becomes another part of the story of the week.

I'm right there in the thick of it. I go close on Macs Joy in the Champion Hurdle. I give him a good ride and he runs a good race. We're beaten by a length, fair and square, by Brave Inca. No complaints. Moscow's retirement is the big story on the Wednesday, but I get on the board with a nice double either side of that. I have a Grade 1 winner in the RSA Chase on Star De Mohaison, and then win the Coral Cup with Sky's The Limit, as good a handicap winner as you could see in Cheltenham; I do all the right things tactically and he wins by an easy four lengths. I ride Forget The Past in the Gold Cup for Michael O'Brien and finish third. When I tally it all up, as weeks in Cheltenham go it's far from the worst; it's a relief. There's a desperation at the start of Cheltenham week when you're trying to get on to a possible winner, but once you've had one, it's easier to take. I ride winners for Barry in the years that follow, but we're never quite as close as we once were.

By the time the last week of the season comes, Ruby is three wins ahead of me in the jockeys' championship, 83–80. When the race is that close, the championship becomes morning, noon and night for the last few weeks. When I go to bed, I'm thinking about it. When I wake up, the same thoughts are still there waiting for me. Every winner is a good one, no matter how it comes, and every blank day the other fella has is just as important. Three wins is a lot of ground to make up in the space of a week, but I'm still hanging in there. Half a chance is better than no chance at all.

I go down to Thurles fired up, ready to throw the kitchen sink at anything and everything. My first ride is on a mare for Thomas O'Leary, Grange Glen. She's 4/1 second favourite in a mediocre maiden hurdle, precisely the kind of result I'm depending on to stay in the championship. We turn into the straight, running down to the second last, right at the point of the race where Grange

Glen is coming out of her comfort zone, and she's starting to feel the pinch. I need her to fly the second last so that we can give ourselves a shot. I should just cut my losses and come back again for the next race, but I'm not thinking logically and I pay the price. I ask her for a hallelujah jump and I don't get it. I get buried instead. It's the end of my day, and the end of my championship.

Grange Glen makes a desperate mistake and unseats me. The gash where I've just split my chin open off her hoof is a sore one, but it's knowing that I've no chance of catching Ruby now that really sickens me. I've just gift-wrapped it for him with a week to go. It's over. When I go inside to get cleaned up, there's a doctor there who says he's worked in plastic surgery before and he can stitch me up there without me needing to go to hospital. My mind is racing with winners and numbers and regrets, and I'm barely listening to him as he's asking me what I'd like him to do. I'm thick as a bull.

'If I put local anaesthetic into this, it's going to swell more and it will scar more,' he explains.

I think he realises that he's talking to a man who is not particularly concerned with anaesthetics or stitches or scars at the moment. I give him a pretty blunt response.

'Grand, just go for it. Stitch away. Whatever you want.'

And that's what he does, eight double stitches in my chin, a loop inside and a loop outside to make a figure of eight, knotted tight, and three stitches down by my eye. A week later, Ruby wins the championship. I've still got the scars to remind me of it.

15

sit down and wait as the computer flickers back to life. It has become a habit, checking the entries again and again. I run my eyes down the list but it's all the same races, all the same names. Nothing has changed. There's nothing there for me.

It's the summer of 2007 and I feel like racing's forgotten man.

Once you lose momentum, it's very hard to turn things around. Racing's a fickle game, and if it's a question of 'What have you done for me lately?', then the vibe I'm getting from a lot of trainers is 'Not much', apparently.

I've never been on a retainer. I've never taken a job as a first jockey. I've always preferred the freedom of being freelance. I want to be on the best horses on the big days – that's why I'm a jockey – and being freelance lets me do that. You trade away the security of a contract job, but I've built a different type of security over the years: strength in numbers, rather than hitching my star to a single yard. I have the best of three worlds when I'm riding for Jessie, Edward O'Grady and Tom Taaffe. It's impossible for them all to be in good form at the same time, but that's okay. I only need one of them to be.

But being a freelance jockey is a high-wire act and this is more than a wobble. I'm on the way down.

You have to be a politician, too. You can't ride two horses in the same race, so if you're letting down a trainer or an owner, you have to do it the right way. Sometimes you ride one horse when you'd much rather be on a different one in the race. You take one for the team and keep everyone sweet. The last thing you need is to end up on the naughty step or fall out of favour. You can't afford to.

Tom Taaffe goes ballistic when he finds out that I'm riding Kazal for Eoin Griffin in the Slaney Novice Hurdle in Naas in early 2007. He has a horse in the race too, Treacle, but I've won on Kazal and he's the one I want to ride. It's Ciaran who tells him, not me, and Tom gives it to him both barrels. The toys and the pram aren't even in the same postcode by the time he's finished. All Ciaran can do is listen because there isn't a hope of us changing our mind.

'The one you're on is the best horse in the race,' he reminds me. 'You ride the best horse in the race.'

Ciaran's a good judge of a horse's potential. His dad, Mick, was a top trainer in his time, won a Gold Cup and the Irish 2,000 Guineas, so Ciaran knows how the game works. Whenever there's a decision like this to be made, the two of us are on the same page about how to handle it: go with your gut instinct, take the decision, and then back yourself. And whatever I decide, Ciaran is always standing right there with me. The only way to be sure that there's no blowback is to ride the winner and then there can be no arguments. Kazal wins, Treacle finishes 15 lengths back in fourth, and there's never another word about it from Tom.

A trainer has to do what's right by them and their owners too, and if you're good and you show any sort of commitment, they'll try to tie you down. Edward O'Grady makes me an offer – decent money, a proper string of horses. It would be a great job for a lad in his mid-30s who's looking for a bit of structure and stability, but at that time he's talking to a young jockey with stars in his eyes and the world at his feet. All I can see is what I'm being asked to give up, the trainers and owners that I'll be forced to say no to, the big weekends in England that I'll miss out on. I'm a bit slow to give him an answer because the answer is going to be no, so he invites me down to his home in Tipperary to discuss it.

'Are you going to accept this offer?' he asks me.

As politely as I can, I try to explain to him the reasons why I'm not.

'Right,' he says. 'I'll double it.'

My answer is the same. It has never been about the money. It's about opportunities and my ambition, and none of the yards were ever big enough on their own to match that.

The risk, as I'm finding out now, is that while I've been out playing the field, they've started to look elsewhere for that commitment. There are other jockeys climbing the ladder behind me – Robert Power in Jessie's, Andrew McNamara in Edward's, and Tommy Ryan in Tom's – and slowly but significantly, their slice of the pie gets bigger and bigger in each place until, all of a sudden, all that's left for me is a plate of crumbs. Everything else is gone.

The 2007/2008 season is a battle right from the start. It's only three weeks old when I fall in Kilbeggan; from the pain in my chest, I can tell that I've broken a rib, and it feels like I've sprained my wrist as well. I ride in the next race as planned anyway, and win, but when I come back in afterwards, I break out in a cold sweat. When I'm stood down for the rest of the card, I don't argue. The recommended treatment for a broken rib is usually to rest up and give it time to heal, but instead I prescribe myself a day of racing in Navan the following day. I'm still sore but I ride another winner, which is enough to make the day worthwhile.

If the injuries aren't severe enough to stop me from going racing in Navan, there's no way they're going to stop me going to the Champions League final. Tickets in hand, a dozen of us head for Liverpool Airport and then on to Greece for the 2007 decider between Liverpool and AC Milan. We've got a great group: Robert Power – Puppy – David Casey, myself and lots of others. The atmosphere when we get to Athens is electric. Every queue is a sing-song. We find a bar with a pool table and rack them up for a game, but as soon as I break the balls, the pain shoots through my wrist. It wasn't sprained – it's broken. So after the football, the European Cup and myself both find ourselves heading for places that we know very well: the trophy to Milan, and me to see Paddy Kenny in his clinic.

Paddy is Fred Kenny's son, and took over as the jockeys' main orthopaedic consultant when his dad retired. I put my cards on the table straight away. I'm booked to ride a couple in Tipperary that evening and there's one of Jessie's in particular that's fancied and I don't want to miss.

'I'm going to put you in a cast,' Paddy tells me.

'Okay, but can I go down and ride one for Jessie and I'll come back and get the cast afterwards?'

'No, not with the way your wrist is,' Paddy explains. 'If you fall on it, you'll displace it and you'll need an operation.'

It's black and white with Paddy. If it was safe to race, he'd let me race. There's no point in arguing.

I'm out for six weeks while my wrist heals, and by the time I'm fit again, there's no hiding from how bleak my book of rides has become. Everything has unravelled. I've been getting fewer and fewer calls from Jessie, Edward and Tom, and now I'm down to the bare minimum with all three. I've been squeezed out by the lads who are there day in, day out. They committed when I wouldn't, they were happy to pick one yard and fight to be the main man, and now they're the ones getting the rides and I'm the one paying the price. I've had great days for all those yards, but yesterday's memories don't buy you much today. I was happy to pick and choose for all those years; now it's the trainers' turn to do what they feel is right for them. Even when things were at their best, I always knew there was a chance that a door would close. I just didn't expect all three of them to slam shut at the same time.

It's easy to get rides when you're winning and your name is in lights. Everybody wants you. That's the way it's been for me for years. I was lucky that I never had to pay much attention to the other side of the story, but now I'm living it. Once those lights go out, it's hard to even find a candle. I'm not riding winners so I'm not in a trainer's head when they go to book their jockeys. I don't get called for the spare ride. I'm forgotten. And it doesn't take much for a career to wither and die. A jockey without horses to ride isn't much of a jockey.

It's hard watching someone else ride horses you feel you should be on. I'm not looking for the next Moscow Flyer or Kicking King. I'm not even looking for good horses. I'm battling to get on average horses, bad horses, just to get a few rides and see if I can make something out of nothing. Ciaran sets me up to go and ride work in different yards on different mornings, hoping that it might help to open a few doors. Paula sees me switch the computer on again and I can tell she's worried. She has already watched me check the entries today. More than once. But I can't accept that there's nothing there. Not again.

Riding a good horse on a big day isn't pressure; fighting to keep your career from going under is pressure, and I'm feeling it. It becomes a compulsion, going back over the entries time and again, convincing myself that I must have missed something, hunting for the one half-decent ride that I might have a chance of getting on. I open the same page later and look again, and the only thing that has changed is the time on the clock on the wall. I think that I'm being proactive, that I'm working and doing everything I can to find my way out of this, but all I'm doing is driving myself mad. It's torture. Every time I look, all I get is a reminder of the fact that it's another day where I've got nothing, and the wound rips open again

The diary is Paula's suggestion. It's stupidly simple, but it's what we need to bring calm back into our lives. I buy a notebook and then I go through the entries once and once only, writing down three or four horses in each race that I might have a chance of getting on. I ring Ciaran and talk through the list, see what he thinks and which phone calls are worth making. If it's a trainer I've a good relationship with, I'll go straight to them and ring them myself. But once I've written my list in the diary and we've made the phone calls, that's it. Even if it never makes a tap of difference in terms of getting me on a horse, it stops me obsessing. Another look at the form of the 6.30 in Bellewstown tomorrow isn't as important as making time to sit down and eat with Paula or helping to put Síofra to bed. The smallest bit of normality is priceless. Tomorrow is another day.

Winter comes, the better racing starts, and my prospects improve slightly. The good horses come back out for their first runs of the new season, but Edward and Tom want their new men to start building up their partnerships from the start. I win three races for Eric McNamara on a young horse of his called Bellflower Boy.

'That was Barry Geraghty at his brilliant best,' Eric says in one of his interviews afterwards.

My brilliant best. It's only one line, but I latch on to it. It's so good to hear.

I'm grateful to Jessie, who leaves me to ride anything I've been riding before. A cupboard stripped bare doesn't quite look so bad when you've still got a horse like Macs Joy that you can reach for.

Macs Joy is a special one. From humble beginnings, Jessie transforms him into a Champion Hurdle contender. He never wins the big one at Cheltenham – he's a touch below the superstar league of Moscow or Kicking King – but he's deadly. He's a gorgeous horse, but it's his personality that gets me: he's a little barrel who jumps brilliantly, who has speed but is still measured, who just has that bit of class. He never lets you down. Anytime I go out on him, I know he'll take care of the running of the race and I can concentrate on the tactics we need to get us there. I just love him.

He hasn't been out of place in a vintage era of Irish two-mile hurdlers, well able to hold his own against both Brave Inca and Hardy Eustace. The day he really announced himself, the Festival Hurdle at Leopardstown at Christmas 2004, he had both of them well held behind him. And to prove it wasn't a fluke, he went out and did it again a few weeks later in the Irish Champion Hurdle, although that one turned out to be a much closer contest. I gave him an ordinary enough ride that day, rode him way too handy, and he still managed to dig it out. The three of them passed the finishing post in practically a straight line: Macs Joy a short head ahead of Brave Inca, with Hardy Eustace a further head behind. Even after losing out to Brave Inca in the 2006 Champion Hurdle, he turned around a few weeks later in Punchestown and beat both of them again. There was so little to choose between the three of them that it all came down to who was right on the day. And Macs Joy was right on plenty of big days.

He's my little star and I'm always looking out for him. I'm down riding work in the Curragh one morning and another one of Jessie's lads is riding Macs Joy in the same lot. It's a piece of work – a good gallop to get the horses fit and ready for their next race – but you're there to do the right thing by the horse. If they're feeling it, great; if not, you try to find out why. What you don't do is take out your stick and hit a Champion Hurdle horse with a couple of smacks. I see this lad go for it on Macs Joy and I'm fit to steer across and pull him off the horse in anger.

'Jesus, go easy, will ya. There's no need for that.'

It happens a bit during pieces of work, lads get overexcited and hear the roar of the crowd and start riding imaginary finishes, but you don't do that to my pal.

I'm hoping against hope that Macs Joy will be back to his best this season. Last year was a mess, broken up by injury with any hope of training on and improving again gone by the wayside. When we get him back out, Jessie sends him straight to the Morgiana for his first run of the season and we finish third. She has a couple of options for him after that and we skip the Hatton's Grace and go to Cheltenham instead for the Bula Hurdle in December 2007.

It's a race that always attracts classy horses and this year's no different. Even if Macs Joy hasn't been at his very best, we're still sent off a 7/2 shot and joint favourites with Sublimity, the reigning champion hurdler. We jump off towards the front and I take a lead in behind Osana and Afsoun, who make the running over the first couple of hurdles.

We're running down the back straight, the race only starting to get going, when I suddenly feel Macs Joy stumble underneath me. We're running on the flat, nowhere near a hurdle, and his leg just gives way on him. It's like getting a blowout when you're driving your car, except this is worse than a blowout – this is like the wheel coming off. I pull him up quickly but I'm already preparing myself for the worst. One look at his leg is all I need. It's broken. I jump down off him and do what I can. I have the reins in one hand, trying to hold him still in case he tries to gallop away in his distress, and with the other, I try to pull the saddle off his back.

For a moment, it's just the two of us, alone out there on the far side of the track. I stay with him, do what I can to mind him, and I cry. I cry for him because I know what has to happen now. The vets arrive and put the screens up around him. When they're ready, I say goodbye to my little friend and I leave him. I walk away, drop down to my knees, and cover my ears. I don't want to hear the bang of the gun.

Buveur D'Air just getting the better of Melon and Paul Townend in a tight finish to the 2018 Champion Hurdle. (© *Seb Daly/Sportsfile via Getty Images*)

Peregrine Run jumping Valentine's Brook in the 2019 Topham Chase. I'm lying on the ground with a badly broken leg three fences later. (© *Alex Livesey/Getty Images*)

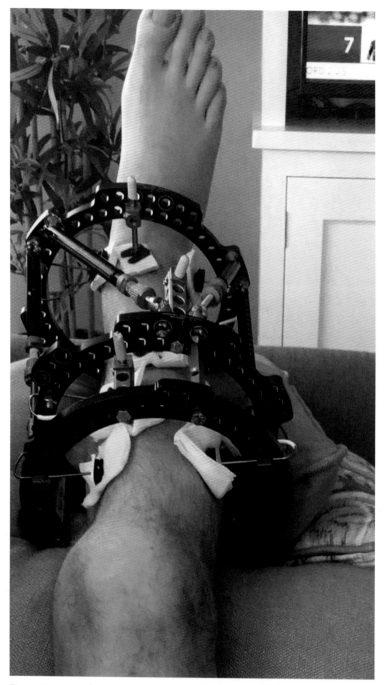

Propping my foot up on the couch with the frame I had on for fourteen weeks. It had three screws going into my leg and four wires going through it.

A spin on a horse and carriage through the Phoenix Park the day of my sister Sascha's First Communion. Ross, me, Norman, Sascha, Jill, Mam, Holly and Dad.

On board Little Tom aged 11 after winning a Grade A showjumping competition at Rolestown Show for ponies 128 cm or less. He was called Little Tom because he was only 118 cm.

With Noel Meade after we were crowned Champion Jockey and Champion Trainer for the 2003/04 season. (© *Healy Racing Photographers*)

Having a bit of fun at Seven Barrows after riding out with Tom Symonds, Ben Pauling and 'Corky' Browne. (© *Fiona Crick*)

Cockney Lad flies the last before beating Theatreworld in the Lismullen Hurdle at Navan in November 1997. My first taste of the big time. (© *Healy Racing Photographers*)

Christmas Hurdle at Leopardstown in 2000. Moscow Flyer jumps the last between Stage Affair (Ruby Walsh) and Mantles Prince (Norman Williamson) as Istabraq (Charlie Swan) crashes out. (© *Healy Racing Photographers*)

Florida Pearl pings the last to win the 2002 Punchestown Gold Cup. (© *Healy Racing Photographers*)

At Sandown in 2004 celebrating Moscow Flyer's second Tingle Creek win with a flying dismount. Of all the big clashes I ever rode in, this one really lived up to expectations. (© *Edward Whitaker/Racing Post*)

The stuff dreams are made of as Monty's Pass stretches away from the field to win the 2003 Aintree Grand National. (© *Phil Noble/PA Archive/PA Images*)

Kicking King and I scramble to stay upright after crashing through the last before winning the 2004 King George. (© *Trevor Jones / Racingfotos.com*)

Spraying Champagne all over a packed 21 Club in Cheltenham, celebrating Kicking King's Gold Cup win and Moscow's second Champion Chase in March 2005.

Jessie giving me a big hug after Macs Joy wins the Champion Hurdle at Punchestown in 2006, reversing the Cheltenham form by beating Brave Inca and Hardy Eustace. I'm still looking the worse for wear after splitting my chin at Thurles a week earlier. (© *Healy Racing/Racingfotos.com*)

Getting a pat on the back from Nicky after Punjabi's Champion Hurdle win in 2009. It was a great way to cap a first season in the job. (© *Glyn Kirk/AFP via Getty Images*)

Punjabi and I returning covered in mud after running in the 2013 County Hurdle. A long way from our glory day of winning the Champion Hurdle. (© *David Davies/PA Images*)

Sharing a joke with the Queen and Nicky before riding Barbers Shop in the 2009 Cheltenham Gold Cup. (© *Samir Hussein/WireImage/Getty Images*)

Giving my old friend Bobs Worth a well-deserved kiss after flying home to win the 2013 Cheltenham Gold Cup (© *Mike Hewitt/Getty Images*)

Staring into space seconds after winning the Gold Cup on Bobs Worth. All I could think about was John Thomas McNamara after his fall the evening before; the Gold Cup didn't feel so important. (© *Michael Steele/Getty Images*)

Sprinter Sacre getting a little bit of practice in at home. He was the most amazing horse to ride; I never rode a horse who travelled and jumped with as much ease as he did. (© *Fiona Crick*)

With Paula by my side as always supporting me as I hold the Champion Hurdle trophy after Buveur D'Air's win in 2018. (© *Ramsey Cardy/ Sportsfile via Getty Images*)

Visiting Monty's Pass at home in Jimmy Mangan's with Órla, Rían and Síofra, my leg frame hidden under a widened tracksuit leg.

Epatante flying the last *en route* to winning the 2020 Champion Hurdle. I was high as a kite afterwards, knowing I had won one of the big ones at my final Cheltenham Festival. (© *Galoppfoto/Racingfotos.com*)

Saint Roi quickening away from the pack to win the 2020 County Hurdle, my last ride at Cheltenham. (© *David Fitzgerald/Sportsfile via Getty Images*)

Debriefing JP for the final time after Saint Roi's win. It was a pleasure to put on his famous silks and ride so many great winners for him over the years. (© *Harry Murphy/Sportsfile via Getty Images*)

Nicky giving me a high five after Dame De Compagnie won the Coral Cup. He was a brilliant man to ride for, especially when it came to the Cheltenham Festival. (© *David Fitzgerald/Sportsfile via Getty Images*)

Celebrating with two great friends of mine, Roger Loughran and Kevin Tuite, after announcing my retirement. (© *Niamh Menton, The Photo Lounge Ratoath*)

At home with my beautiful family a few hours before announcing my retirement. It was our little secret. (© *Niamh Menton, The Photo Lounge Ratoath*)

16

'You're not lucky for me,' Paddy Monaghan says.

That's his explanation. That's the reason why I'm being dropped. This is the week before the Champion Hurdle in 2008 and, thanks to Paddy and whatever superstition has suddenly taken hold, I've no ride in the race. I meet him plenty of times in years to come, and any time I do, he still jokes about how that moment was the lifeline that turned my career around.

I've known Paddy for years; his sons are part of a group of friends that I've met through Paul Carberry and Niall and Adam Lord. Paddy's a real character, a great racing man. I'd jump on the train with Paul to go down to Mallow to go racing, and we'd often bump into Paddy somewhere along the way and there'd be a bit of craic and a story. I'm not sure what particular piece of bad luck he's taking issue with here, not that it really matters. Catch Me is the horse we're discussing, a 12/1 shot for the Champion Hurdle next week – the horse I thought I was riding, but apparently not. Paddy is involved in the horse alongside James O'Shea, a businessman from Tralee, for whom I've ridden plenty of winners over the years. I've won on Catch Me for them as well, a couple of times during his novice season.

Maybe it's the run in the Deloitte last year that Paddy's still not happy about. It was all set up to be a proper Cheltenham trial, Catch Me against Aran Concerto, a good one of Noel Meade's. The race was just starting to take shape. Leading Run, Noel's other one in the race, was taking us down to the second last and I'd just moved into a challenging position. I'd been watching Leading Run throughout, I'd seen that he was jumping right at every hurdle and, in hindsight, trying to pass him out on the right was maybe not the smartest idea. I deliberately left plenty of room between us to allow for him jumping right again. Just not enough, obviously. He jumped way right at the second last, bumped Catch Me, turned him sideways, and he unseated me.

If that was Paddy's issue, it didn't cost me the ride – at least, not immediately. I rode him in the Ballymore at Cheltenham, where we finished a close third, and again in Punchestown in his last race of the season. We were right there, revved up for a fight to the finish, when we fell at the final hurdle. There's a fine line between winning all three of those big Grade 1 prizes that spring and winning none, and in Paddy's eyes, it seems I was the common denominator. I was the unlucky one.

I never expected him to hold it against me when it came to the Champion Hurdle. Once Andrew McNamara took the job with Edward O'Grady, he automatically moved to the top of the queue, but he's chosen to ride Sizing Europe for Henry de Bromhead instead. They leave the decision right up until the last minute, and I'm waiting for the call that never comes. James O'Shea is happy for me to ride the horse. Edward is happy for me to ride the horse. Everyone's happy bar Paddy, and he's the only one who's willing to dig his heels in to get what he wants. When I do get the call, it's to tell me that Ruby's riding the horse.

A couple of days out from one of the biggest races in the year, and it looks like I'm going to be sitting watching it from the weighroom, until Ciaran O'Toole comes through for me again. Nicky Henderson has two entered and Mick Fitzgerald is sticking with the horse he finished third on in the race last year, Afsoun.

The other horse, Punjabi, is a five-year-old, typically a year or two too young to really be a contender. He's not an impressive horse, doesn't move brilliantly or work brilliantly. He finished fourth in the Triumph Hurdle a year earlier, which is a good bit of form and, at least with Nicky, you know he'll have his horses primed for Cheltenham. On the face of it, it's a straightforward choice for Fitzy but I don't really care if Punjabi has no chance; I'm delighted to get on anything. When we get there on the day, he surprises me and stays on well to finish third; Ruby and Catch Me are sixth, and Fitzy and Afsoun finish a half-length behind them in seventh.

We're not long awake the next morning when the news comes through. They're forecasting winds of up to 50 miles an hour for Cheltenham that afternoon. Racing is abandoned for the day.

'We'll just go for lunch,' I tell Paula, trying to reassure her. 'I won't have much to drink, if that's what you're worried about.'

I've never been the lad that you find in the pub every Monday, Tuesday, Wednesday; but on the other hand, when I do go out, there are nights when I can go all out. When I started out in the weighroom, I didn't need much encouragement to embrace that side of the culture. It was all just part of what it meant to be a professional jockey. The big racing nights out, they were always celebrated at home when we were growing up – work hard and play hard – and you'd never hear a cross word if you stumbled in with one or two too many on you. I know Paula is worried when we go for lunch in Cheltenham town, but it's okay to have a glass. We won't be going out partying.

'I won't,' I tell her, 'I won't. I've Finger Onthe Pulse and Kazal to ride tomorrow. I can't go mad. No way, no way.'

That's the trouble with lunches, though. It's early when we finish up and then it's on to a bar and on to another bar and I'm getting drinks from two different sides of the room and I'm full as a bingo bus and there's a bit of a row with some lad in a check shirt and the next thing I know I'm waking up and it's Thursday morning.

If I don't get my weight down to do 10st 12lb, I won't be riding Finger Onthe Pulse in the Jewson. This is the situation I've put myself in and now I just have to get on with it. I put my headphones on and I go running. Running to sweat the drink out, running from the fear. When I arrive at the course, they have the breathalyser ready to test everyone before they go out riding. I've been running so much that I sail through it. Not a bother.

And a few hours later, Finger Onthe Pulse hits the front with three fences to jump.

Fitzy comes to beat me on Barbers Shop, the Queen's horse, after we jump the last. He's closing with every stride, his horse eyeball to eyeball with mine, but Finger Onthe Pulse holds on to win by a neck. As Fitzy crosses the line behind me, he lets out an almighty roar – 'Fuuuuuuck!'

Barbers Shop was one of his fancied rides of the week for Nicky, and now he's been beaten by a lad who couldn't even put himself to bed last night. I turn around to him.

'Sorry, Mick' – as cheeky as you like.

Not for the first time, I feel like I've rolled the dice and got away scot free. Finger Onthe Pulse turns out to be my only winner of the festival but, as I soon discover, it's another one of my rides that ends up being the most important one of the week.

∩

Punjabi's third in the Champion Hurdle is a better run than anyone expected, but in the grand scheme of things it's pretty unremarkable. That would be the end of it, nothing more than a footnote in the record books, forgotten about, if Fitzy's career hadn't come to such a sudden, scary end a few weeks later at the second fence of the Grand National. The description of his injuries is frightening enough – four broken vertebrae in his neck, severed spinal cord, and eight hours on the operating table just to try to realign and reset everything back to the way it should be. At 38 years old, getting back to full health is his only priority; getting back in the saddle is not.

Fitzy doesn't retire until later in the summer, but the rumour mill waits for no man and no official announcement. When Punchestown comes, there's a close eye on Nicky's runners to see who he's bringing over and, more important, who he's booking to ride them. My career in Ireland is sinking, and if Nicky is looking for someone to take over from Fitzy on a permanent basis, I need to be on that life raft, and quickly. But instead of picking up the phone to ring Nicky, to ask the question and make sure he knows that I'm interested, I'm like the shy lad standing over against the wall at the dance. I let Ciaran O'Toole do my talking for me instead, and I know exactly what he's saying:

'Barry's available to ride whatever you're bringing over, Nicky, and sure isn't he the man you're going to want on your horses next year? He has no commitments here, he's free to travel, he can be over there whenever you need him.'

Ciaran has every big race I've ever won, every good ride I've ever had, on the tip of his tongue and he'll talk Nicky through every last one of them if that's what it takes to convince him. When the Punchestown declarations come out, AP McCoy rides two or three of Nicky's good ones that week but I keep the ride on Punjabi for the Punchestown Champion Hurdle. I only get one opportunity to back up all Ciaran's talk and impress, and I take it.

Punjabi's a horse with more stamina than speed. A sprint from the back of the last isn't going to do us any favours. I let him go as we're coming round the bend into the home straight and hope that the five- or six-length advantage that we open up will be enough to see us home. It's bold, it's brave, and it pays off. We don't get the cleanest jump at the last, but Sublimity can't chase us down. We win by three lengths.

The June sale at Goffs is a place where deals get done, but nearly all of them are for assets that are a lot more valuable than a 28-year-old jockey who is trying to patch together bits and pieces from a career in freefall. We're both there to do our own buying and selling, but we need to talk and David Minton makes sure that neither of us let the opportunity slip by. Minty is one of the men behind the Highflyer Bloodstock agency and when it comes to the sales, he's the agent who helps Nicky whittle down his shortlist of horses to have a look at. I meet him at Goffs and we talk horses for a while, but before he leaves, he encourages me to go and talk to Nicky.

'He's here,' Minty tells me. 'Find him and the two of you can have a chat about what you want to do next season.'

It's hard to find a quiet corner in Goffs, so myself and Nicky go for a walk down to one of the back yards. There's a row of stables down near the horse car park and we nip around the back of one of them like two teenagers sneaking a cigarette.

'We'd love you to come and ride the horses,' Nicky says.

'And I'd love to come and ride them,' I tell him.

It's as simple as that. There's no negotiation and no back and forth. We leave the finer details until a later date and the deal is done in a five-minute chat. All my prayers are answered. For the first time in my career, I have a job: first jockey to Nicky Henderson at Seven Barrows in Lambourn.

And I forgive Paddy Monaghan as well. When I meet him again a few years later, my career is in a much better place and he's in like a flash to break the ice.

'Say thanks,' Paddy tells me.

'Thanks for what?' I ask him – and in my head, I probably add, 'ya bollix'.

'For getting you the job with Henderson,' he says.

You'd never know if Paddy is winding you up or being sincere, and before I can ask, he explains it himself.

'Sure didn't I jock you off Catch Me and you rode Punjabi? I got you the job with Henderson.'

If that was the sliding doors moment of my career, I'm glad I never found out what was on the other side. I've always had enough self-belief to keep myself afloat, even in the worst storms. No matter how bad it got, I never lost my love for it, never thought I might be better off quitting. But by the summer of 2008, I was hanging on for dear life, desperate for any opportunity.

So thanks, Paddy, I suppose.

17

Corky Browne might just be slagging or he might be deadly serious; it's hard to tell. He's Nicky Henderson's head lad, right-hand man, adviser, assistant, and everything else in between. He's been part of the furniture in the yard for over 30 years but he's Carrigtwohill born and bred, hence the nickname, and he's never lost that bit of Cork mischief. He's telling me a story about the summer of 2008, after I'd won on Punjabi in Punchestown and I was in the running for Nicky's job.

'I asked round about you at home that summer,' he tells me. 'What about Barry Geraghty? And do you know what they told me? He's gone.'

Maybe Corky's right. Maybe things had slipped so far that people doubted if I could ever turn things around. Maybe there were more people out there like that punter in Listowel who shouted over the rail to me, 'Geraghty, you'd be nothing without Moscow Flyer.'

Maybe they thought I was a jockey who rode good horses rather than a good jockey. That I was a cocky little fucker when everything was going my way, and that I wouldn't be able to hang tough when the shit hit the fan, that I wouldn't have the strength, the belief to persevere. That I'd cover up, give up, when my back was against the wall instead of taking a deep breath and coming out swinging.

If that's how people feel about me, then Cheltenham in 2009 is my opportunity to set the record straight. I've always relished the big race and the big day, thrived on those moments, and this is four full days of it: shrug off the expectation, tell them pressure's for tyres, block out all the noise, and go and ride my race. Except this time, it's not that easy.

Because I'm not coming from a strong position, there's a little bit of insecurity in the weeks leading up to the festival. Colm Murphy asks me if I'm available to ride his horse, Big Zeb, in the Champion Chase but I tell him I'm booked up. Nicky has a horse entered, Petit Robin, that I've finished second on a couple of times during the winter and, as first rider, I assume that I'll be needed to ride him. But no sooner than I've said no to Colm, Nicky comes to me with a bit of a problem: Petit Robin's owners have asked for AP to ride the horse instead. He asks what I'd like to do and I explain my situation to him, tell him that I'm after turning down Big Zeb to ride the horse. Nicky's very apologetic.

'That's what the owner has asked for,' he says. 'I'll leave it with you to have a think about it.'

When I get home that weekend, I tell Paula what's after happening and we talk it all through.

'You're Nicky's first jockey now,' she reminds me as we chat about all the different possibilities. 'If you stand aside for this one, that's going to open the door for the next owner to say that they'd like to have another jockey instead of you. You can't do that.'

In any walk of life, you have to have someone who you trust, someone whose opinion you really value and who you can bounce ideas off. I've been lucky to have Paula by my side for so much of my career. Through all the ups and downs, for any of the big decisions that have come my way, she's always been there for me and rock solid.

I go back to Nicky after discussing it with her and tell him that it's important to me that I ride the horse, and Nicky sorts it out with the owner, John Poynton. Petit Robin runs a cracker and finishes third in the Champion Chase; more important, I feel a lot more secure in my position.

Through all the years, and all the good horses I've won on and lost on, I've never once felt pressure at Cheltenham, until now. I'm so aware of it that I even say it to Ruby – 'This is the first year that I've ever felt pressure here.'

It's not the pressure that comes when you're on the rebound from being a sinking ship or when you're so desperate to seize a lifeline that your determination turns to anxiety. It's nothing to do with that. It's not coming from Nicky either. As a trainer, he's cut from the same cloth as Jessie. He doesn't want me second-guessing myself or doubting my instincts. He trusts me to ride the race as it happens. Nicky would never do anything to add to the pressure.

It's the job; that's where the pressure is. I'm now first jockey to one of the biggest, most respected yards in horse racing. For the first time ever I'm heading into the week with a huge book of good rides, all for the same trainer, and that volume brings expectation. The beauty of being freelance was that the expectation was collective. It was shared out between me and Jessie and Tom Taaffe and Edward O'Grady or whoever else I was riding for, and it was barely noticeable. If I had a blank week at Cheltenham for one of them, there was a good chance that I'd ride a winner for one of the others. But now, understanding and supportive as Nicky is, I have to answer to the same person after every race. And that person just so happens to be a man who has made a habit of winning races at this festival. I have to deliver.

The job has been a godsend for me, there's no hiding from that, but I want to prove that I can still stand on my own two feet. I hope to have lots of great days with Nicky, but it would be nice to show that I'm still good enough and sought-after enough to win without him as well. That's what makes my first ride of the week so satisfying. Tom Cooper's Forpadydeplasterer is one of my own rides, one that I've worked up myself – an Irish ride too – and he stays on under pressure to win the Arkle for me by a short head. On a personal level, it means a lot. I might be Nicky Henderson's first jockey now, but that's just one string and not the entire bow.

I weigh out for the Champion Hurdle a little over an hour later and go down to meet Nicky in the parade ring. He has three horses in the race and I'm not even riding the best of them. Binocular was one of the star novices of the previous season and is hot favourite to take his place as the two-mile champion, but because he's owned by JP McManus, it's AP McCoy who rides him as JP's first jockey, not me. Of Nicky's other two, Punjabi is the obvious second string, so for the second year in a row, he's my Champion Hurdle ride.

We've had a mixed season together. It got off to the best possible start when we got up on the line to win the Fighting Fifth Hurdle at Wetherby, which is one of the best early-season barometers in the two-mile division. But after falling in the Christmas Hurdle and then disappointing in the Kingwell Hurdle at Wincanton in February, the bookies and punters aren't having much difficulty making a case for others ahead of us. Still, I'm very hopeful for a big run and I've a sneaky suspicion that he might catch a few people by surprise.

I can't shake the memory of his last piece of work on the gallops in Seven Barrows, and I've only just managed to shift the smile from my face. Punjabi, not to put too fine a point on it, is not a good workhorse. He wouldn't show much at home and he'd never impress you or excite you. When I pulled him up after his last piece of work and Sarah, Nicky's daughter, saw me grinning from ear to ear, she knew that he was as good as he could be. This was a different level from anything I'd ever seen from him before. Ten days before the Champion Hurdle, he was tuned to the eyeballs.

I don't get too carried away. Even in frightening form, there are still a lot of horses better than Punjabi among the 23 that are entered, but he finished third in the race last year and he's coming back a year older and stronger and, on the face of it, at the peak of his powers. Dessie O'Halloran, who played with Sharon Shannon's Big Band, asks me if I've any tips for the week.

'Punjabi each way at 33/1, Dessie.'

No sooner than the words are out of my mouth, I'd say every sinner in Tigh Chóilí pub and the Crane Bar in Galway has us backed. To even have a chance, I have to get every single decision right and, as soon as we jump off, they start coming at me thick and fast. Last year's runner-up, Osana, leads us out at a good clip and in a championship race at a good pace, the margins are tiny. It's pin of the collar, walking the fine line between going as fast as you can and not going too fast, and that's where I can make my judgement really count. I leave him to sit in the middle of the pack, not too far behind the leaders, and as we start our run down the hill to the third last, I close what's left of the gap.

Ruby leads us over the third last on Celestial Halo with Hardy Eustace right there beside me and Binocular sitting on my tail. That's the four. Punjabi is already going flat to the boards just to stick with them and not lose ground but I know he's got the stamina to stay and keep on running for me. I hang on to that last little bit, the final three per cent, and hope that it's enough to give us a shot.

Hardy Eustace fades away and it's a three-horse race as we jump the second last. I draw up alongside Celestial Halo as we come round the bend and into the home straight. If he's the main threat, and Punjabi can stay with him without burning that last little reserve, that's the bit that's going to win the race. There's no time to look round. Binocular is still snapping at our heels and if he finds a gear and comes from behind us – whoosh – it's game over and there's not likely to be much that either Ruby or myself can do to stop him.

Celestial Halo and Punjabi jump the last together, a length ahead of Binocular, who's closing in third, but neither of us gets a great jump. Ruby misses it a little, and my lad gets in a little bit too close and rattles through the top of it, but we're the ones who get away from it quickest. I get down low on Punjabi and I go for it, empty out that three per cent onto the altar of Cheltenham's hill and pray that it's enough. Celestial Halo has been at the front practically since flagfall but he won't give up. He matches us stride for stride, every inch of the run-in, until about 50 yards from the line when the slightest crack appears in his resistance. It's barely noticeable – how could it be when the margins are so fine? – but that's all it takes. AP and Binocular come at us on the other side, finding more and more with each of their last five strides. I'm still in front of him, but only barely. I can't hold on. I need the line. It's right there and I need it before I...

Ruby stops riding as he hits the line. He knows he hasn't got up to beat us. AP rides past me. He gets there, heads me, but it's two strides too late. The three of us were still bombing as we flashed past the line together, but I don't need to wait for the photo for the result. Punjabi wins the Champion Hurdle by a neck, a rapidly diminishing neck, with Celestial Halo second and Binocular a head back in third.

I stand up in the irons as Punjabi slows himself down. I don't even manage a salute. All I can do is breathe a sigh of relief. I don't need anyone there to remind me to savour the moment.

This time last year, I wasn't sure if there would ever be another moment like this to savour. My career was on the floor. Barry Geraghty? Gone. Washed up. Finished.

If I can ever repay Nicky what I owe him for giving me this opportunity, the Champion Hurdle is the right place to start. It's his first win in the race since the great days of See You Then more than 20 years ago. My first win in the race full stop. I've been second. I've been third. In my quieter moments, I made my peace with the fact that maybe this was the one race I was destined never to win. And I've done it – I'm the first jockey to complete the set by winning the Aintree Grand National and Cheltenham's four big championship races.

I'm back where I've always felt I belonged and I'm not done yet. Once I've ridden a winner for Nicky, his instructions for every race finish with the exact same message: 'Have a nice time.' Wednesday and Thursday are two blank days but I'm back on the board in the first race on Friday when Nicky's good young juvenile, Zaynar, gets up to win the Triumph Hurdle.

But by Friday evening, I've something far more important than racing on my mind. I find my phone and make a call that I've been thinking about for a while now. I want to do this the right way. When it rings at the other end, Paula's mother answers it. I explain to her why I'm calling out of the blue like this. She has been an amazing support to us since the beginning and I want to ask her permission. I want her to be the first to know that in a few minutes' time, as soon as I can get a moment's quiet in the madness of the weighroom, I plan to ask Paula to marry me.

There must be about 200 people in the weighroom that evening. It's tradition at the end of the week, a big party for the jockeys, their families and friends. At least I didn't have to worry about finding a bottle of champagne at short notice;

there's plenty here to go round. I've been waiting for the right moment and this is it.

I enlist Ruby's help. He jumps up onto one of the tables and taps his glass and the room falls silent for him.

'Before I say anything,' Ruby announces to the room, 'Barry has a few words he'd like to say first.'

And as Paula turns to face me, I'm down on one knee.

'Yes,' she says.

t's not every day that you ride your 1,000th winner. Monday 2 November 2009 should be a landmark moment in my racing career. Duc De Regniere's name should roll off the tip of my tongue. But in years to come, when I'm asked, I can't even be certain what horse I was riding. We pass the finishing post and I put on a brave face and say all the right things but there's no great joy in it. I left my mind in Wetherby two days ago.

My Petra should be my 1,000th winner, not Duc De Regniere. Coming off the bend into the top of the straight at Wetherby, it looks for all the money in the world as if she will be. I've given her a nice positive ride the whole way around, she has jumped nicely for me, and as we move to the front to take up the running, she's the one to beat. I know I have loads in hand, I can feel it in the way she's travelling. The longer we can sit here like this, the better. The later the others leave it before challenging us, the more we'll have left in the tank to hit the line running. I keep in tight to the running rail as we make the turn, watching out of the corner of both eyes to see if anything is going to come from behind and try to join us. That's what I'm focused on.

By the time I hear the shout, my race is already over. Everyone else behind me peels away to the right of the marker in the middle of the track, but I've gone too far to do anything about it. I know immediately that they're right and I'm wrong. It's my mistake. I've taken the wrong course.

I know the track at Wetherby inside out. I walked it this morning, same as I do most days before racing. I know that when you come off the top bend, the hurdle course is to the right and the chase course is to the left. It's such a basic thing to get right, such a simple, stupid mistake to make. Racecourses aren't laid out to trick you or to catch you out; the running rail leads you to where you want to go. Most of the time. But on this occasion the marker was set way off course, and following the rail only led me into trouble. My mind was on winning the race and not on where I was going. It's like missing a turn on the motorway. I was watching my wing mirror the whole way, ready to indicate and turn off, and the next thing I knew I was past the exit and looking at it in the rearview mirror. At that point, there's nothing left to do except pull up the horse and get ready to face the music.

The embarrassment is the worst of it. Punters won't forgive a silly lapse in concentration like that when you're riding the favourite and coming to win. If they want to lean over the rail as we come back in and shout and roar and try to outdo each other with every kind of insult, tell me that I'm fucking useless, a clown, a shit jockey, I don't have much to fight back with. Never mind the punters – what must Nicky be thinking? Or the owners? This wasn't a nothing mistake; there was more than £20,000 in prize money for the winner. The shame I'm feeling, it's the shame of having to stand in front of them and apologise for costing them with something so stupid.

I go in to the stewards' room for the enquiry and hold my hands up. There's nothing I can say. They ban me for 12 days for taking the wrong course. When I ring Nicky afterwards, he's nearly doing more apologising than me. It's a mistake and mistakes happen, and he feels that the embarrassment was punishment enough without the stewards putting a 12-day suspension on top of it as well, but they're the rules. He has already spoken to the owners too, Richard and Lizzie Kelvin-Hughes, and their only reaction was understanding and sympathy. It's a bad mistake to make but nobody, not Nicky and not the owners, is hanging me out to dry.

My ban doesn't kick in for another two weeks, so I get back to work and ride out my rest of the races on the card. Two days later I ride Duc De Regniere to the simplest of victories in Kempton, my 1,000th National Hunt winner in Ireland and Britain. It has been 12 years in the making, and I can't even properly enjoy it when it happens. The gloss is gone off the moment.

I never suffer from that particular lapse in concentration again, thankfully, but there are plenty of punters out there who don't need the mistake to be anywhere near as egregious to let you have it with both barrels. Or worse. When I arrive at Newbury one day for racing, the head of security comes down to meet me and tell me that he'd like a quick word. He explains to me that he has been speaking to my father and that somebody had made a call to my parents' house the night before to threaten me. Whoever it was got their number and rang them – 'You tell Barry I'll see him in Newbury tomorrow.' Rather than worry me, Dad called the racecourse to let them know, but some gobshite with a big mouth is hardly going to worry me. It wouldn't even be that uncommon for a jockey to get a call like that. I tell the security guard not to worry, that I'll be grand, but I understand that it's his job to take it seriously. He stays with me for the day, right up to the point where he walks me back to my car in the car park after racing.

Another time, it's a letter to Tralee Racecourse rather than a phone call. I bring it into the weighroom with me and pass it around, show Paul and Ruby and the boys so that we can all have a bit of a laugh. It never bothers me. If someone wanted to threaten you in the days before Twitter and social media, at least they had to get a bit creative about it and spend a bit of time on their arts and crafts. As for Twitter, Ruby sums it up perfectly: if you're going looking to see what's being said about you, you're looking for the compliment, and if you're looking for the compliment, you have to be ready to take the stick as well. I find it's easier to keep it all at arm's length. Even when it comes to criticism in the media, I let it wash over me unless it comes from someone who's qualified to comment, someone who understands racing and doesn't have an agenda; then I pay attention.

My Petra is a rare blip in my seven seasons riding as Nicky's first jockey. I'm made to feel like I'm part of the team from the moment I arrive in Seven Barrows. I grew up admiring his amazing horses, Travado, Remittance Man, unbelievable jumpers that had come through Nicky's hands in the 1990s, and now I'm here to work with the latest generation. It's a privilege.

Nicky's a genius when it comes to schooling horses. He develops these magnificent jumpers who know how to adjust and pop and measure. It's rare to see one of Nicky's flying down to a fence, revved to the max, thinking they're an aeroplane but ending up in a crash landing. It's equally rare to see one fall at the last, even if they've had a hard race and they're tired and they're being scrubbed along. They've been through so many good schooling sessions with Nicky at home over the years that it's second nature, muscle memory. It's not just the horses – working with him brings me to the next level as a jockey too. His team of horses is as good as anything anywhere in Britain or Ireland, and now they're my team of horses too. I try to be as involved as possible. If I have an idea for a particular piece of work, if I spot something that could do with a bit of fine-tuning, I say it. I'm all in.

There are days when I'd fly down to Plumpton with a couple of good chances for Nicky but come home empty-handed. Plumpton is one of the most southerly tracks in England and it's always nice to justify the trip with a winner. I'd be kicking myself on the way home, annoyed that I went too soon on one of them and didn't go soon enough on the other. But when I'd ring Nicky to talk it through, I should have done this or I should have done that, he'd brush it off and tell me not to worry. Next time out, if I gave the horse the worst ride in the world, he wouldn't be beaten.

'A few of them just weren't right in their coat the last ten days,' he'd say. 'They've just come in their coat now.'

So many trainers focus on weight and fitness and they never really understand their horses the way Nicky does. They think they have their horses primed and in the form of their lives, they can't see any possible way they could be beaten, and then when they do lose, somebody else has to take the fall. The jockey, usually. That's the difference with Nicky. He sees things that other trainers don't. He has a natural feel for a horse, and you can't teach that.

Taking the job with Nicky means a new routine, a new rhythm to my week. Meath is home for me and Paula and Síofra, and it doesn't make sense for the three of us to move our entire lives to England, so I commute cross-channel instead, travelling over and back to Lambourn whenever Nicky needs me. I fly out of Dublin on a Wednesday night, school for Nicky on Thursday morning, race Thursday, Friday and Saturday, and then fly home again on Saturday evening. Nicky has built a rock-solid team in Lambourn and I'm made to feel at home there straight away. I get on great with Tom Symonds and Ben Pauling, his two assistant trainers, and the lads make sure that there's a spare bed there for me on any of the nights I'm staying in England. I couldn't ask for a better welcoming committee. In later years, I stay in Luke Harvey's house – or 'Hotel Harvey', as he likes to call it – which is only a couple of miles down the road from Nicky's yard. There's always great company with Luke and his friends, and he's more than happy for me to come and go as I please, which makes my weekly commute and life in England very straightforward. I come in from racing most Friday evenings and flick the TV over to At The Races to watch Luke on *Get In*, but even though he was a jockey himself before becoming a broadcaster, our racing chat is never taken too seriously which suits us both down to the ground.

But my move to England is not without its complications too. Paula and I were both young when Síofra was born, and with me being away a lot and Paula three hours from her family in Kerry, it's certainly hard at times. We've always had a loving relationship and very strong commitment to make it work, but when I'm in England, it's easy to fall back into bad habits. I don't have anywhere to be or anything to do when my day's work is done. The thousand little bits and pieces of the day that make up a family life, they're all back home in Meath. The pub fills the empty space. We go there for dinner, myself and Tom and Ben, and there's no dinner without drinks. I have great nights with the two lads, brilliant craic, but then when I come home on Saturday night, back to Paula who has been on her own minding Síofra while I'm away, I'm wrecked after three days' racing and two hard nights out. It's not fair on either of them.

I come home one Saturday night, a little over a month before we get married, and Paula tells me that we need to talk. She plays me the video of the previous afternoon's racing, the second day of the Hennessy meeting at Newbury. I won the Grade 2 novice chase on Punchestowns for Nicky, and when the cameras cut to the presentation, I'm going a mile a minute on a piece of chewing gum before I go up to collect the trophy.

'Look at yourself,' Paula tells me. 'You've got back, you've got your break, you've got the good job, and you're going to throw it all away because of your partying.'

She's worried that I'll show up for racing one morning and my good luck will finally run out, that I'll fail the breathalyser and not only will I be banned, I'll probably be sacked as well. 'You're going to lose it all,' she warns me.

I promise her that I won't let that happen. Getting the right balance between mind, body, diet, wellbeing and emotional connection has always been Paula's passion, and over the years, it rubs off on me too and shapes how we live our life as a family. When you believe in that holistic approach to tackling the problems that present themselves in your life, it completely takes away the stigma around going to see a counsellor or a therapist that unfortunately still exists for some people. If I need to talk to someone to help me figure out this problem, that's what I'll do.

Paula finds that she's pushing an open door when it comes to getting me involved in a more holistic lifestyle. She studied naturopathy in college, and then went on to study nutritional therapy. Having a nutritional therapist as a partner is no bad thing when you're a jockey trying to make weight four or five days a week, but I've always been particularly good about my diet, even without Paula's help. When it comes to food, I find it easy to be disciplined; I eat at set times and that's it. As for homeopathy, I've never liked painkillers, never really took them because they never agreed with me; I'd much rather suffer through the pain in my arm or my leg or my back than have my stomach in bits from taking medication. The lads in the weighroom see the homeopathic remedies in my bag and there's a bit of slagging. Arnica is my go-to for any bumps and bruises, but Mark Enright, Mark Walsh, they hear me talking about it so often that it becomes a bit of a running joke. When someone comes in after a fall, no matter what's wrong with them, that's the answer – arnica.

Another busy Christmas creeps up on us quickly – busier than usual as the two of us take care of the last little details before we get married on 4 January. The day before New Year's Eve, I'm over in Nicky's to do a bit of schooling before racing in Taunton that afternoon. I get a fall riding Oscar Whisky schooling over hurdles and come down heavy on my left shoulder. It's Wednesday, I'm getting married on Monday, and the last thing I need is to be showing up crocked on my wedding day. I'm okay, though; it's sore but it doesn't feel like anything more serious than a bad bruising. When I go inside for my breakfast, Sophie, Nicky's wife, takes a bag of frozen peas out of the freezer and hands them to me, tells me to keep the cold on my shoulder for a few minutes and see if it helps.

It's about a two-hour drive from Seven Barrows to Taunton. Tom drives us, but he's been up since about five o'clock this morning getting the yard ready, so I spend most of the two hours chatting away to make sure he doesn't get tired. I can't even offer to drive myself. My left arm is completely useless; I wouldn't even be able to use the gear stick. I give my arm a bit of a test run when we get to the track, try to see how bad it is and what I can do with it. I've no problems moving it when it's down low or by my side – I can get a good hold on the horse's reins – but I can't raise it at all. Even getting up onto the horse in the parade ring, I have to use my right arm to lift my left and put it up on the horse's neck, and then get Tom to more or less lift me up onto the horse. At worst, I'll be able to get down low and ride a finish if I need to, but I'd be as well off leaving my whip in the weighroom because there's no way that I'll be able to use it.

My shoulder's still sore on New Year's Day, but sore doesn't stop me from going to Cheltenham and riding a treble. If I'm able to function that much, it's okay for the moment. I'll worry about it after the wedding. It's only when I look back at our wedding photos and see myself struggling to put my arm into my suit jacket that I realise how pokey I was with it.

We get married on a perfect January day – crisp, dry, clear skies – in a beautiful spot near Killarney known as the Black Valley, a bit more than an hour down the road from where Paula grew up in Kerry. The only trouble with the January racing calendar is that it doesn't leave much time for a honeymoon. We fly out to Paris the following day for four days, knowing that I have to be back to work at the weekend when Punjabi goes in the Welsh Champion Hurdle in Ffos Las. We check in to an incredible hotel just across the river from the Eiffel Tower. The Hôtel Plaza Athénée looks like something straight off the television, which, it turns out, it is; some episodes of *Sex and the City* were shot there. Neither myself nor Paula had a clue where to start when it came to booking a nice place to stay, so I asked Nicky to check it out for me with one of his owners, John Jarvis. John certainly didn't put us wrong.

It's baltic in Paris; baltic everywhere, by the sound of things. Word comes through on Thursday morning that the track in Ffos Las is frozen solid and the weekend's racing has been cancelled. It couldn't work out better for us. We book flights for Paula's mother and Síofra to fly out to join us the following day, and the four of us spend the weekend in Disneyland Paris before flying home. It's the perfect end to a perfect week.

And when we get home from our honeymoon, I finally go to see Paddy Kenny to get my shoulder checked and X-rayed. It turns out I was wrong; it was fractured the whole time.

19

Buying and selling horses is a bit like going fishing. There's an art to it, but that will only get you so far. You need money, luck and patience as well – and if you're short on the first of those, you can be sure that you'll need lots and lots of the other two. When I start to dip my toe into that world, I learn as I go, but it's not Monopoly money that's changing hands. It's an expensive game to play and mistakes can be costly. I have to learn quickly.

Only a fool would step into the sales ring without doing their homework. I study the sales catalogue, doing the same thing that everyone else is doing, scouring and scouring in the hope of finding that little gem of information that everyone else might miss. Anyone can spot the obvious star; that's why they go for so much money. I work my way down through the book, take my notes, make my list and then I go to see them in their box. I watch them trot up and down, see how the pedigrees and the black type on the page look when they become flesh and blood. I want something I like, something that might have a bit of value. This lad, Lot 426, isn't particularly impressive. A bit of an ugly duckling. But that's the beauty of National Hunt racing. Every so often, one turns into a swan.

Norman and myself stop to take a good long look at this fella, size him up, check him out from one side and then from the other, looking for any obvious faults. I look at his listing again. He's got a great pedigree on paper, by Bob Back out of Fashionista, a daughter of King's Theatre. Two good lines. But now that he's here in front of us, there's not much to get excited about. He's a nice horse, has a nice way about him, but nothing more than that really. He's built nicely at the front, got a great shoulder, but other than that, he's not the biggest horse. He's missing that bit of power behind. His back end – his arse – which is his engine, is not the most robust. It could do with a bit more muscle. Without that, he just looks a bit too small.

We move on to take a look at the next one on the list, but this is the kind of league we're shopping in. I've money to pick up a couple of horses in and around the €15,000, €20,000 mark, and Norman is keen to go in on one as well with me. Once the bidding goes above that on anything we like, it's time to bow out. Before the sale is out, there are a good few foals and yearlings that sell for €100,000 or more, but I have my budget and the good sense to stick to it. When you're looking to buy at that level, you choose your risk. You can either buy a horse that has a good pedigree or a horse that has good conformation, one that looks impressive when he's there standing right in front of you. The ones that have both pedigree and conformation, they're a safer bet. That's why they're the ones that go for the big bucks.

When Lot 426 is called into the sales ring, myself and Norman are still interested enough to follow him inside and see how things play out when the bids start coming in. Maybe nobody else will fancy him. Maybe somebody with deep pockets will. If he's there to be bought at a good price, we'll take him and we'll split the cost. We pay €16,500 for him, happy that it's good value, and we bring him home to the farm.

The Bob Back yearling that we buy in November 2006 isn't the first time I've got involved in buying and selling horses. I started in my early twenties, another one of the many little earners that myself and Barry Callaghan had on the go. He was into it in a small way and got me involved too at the start. I bought and sold my first horse with him, a Roselier who went on to a win a bumper for Frances Crowley. From there, once I bought the farm and had a little bit of land to keep a few on, it was a natural enough progression for me to start buying and selling by myself. Bullock Harbour, a horse I buy as a yearling and sell again as a four-year-old for a small profit, wins races too, while in later years, Brain Power turns out to be good enough to run in a Champion Hurdle before finishing second in the Arkle.

I don't have much interest in buying horses for myself with a view to sending them training and racing. I try to spot a bit of value at the sales, hang on to them for a couple of years, and sell them on again. I enjoy bringing on young horses, and it's great to see them go on and progress. Any young horses I buy start out on the farm in Drumree and then as they get a bit older, I bring them up to the fields behind our house to keep working on them there. We break some horses before we sell them – a horse needs to be trained before they'll allow someone sit up on their back and ride them – while others, like our Bob Back, are sold unbroken. Our job is to exercise him, trotting him around on a piece of equipment called a lunge to work on his fitness and muscle tone so that he's in the best shape possible when we bring him to the sales. We keep him for 18 months and bring him to the Land Rover sale at Goffs as a three-year-old in 2008, but nobody has ever ridden him and he's never had a saddle on his back. You're very much dealing with raw material.

If sales are competitive as a buyer, it's every bit the same when you're there trying to sell. There are hundreds of horses, some good and some bad, and every one of them has a consignor jostling for position, trying to get their horse noticed and sold at the best price possible. Minty – David Minton – probably has 20 or 30 horses already on his list for Nicky Henderson to look at but he humours me and agrees to have a look at one more. The bidding goes up to €24,000 but Nicky and Minty aren't interested at that price, don't think he's worth the money. In the end, we don't sell him to anyone. Nobody goes any higher than €24,000, which is lower than our reserve price, and we keep him.

I leave Goffs that day without doing the deal that I was expecting, but that very same afternoon, myself and Nicky come to our own arrangement that sees me take the job as his first rider. A lot has changed by the time we bring him to the Doncaster Spring Sale in May 2009. The world is in the grip of a global recession. Families, small businesses, big industries, entire countries are on their knees and the bloodstock trade is not immune. Prices plummet. We bought this horse at the height of the Celtic Tiger and now we're trying to sell him at the bottom of the bust. Nicky goes to the sales with orders from a few syndicates for horses in the £20,000 price range. He buys two or three, and our Bob Back is one of them. It's less money than we could have sold him for a year ago but times have changed. We're happy with the price we get for him on the day, and we wash our faces and move on to something else.

The horse is bought on behalf of a group of friends – The Not Afraid Partnership, headed up by Malcolm Kimmins and John Jarvis. They decide to keep part of the sire's name when they send him into training with Nicky that season. They call him Bobs Worth.

∩

There's a buzz in Seven Barrows that winter, but it's not Bobs Worth that's causing it. The first time that I sit up on Sprinter Sacre, the day of his Ascot bumper in February 2010, it's easy to see what all the fuss is about. When his owners, Raymond and Caroline Mould, agreed a few years earlier to buy him from a job lot in France, they knew they were taking a punt. As it turned out, their numbers came up; their prize was the horse of a lifetime.

It's love at first sight for me. I take one look at Sprinter Sacre and he takes my breath away. He's only four years old and he's already built like a superstar in the making. Visually, he's the most impressive horse I've ever been lucky enough to ride and in terms of ability, as I soon discover, he's every bit as talented as Moscow Flyer at his best. From the second I sit up on him in the Ascot parade ring, he's got grace. I can feel the power coiled beneath me. When we break into a gallop, he's got speed. When we take him over jumps, he's got scope and accuracy. He's got that enthusiastic personality, loves racing, is ready for any challenge. He's all class. It oozes from him.

It has already been a day to remember by the time I get up on him to ride in the bumper. I win the first race on the card, a novice hurdle, on Finian's Rainbow. The Reynoldstown is up next and I make it a quick double for the day when I win that one too on Burton Port. An hour later I win the feature race of the day, the Grade 1 Ascot Chase, on Monet's Garden. It could have been even better. Nicky has two horses in one of the later novice hurdles that afternoon and he wants me to ride Osric for Richard and Lizzie Kelvin-Hughes. I don't argue, although it's hard not to see it as one that got away when we're beaten by 43 lengths and Nicky's other one, Lush Life, wins instead with Ruby on board.

I should be going out on Sprinter in the last race looking for my fifth winner of the day, but I won't turn up my nose at a four-timer either. All the talk in the yard doesn't seem too far off the mark in the early stages; he travels every bit as well as he looks. I ride a typical Nicky ride on him: drop him into the middle of the pack, get him relaxed, creep along, and then make a move in the last couple of furlongs, somewhere between where the last two hurdles would usually be. I'm sitting swinging when he gets to the front, thinking this is easy peasy, only for Ruby to arrive up alongside me on the second favourite. I give Sprinter a squeeze to go on again. I think that I'm in a Ferrari and not on a four-year-old running on the racecourse for the first time. I expect him to take off on me but he's slow to pick up. When you ride a young horse bursting with potential, you have to be so careful. The last thing I want to do is to give him a bad experience that could ruin him for ever. I ride him hands and heels, hands and heels, hands and heels, waiting for him to pull away and move a few lengths clear of Ruby's fella, but he never does. He wins, but only by a nose.

It's not anywhere near as impressive as I expected him to be, but the penny drops quickly with him. We get him out for one last run before the end of the season and I see the real Sprinter in action. He hoses up in his second bumper, wins by the easiest four lengths you'll ever see, and I leave Ayr knowing that the buzz was legit. We've got a serious talent on our hands. When we start him out over hurdles the following winter, there's only one target in anyone's mind. That's what makes it such a hard decision for me to get off him and ride something else in that year's Supreme Novices' Hurdle.

Sprinter's novice season isn't perfect. He runs a bit flat in his first race back, so Nicky decides to give him a break again for another couple of months. It's hard to argue with the results because when he comes back the following February ahead of Cheltenham, he's electric. He bolts up in Ffos Las and then bolts up again in Ascot a fortnight later.

'Jesus, that horse is unbelievable,' Noel Meade tells me when we're chatting one day. 'I've never seen anything like him.'

Noel has always been a great judge of a horse and when he sees it, he says it. It's high praise coming from him, and yet I'm still not certain that Sprinter is the horse I want to ride in the Supreme. Spirit Son's performances on the racecourse don't hold a candle to Sprinter's, but every time I ride him in a piece of work, he rips up the gallop and annihilates everything else that comes up against him. He looks the real deal at home, always really impressive, but even though he's won a couple of novice hurdles as well, he just hasn't managed to travel and excel at that same level on the racecourse.

Ten days or so before the race, I arrive to ride out in Nicky's and I know that it's decision day. I'll ride one piece of work on each of them and then I'll have to pick one. I ride Spirit Son first and, same as always, he blows me away. It's an unbelievable piece of work. Sprinter works nicely too, but when we're done, he gives a big blow. If Spirit Son is 100% ready, Sprinter doesn't even feel 90%. It's a good piece of work but he's just not as fit or as forward. I know Nicky's not going to work him any harder than he has already done, put pressure on him and gun him for this race. With a big horse like Sprinter, he's always thinking of the bigger picture. That's what makes him such a brilliant trainer. Nicky, Corky and most of the team at Seven Barrows think I should be riding Spirit Son. It's a huge call to make but on the basis of the two pieces of work alone, it's cut and dried. Once I feel Sprinter give that blow as early as he did, my decision's made for me. I'll ride Spirit Son. When I tell Noel that I'm getting off Sprinter, he can't believe it.

There's real depth to the 2011 Supreme and Nicky's pair aren't the only top-level prospects in the running. Cue Card, last year's bumper winner, is there, and so is Al Ferof, the latest rising star to wear the yellow silks and red star of John Hales. I let Spirit Son drop in around fifth or sixth, not too far off the early pace. AP McCoy rides Sprinter and they sit just in behind us, never too far away. AP makes the first move as we come down the hill on the run to the third last. Sprinter has never fully settled and he's keen to get on with it. AP lets him hit the front, daring the rest of us to come and try to beat him. I'm right there beside him on Spirit Son, biding my time as Cue Card looms up between us and throws down the first challenge to Sprinter.

Cue Card starts to run out of steam as we turn into the home straight and come down to the last, while Al Ferof is still making good ground behind us in fourth, full of running for Ruby. Sprinter is first to rise at the last, but he clips the top of the hurdle and it leaves the door just slightly ajar for me. Spirit Son takes the lead on landing but only briefly before Ruby and Al Ferof come charging up the home straight, freshest of all, to beat us on the run to the line. Spirit Son chases home in second, two lengths back, with Sprinter a little over three lengths behind us in third.

That race is the making of Spirit Son. It is the day he becomes a racehorse. He steps up to two and a half miles a few weeks later and franks the Cheltenham form by trouncing Cue Card, beating him by 13 lengths in the Mersey Novices' Hurdle in Aintree. Unfortunately, we never get to see how good he might have been; his young career is cut short by injury, forcing his owner, Michael Buckley, to retire him with a record of four wins and a second from five races. As for Sprinter, I promise myself that I'll never get off him again if I have the choice.

Finishing second is the story of my week in Cheltenham that year. Spirit Son is second in the Supreme; Finian's Rainbow is second in the Arkle; Carole's Legacy is second in the Festival Trophy. They're the first three races on the opening day of the festival, and I finish second in all three of them. I finish third in the Champion Hurdle, second in the Champion Chase. When Friday comes, I still haven't had a winner. My whole week is now riding on Bobs Worth in the Albert Bartlett Novices' Hurdle; I just hope we've picked the right race for him.

Bobs Worth is the same on the gallops in Seven Barrows as he was on the day Norman and I bought him. There's nothing flashy or impressive about him. He's not doing anything wrong, but he doesn't do a whole lot to get me excited about him either. I've ridden plenty like him in the past – nice horses who won't have the biggest future but who should win a couple of races and have a bit of fun along the way.

Nicky gives him his first run in a Kempton bumper to test the water and see where he stands. Kempton's bumpers are generally a pretty good yardstick, and the going is good-to-soft, which we expect to suit him down to the ground. Nicky has the favourite in the race as well, a horse called Prince Of Pirates which is owned by John Magnier and ridden by John's son, JP. He makes the running from the start and I follow him round. We head him briefly to take the lead with about two furlongs to go but Prince Of Pirates steps up another gear in the last couple of hundred yards to win by a length and a half. I'm pleasantly surprised leaving Kempton that evening. It's not a performance to make the hairs on your neck stand up, but it's certainly more impressive than anything we've seen from him at home. He goes back to Kempton again for another bumper a couple of months later, and this time he wins.

It's only when he starts racing over hurdles that I'm forced to admit that maybe I've been underestimating him slightly. If that's the case, I'm happy to be wrong every day of the week. Nicky decides that something about Kempton obviously suits him, so we go back there again for his novice hurdle debut. I adjust my expectations accordingly. Kempton is a sharp two miles, and the going is good, and I've yet to see anything from Bobs Worth on the gallops at home to suggest he'll be able to handle that pace. But as he turns into the straight, he's still tanking along and he wins, going away from the others by nine lengths. It's too good a performance to ignore, made even more encouraging by the fact that the runner-up, Sire De Grugy, is no slouch and a future Champion Chaser in waiting himself.

After that, there's no denying that we've a really good prospect on our hands. I'm even more excited because I know from him that he'll be even better when we step him up in trip to race over a longer distance, and that proves to be the case. He wins over two and a half miles in Cheltenham on New Year's Day and then really puts himself on the map by winning a Grade 2 over the same distance a few weeks later on Cheltenham trials day. It turns into a really good scrap against a really good horse, but when Paul Nicholls's Rock On Ruby serves it up to him after the last, Bobs Worth is ready for the fight. They go toe-to-toe but Bobs Worth refuses to let Rock On Ruby past. He runs all the way to the line, winning by a little more than two lengths, and from that point on, there's not much we can do to keep a lid on the Cheltenham chatter.

All that's left to decide is what race he should go for. Nicky's instinct is to stick with a similar trip and go for the Neptune, the big novice hurdle over two miles and five furlongs. The alternative is to step up again and go for the Albert Bartlett, a slightly longer race run over three miles. That's my preference. I have no doubt that Bobs Worth will be able to handle the extra couple of furlongs. It's generally the way with horses like him who aren't that impressive or flashy in their work. If they don't show speed at home, they're probably going to develop as more of a stayer. The pace over three miles will just be that couple of notches slower, which I think will work in his favour too. He's not a bad jumper in any sense but he's not as slick as I'd like him to be at times. I worry that he could just be prone to making a mistake at the wrong time. If he's going at speed, one of those could be enough to cost him the race, but if the gallop we're going at is a beat or two slower, that might be all he needs to get a leg out.

In the end, we go for the Albert Bartlett and he jumps off the 15/8 favourite. Friday afternoon is a long time to wait to get a score on the board and I'm not the only one facing the pretty bleak prospect of a blank week; Nicky is still waiting for his first winner too. Bobs Worth makes a mistake at third last just as we're starting to move up on the outside and get into a position to challenge, but it's nothing catastrophic. He gallops away and gallops away and gallops into the lead in the home straight and all I have to do is give him a couple of taps on the neck to make sure he keeps his concentration at the last. He jumps it like a fence, brushing the top of it with his hind legs as he lands, and takes off up the hill. I hear someone running on behind us, throwing the kitchen sink at us as they try and chase us down. I'm not sure who it is. And they never get close enough for me to find out.

20

'Mate, I've never seen you like this,' Ben Pauling says to me. 'You're a wreck.'

That's putting it politely, but at least Ben can see that I'm not messing around here. I'm up to ninety with worry and I need to make sure that he's hearing what I'm saying. Because if anything were to happen to Sprinter Sacre up in Doncaster, I really don't know what I would do.

As impressive as Sprinter was over hurdles, we've always suspected that he could be a completely different machine when we send him chasing. It's a frightening prospect, but I'm more frightened by the fact that he's making his debut over fences and I won't be the one to ride him. I'll be 150 miles away riding another horse. Nicky decides that he needs me in Cheltenham for the first day of the December meeting and that David Bass, one of the second jockeys in the yard, will ride Sprinter in Doncaster. Nicky won't even be there himself – he'll be in Cheltenham too – so Ben is going as his representative. I go over the instructions with him again.

'Just make sure that David takes him down to the start quietly and keeps him nice and relaxed,' I tell Ben. 'There's no need to be asking any questions at the fences. He can just let him pop away and it'll be grand. The last thing you want is to set him alight. And don't get to the front too soon. Just try to keep it all nice and calm.'

I could do with taking a bit of my own advice, but I'm totally wound up. David's a very good jockey; it's got nothing to do with that. Sprinter's the most exciting horse I've sat up on since Moscow. He's my baby and I want to mind him. I don't want David to be worried or nervous going out on him, so I try not to let him see how anxious I am.

'Just ride him quietly and take a lead if you can' – that's the only advice I give him – and it's poor Ben that gets it both barrels instead. After that, it's out of my hands, whether I like it or not.

I win the first race at Cheltenham, and as I'm leaving the weighroom to head out for my next ride, I see Sprinter tucked in behind the leader on the run down to the first fence. He jumps it safely. Only 11 more fences to go. As I'm crossing the track to head down to the start for my next race, I catch another glimpse of Sprinter on the big screen. He pops up over the last, a good five lengths clear of the only other horse that's managed to stay anywhere close to him, and he takes off like a rocket when David lets him go, winning by 24 lengths. It's over. Job done. He'll be back home soon. I breathe a huge sigh of relief and get back to concentrating on the task at hand. When I get back to Tom and Ben's that evening after racing, he's thrilled with how he jumped, quick and slick. We sit down to look at the replay together. Watching through my fingers, even though I know how it ends, I manage to see most of it.

Sprinter didn't beat much, but it's the way that he beat them, and there's no doubt that he's ready to step up into a higher class of company. Nicky enters him into the Wayward Lad Novices' Chase, the Grade 2 at Kempton two days after Christmas. It's only a three-horse race but we've got company. Peddlers Cross, who chased home Hurricane Fly in the Champion Hurdle a few months earlier, is the odds-on favourite. He's the favourite for the Arkle in most places too, given that he's barely made a mistake in his two runs over fences so far. The third horse in the race, Harry Hunt, isn't in the same league at all. This is a match between the two of us.

I spot Donald McCain, Peddlers Cross's trainer, while I'm waiting for Nicky to come and weigh me out for the race. Donald's a lovely fella, someone I get on very well with, and I go over to wish him the best of luck. I know how Donald likes to have his horses ridden and I'd make a good guess that I know what his instructions to Jason Maguire will be: go hard, be aggressive, win the race.

'This isn't their most important day,' I remind Donald. 'We don't need to cut each other's throats here.'

I say it as much for my own benefit as for his. It happens all the time; two good horses meet in a match, the public and the media get hyped up for the showdown, and one horse or both ends up sacrificing their whole season for what's ultimately a pretty meaningless race. But Donald thinks he's got a good thing, and they're here today to prove it.

'You look after your fella when he comes off the bridle,' he says to me, warning me that Sprinter might run out of gas before the finish and need to be pushed to the line. And before the words are out of his mouth, I let him know exactly how this one is going to go.

'Donald, he won't be coming off the bridle.'

I'm bullish but I've no reason not to be. Sprinter was as good as any of his class of novice hurdlers, and any time I've schooled him at home over fences, he has jumped them like they're not even there. It's not just the scope he has when he's jumping; it's the grace. But I can't be complacent either. It's hard to know how good he's going to be until he's forced out of his comfort zone and that hasn't happened yet. It will today. This will be his first big jumping test. The speed we'll be going – two miles on a sharp track in good company – will be new to him. Against lesser horses, he's always been able to do things at his own pace. He doesn't really have any experience of jumping at speed. It's easy to make a mistake. Shit could hit the fan. But once we get out there, there's no need for me to worry. He floats around.

There's only one of us that comes off the bridle in Kempton that day, and it's not Sprinter. He leads Peddlers Cross the whole way around, and even though we jump the third last together, the race is already over. Jason is down low on Peddlers Cross, driving him just to keep in touch, while I'm sitting up in the saddle, barely moving a muscle on Sprinter. I give him a little squeeze when we land at the back of the last, let him know that if he wants to stretch his legs, that's fine by me, and he runs away to the line. He wins. By 16 lengths.

Sprinter passes the test with flying colours. If jumping precisely, clinically, at speed isn't a concern for him, then there's never going to be a concern. He's only had two runs over fences but it's quickly becoming clear that there's no horse out there that he needs to fear. He's as good as any of them. Nicky has two choices now. He can wrap him up and send him straight to Cheltenham for the Arkle and nobody would bat an eyelid, or he can give him one more run and a little bit more experience before his big day. We decide to go for the Game Spirit Chase in Newbury. It's a Grade 2 in open company; he'll be up against seasoned horses who have been running over fences for years. I love the thought of it.

Sprinter's so good, so enthusiastic, that he could turn out to be his own worst enemy. I want to try to teach him how to relax a bit, to settle and save his energy, and the easiest way to do that is to find a race with a bit of pace and let him take a lead. It might have happened in Kempton, only Peddlers Cross made a mistake at the first fence. Chances are there aren't novices out there that will be good enough, that will go off strongly enough, that he'll be able to take a lead. When he's left out in front by himself, he just lights up and takes off and burns around and blows his brains. But if we send him out to race against more experienced horses and I can get him settled off the pace, I can try to teach him how to make his own life a bit easier.

We don't know what calibre of opponent we'll run into in the Game Spirit. In the end, it turns out to be an average enough renewal. Nicky also has French Opera, who won the race last year. We know he'll make the running and Sprinter can follow until it's time to challenge. The plan works perfectly – until we get to the seventh fence, Sprinter says sod that, and jumps out in front to take the lead.

Everything has to be done so quietly when you're trying to teach a keen horse to settle. Every time he jumps a fence, I drop my hands and leave my reins sitting slack. That's my sign to him that we're taking it easy. I don't want him to stick his head out and take up contact or start straining to go on. But every single time, within two strides of landing at the back of the fence, Sprinter is back in my hands again and pulling away from me – let's go, what are we waiting for? We jump the next and I do the same thing again, drop my hands, sit dead still. Don't pick up, don't pick up, and then boom, he grabs me again, switched on, dying to get on with it. That's how enthusiastic he is. He'll get away with it today – there's nothing good enough to really challenge him – but against better horses, I don't want him burning the candle at both ends.

We jump the last fence three or four lengths clear of French Opera in second and, for the first time all day, Sprinter doesn't grab hold of me. He coasts home, completely on the bridle, beating far more experienced horses in only his third run over fences, and breaks the track record that has stood for more than 23 years.

It's an incredible statement. We knew how good he was. Now the rest of the world does too. The second coming has arrived.

It hits me as we go down to the start of the Arkle. It's only for a second and I don't dwell on it, but still, it hits me. The anticipation, the excitement, it's gone into overdrive for the last few weeks and I've tuned it all out, but now we're here, I can't ignore it any more. The whole year has been building towards this one moment. For me and for Sprinter. Everyone's watching. Everyone expects. This is it.

I take a deep breath, snap myself back to reality, take all of the emotion out of the situation. It's only a horse race, same as any other day of the week. Two miles, six horses, 13 fences – I've done it a thousand times or more. Yes, the prize is bigger. Yes, I'm on the best horse in the race. But the fundamentals are still the same. I know my horse. I know my instructions. I know my opposition. I know what I need to do.

Sprinter has been even money to win the race since his performance at Newbury; now he's odds on. Al Ferof and Cue Card, the best of last year's Supreme Novices, are back to do it again. They're the ones who set the pace up front. It looks like it will be between the three of us from a long way out. But even in a competitive year, the reality is that one horse is head and shoulders above the rest.

It's as easy as a schooling session for Sprinter. I never even have to take him out of third gear. The year Moscow Flyer won his Arkle, they went off flat to the boards and I only had two horses behind me for most of the first half-mile. Al Ferof and Cue Card set a similar pace here. The only difference is that Sprinter is on their tails, galloping all over them without even trying. He pulls me down the back straight. He wants to go. Wait, I tell him. We'll get our chance.

A young chaser has a tendency to be a bit more exuberant with their jumping. Sprinter takes it to the extreme. Al Ferof and Cue Card jump nicely, measure their arc across the brushes of the fence. A black shadow soars over them like an aeroplane as Sprinter puts in huge leaps, putting plenty of daylight between himself and his obstacles. Al Ferof stands way back off the ditch at the end of the back straight, so far back that he nearly comes down on top of the fence. It's a bad mistake. Sprinter jumps it two lengths behind him, lands two lengths in front of him, and takes off down the hill. There's no stopping him now. He's five lengths clear jumping the third last. These are top-level horses he's racing against and he's barely breaking out of a canter to pull clear of them. Joe Tizzard has been saving a bit for the fight on Cue Card. He closes the gap on the run down to the second last but it takes all he's got just to eat into Sprinter's lead and try to get back on terms. Finishing seven lengths second is by no means a disgrace. Sprinter is simply that much better than everyone else.

It's the opening act of another one of those incredible Cheltenham weeks, a five-part play that I don't ever want the curtain to come down on. Just like Bobs Worth a year earlier, Nicky is torn between two options for Simonsig, another classy novice hurdler who is going places in a hurry. For a horse that works like a miler on the gallops at home, the Supreme Novices' is the obvious option, but we find ourselves weighing up the exact same question: would the slightly slower pace over the Neptune's two miles five furlongs be a bit more forgiving for his jumping? We settle on the longer race and when Simonsig's main challenger runs out at the second last hurdle, it's easy up the hill to win by seven lengths.

I jump down off Simonsig and up on to Bobs Worth, win the RSA Chase – the Gold Cup for novices – and then jump down off Bobs Worth and up on to Finian's Rainbow, the second favourite for the Champion Chase. It has already been the most surreal 90 minutes of my career and it's about to get even better.

Finian's Rainbow is improving all the time but we've our work cut out for us up against the defending champion, Sizing Europe. He has three wins from four this season, his only defeat coming when he stepped up to three miles on soft ground for the JN Wine Chase at Down Royal. He won't be knocked off his perch without a fight, but if there's a chance, even half a chance, I'm on the right horse to take it.

Wishfull Thinking and Richard Johnson lead us out over the first few fences. We're a stride or two behind when they fall at the fourth, the fence in front of the stands, and crash out through the rail and into the small group of people that have gathered there. We hear the gasp of the crowd but we're gone past it and off out into the country before we know what's happened or if any damage has been done. We follow Sizing Europe down the back straight, first and second the whole way along, and as we come to the top of the hill, Andrew Lynch bombs down the hill towards the third last. It's not a move I'd ever make if I could avoid it. That particular part of Cheltenham can break hearts just as easily as the long run to the finish. A horse will take off down the hill like a snowball if you let it, his legs going faster than he wants them to, and unless he's got buckets left in the tank, he'll bottom out when he comes off the down slope and meets the rising ground again. You have to be so careful.

I leave Andrew at it, let him pull a few lengths clear of us. If I go with him now, I'll throw away my only chance, so I sit and wait instead. Up in the owners' and trainers' bar, my brother Norman is watching the race. Jamie Spencer, the top flat jockey, turns to him as we come down the hill, a half-mile from home, and calls it there and then – 'Your man wins.'

Sizing Europe misses the third last, gets in a little bit close, and we fly over it behind him, jumping right back up onto his tail. As we land, I feel Finian's Rainbow contract and expand again; he lets out a huge blow and then fills right back up again in the next breath. I don't know what Sizing Europe has got left but I know my lad is ready for a race. We turn into the home straight, jump the second last, and that's where the confusion starts.

I'm not thinking about the last fence or even looking at it until we're on the run down to it. I'm riding my race, trying to win a Champion Chase. And then I see the chevrons, pointing us away from the last. It's dolled off. Don't jump it. Go around. I'm on the outside and Andrew's on the inside, so he's the one who moves first. He grabs his reins and steers Sizing Europe away from the fence and across my racing line, but then steers back towards the fence and straightens up again. The chevrons are only covering half the fence, though, the half over by the rail where Wishfull Thinking and Dicky fell a few minutes ago. There are no chevrons on the half nearest us, nothing to stop us from jumping it. The old rule was that if the markers are only covering part of the fence, you're not supposed to bypass it entirely, but me and the rulebook wouldn't exactly be close friends so there's a split second of uncertainty where I'm not sure what we should be doing. I'm ready to jump it if we're jumping it. Andrew steers back across me again. He wants to go around. I roar at him: 'Make up your fucking mind! Make up your fucking mind!'

We go round it. It's a long run to the line when there's no fence there to jump, but Finian's Rainbow digs in and won't be shaken off. Fifty yards from the line, he sticks his nose in front and Sizing Europe's resistance is broken. His reign is over. Finian's Rainbow wins by a length and a quarter, and for the third time in as many

Grade 1 races this afternoon, I'm on my way back to the winners' enclosure.

There are a dozen different ways to lose the Ryanair Chase on Riverside Theatre, my fifth winner of the week, and somehow I manage to dodge every snake and find every ladder. He's made favourite for the race on the back of his win in the Ascot Chase a month before the festival but he's a horse that runs well fresh and, for most of the run round, I have a sinking feeling that Cheltenham might have come a bit too soon for him. He's on the back foot from the start. His jumping is off. I need to give him a bit of a shake, just to keep him interested and involved and stop him falling off the back of the pack.

With five fences left to jump, we're struggling to hold our position. I need a gap to open up somewhere for me. Sam Twiston-Davies has been at the front from the very start on Little Josh, a 66/1 outsider. It's been a good pace and I can see that he's just starting to feel the pinch. I give Sam a shout: 'Any chance of a bit of room there, Sam?'

And in an instant, it's like the Red Sea parting in front of us. Riverside Theatre spots the space and jumps up into it. There's a lot of race left in front of us and I'm chasing away and chasing away just to keep Riverside Theatre moving forward, however reluctantly. But without that gap, we wouldn't have been going anywhere. It's a massive break for us at a moment when I was crying out for anything. Sam didn't have to move over or make life easy for us, but he knew his chance was fading away. That's him to a tee, a great jockey and a sound man.

I ask Riverside Theatre for a hallelujah jump at the fourth last and I get it from him, and as I pull him out wide on the run down to third last, we're on the same long stride again. I let him know that this needs to be another big one and he comes up trumps again. Andrew Lynch and Rubi Light are just in front, AP looming large on Albertas Run in behind them. There's a lot of chances still alive and if we can just hang on, we'll have one too. Albertas Run takes it up after the third last, AP hoping to steal a few lengths and run the finish out of the rest of us. Medermit, the grey, runs on well from behind me for Robert Thornton, sticking tight to the rail. The three of us jump the last in a line, Albertas Run still there to be shot at, hanging on for dear life, but it's not enough. With one last burst from somewhere deep inside him, Riverside Theatre squeezes past him and wins by a half-length. We had no right even being there in a fight to the finish. The way he was travelling, he should have been out on his feet long ago. I don't know how he's done it but he has. He just didn't know when to give up.

He's a very popular winner. His owner, the actor Jimmy Nesbitt, is there to greet us when we come back into the parade ring.

'You got Conor's bet up,' the lads from the yard tell me as the party breaks out around us.

'What do you mean, Conor's bet?' I ask. It's the first I've heard of it.

'He was the last horse in Conor's bet,' they tell me. 'All five of them are up.'

Conor Murphy is nowhere to be seen. He's one of the head lads in Nicky's, from Cork, and someone I've always got on great with, even before the calculator starts spinning in my head and my eyes start to water at the amount he's just won. Back before Christmas, he picked five of the best horses in the yard and had a £50 bet that all five of them would win.

Sprinter Sacre.

Simonsig.

Bobs Worth.

Finian's Rainbow.

And Riverside Theatre.

I can't believe what they're telling me. With a bet like that, it's all or nothing. If one part of the bet goes down, it all goes down. If Simonsig had gone for the Supreme rather than the Neptune, Conor would have ended up with nothing – even if Simonsig had won the race. He could have cashed out on Wednesday after the fourth winner, taken a smaller payout, but he let it ride all the way to the end. I can't even imagine what he must have been thinking as Riverside Theatre scrubbed around.

Wherever he is, the ticket he's got in his hand isn't worth £50 any more. When he cashes it in, Conor Murphy walks away with £1 million in his bank account.

The two of us had been discussing the horses all through the winter but he never said a word to me about the bet. When I finally get through to him later on that evening to congratulate him, it sounds like he's still in shock. There'd been a big celebration the night before after Finian's Rainbow's win – so big that Conor tells me he couldn't even get off the couch to cheer home Riverside Theatre. It's a life-changing win for him; he uses the money to move to the United States where he sets up his own training operation in Kentucky.

I chat to Conor on my way into Cheltenham town that evening for dinner with some family and friends. Paula's sister Liz is with us, as is Liz's husband Seán, and so are the Molony family of Thurles Racecourse. No matter where we are – whether it's Galway, Killarney, Listowel, Aintree – the Molonys are there to celebrate with me and Paula. We have incredible craic together and a lot of very fond memories of the chatting and laughing and singing and dancing we've done at different parties over the years. Annemarie is married to John Cullen, who I've got on great with since we started racing together, and when I first started going out with Paula, it was Annemarie who was always looking out for her at the races. When our second daughter, Órla, was born in May 2011, we asked Annemarie to be her godmother.

There's never any doubt that a night out with the Molonys will be a good one, and after five winners, we've plenty of reasons to celebrate. We start off with dinner in Zizzi's, which is in an old church that has been transformed with a big wood-fired pizza oven, and then move on to finish up in the Queen's Hotel afterwards. Jimmy Nesbitt joins us, soaking up every last bit of Riverside Theatre's win, and I bump into David Walsh, the chief sports writer of *The Sunday Times*, and we have a great chat.

I don't have any more winners on Friday – I'm in front jumping the last fence in the final race of the week only for Paul Carberry to arrive with his trademark timing and get up to beat me a few strides from the line – but I finish the festival as leading rider for the first time since 2003. In this game, you learn to appreciate the good days; this week has been up there with the best.

21

Bobs Worth might not be the most spectacular or flashy horse, but he's easy to fall in love with. He always tries to please. He's been that way since we had him at home, a real genuine personality, a horse that wants to work with you and not against you.

When we go chasing with him after winning the Albert Bartlett, those traits shine through in his jumping. He's nimble and he's neat. He knows where to put his feet. Everything is measured. We send him to Newbury first time out for the Berkshire Novices' Chase where we come up against Cue Card. Straight away, we've a high-class horse to pitch ourselves against; we'll get a good sense of where we stand. Bobs Worth travels nicely for me into the straight, but as we meet the fourth last, he jumps a little left and bumps into Cue Card. I feel him give a blow and I know not to push him immediately, to give him a couple of strides to recover and fill back up again. Cue Card pulls four lengths clear of us, but when Bobs Worth gets going again and his stamina kicks in, he flies home. We get up just in the nick of time, beating Cue Card by a short head on the line.

I mention his wind to Nicky when I come back in. He wasn't at peak fitness for the race – Nicky's horses generally improve after their first run of the season – but I could tell that he was struggling to get air into his lungs. You can hear it from a horse as well as feel it, a little whistle or a gurgle that they make if their throat is narrow or their airway is impeded. It's no surprise that he's beaten in Kempton next time out on St Stephen's Day. Racing three miles in top gear on a sharp track is a real test; he needs to be able to fill up fully and when he can't, he's outpaced on the run-in. Nicky sends him for a wind operation and he finishes second on his first run back, in the Reynoldstown at Ascot, but we only really see the full benefit of it when he arrives at Cheltenham for the RSA Chase that March. It's a long, hard race but he's still full of running after the last and wins going away from a very good horse in First Lieutenant.

Bobs Worth only runs twice the following season. We need to save him from himself, as much as anything. When he runs, he empties himself, leaves it all out on the pitch. That's just the type of horse he is. His races really take it out of him, he's a shell of himself for a while afterwards, and Nicky knows that how we time his campaign could easily be make or break. Bobs Worth wins a good renewal of the Hennessy Gold Cup in December and puts every other horse in the three-mile division on notice – and that's it. He goes straight to the Gold Cup, the holy grail.

As Cheltenham gets closer, everybody wants to tell the same story, everybody reaches for the Disney script: take us back to 2006 – you bought this horse when he was only a yearling, reared him at home on the farm, and now you're riding him as the favourite for the Gold Cup. When you sum it up like that, it's easy to see the fairytale, the unique beauty of how this particular adventure has unfolded. It will be one to tell the grandkids in years to come, I'm sure. But there has been a lot of life and a lot of living in those six years. The journey takes place in slow motion, not in a single sentence, and it's hard to step back and appreciate the big picture while you're in the thick of it. Nor do I want to. There's a whole week of racing to get through before then. The Gold Cup is not until Friday.

And by the time Friday comes, everything has changed.

I always got on really well with John Thomas McNamara. He was a horseman, in every sense of the word. A gifted rider. Someone who understood his horse and how to get the best out of it. John Thomas rode as an amateur, so we wouldn't have bumped into each other in the weighroom every day, but he was someone I had great time for; he was a man to speak his mind, a bit like me, which helped. I had huge respect for him, his work rate, his style, his skill. He rode Monty's Pass a couple of times when Monty was starting out over fences. I always felt that there was a little bit of John Thomas's legacy in the way Monty jumped.

The race in which John Thomas had his accident at Cheltenham in 2013, the Kim Muir, is a race for amateur riders. I had already finished for the day and was up in the owners' and trainers' bar when I heard the helicopter coming in to airlift him to hospital. His horse, Galaxy Rock, had fallen at the first fence. I didn't realise how seriously John Thomas had been injured. I'm not sure that any of us really did. By the following morning, everyone's worst fears were confirmed. John Thomas had broken his neck. He was in an induced coma with two broken vertebrae and was being prepared for surgery. Racing carried on while we hoped and prayed for good news, but Cheltenham felt empty that Friday morning. I met John Francome when I arrived at the course. It was Gold Cup day, a day that should have been full of celebration and excitement, but racing was the last thing on our minds. Whatever won the Gold Cup, it didn't matter.

I was 17, still a seven-pound claimer finding my place in the weighroom, when Shane Broderick fell in March 1997 and broke his neck, leaving him paralysed for life. I remember the impact it had, the toll it took on everyone, particularly those who knew him best. I remember the day of Kieran Kelly's funeral in August 2003, the packed church in Carbury, and how the tears I had been bottling up for days couldn't be hidden away any more. Kieran was 25, my friend, and he was gone.

I was sitting beside Kieran in Kilbeggan on the day he had his fall. He was a couple of months older than me, but we both started out racing around the same time. We got to know each other well, days in the weighroom and nights on the town. Kieran was living with Paul Moloney, and I was a regular visitor, always ready to park myself there for the night and enjoy the party. The day I won my first Champion Chase on Moscow Flyer, Kieran won the old Royal & SunAlliance Novices' Hurdle on Hardy Eustace for Dessie Hughes. It was the biggest day of both of our careers. Five months later, Kieran was in hospital with serious head injuries, fighting for his life.

I was racing in Gowran Park on the evening Kieran died. I was getting ready to go out for my next ride, and the last little bit of hope that we'd all been clinging on to was extinguished with a couple of words. Dave Fox, the jockeys' valet, had heard the news and he was the one who told us. I sat back down at my peg and thought about Kieran, the good times that we'd shared together. The fact that we wouldn't share any more. It just didn't feel real. The last two races on the card were abandoned as a mark of respect. I couldn't bring myself to go back out racing, couldn't pretend to concentrate or care. None of us could. Racing was the last thing on our minds.

Every jockey knows the risk they're taking when they go out to ride a horse. One bad fall can end a life or change it for ever. But we do it because we love it. Shane Broderick loved it. Kieran Kelly loved it. John Thomas McNamara loved it. The worry and the fears are real, but we block them out because we have to.

212

Accidents happen, but you never think that it will happen to you or the guy sitting next to you. The sad truth is that it's a lot closer than we'll ever allow ourselves to admit.

The rain comes on the morning of the Gold Cup and with that, I feel Bobs Worth's chance sink away into the softening ground. In 11 races, he's never run on anything heavier than good-to-soft, and now is not the day to see if his stamina can hold up to the extra scrutiny. Even if he handles it, there are sure to be one or two others that it will suit better. Long Run, Nicky's other runner, won't be too put out by it. He had good ground when he won his Gold Cup in 2011, but he also won this season's King George over three miles on heavy. Ruby's horse, Silviniaco Conti, has won a couple of top staying chases this season on soft ground. Sir Des Champs had no problems with three miles on soft or worse around Leopardstown when he won the Hennessy Gold Cup a month ago. Davy Russell, who'd normally ride him, is recovering from a punctured lung so AP McCoy is on board instead today.

In a good race like the Gold Cup that's run at an end-to-end gallop, you don't really know what you have until you've gone two miles. That's where the cracks begin to show. If the soft ground is sapping the energy out of Bobs Worth, that's when I'll know. Before we even jump off, I can picture the point of the race in my head – halfway down the back straight on our final circuit. That's where he could start to struggle.

By the time we jump the first ditch in the back straight, he's flat to the boards. He's sitting sixth and already stretched, but he's not done yet. It's just a question of how long he can keep it going. Long Run leads with Sir Des Champs in second. There's only three or four lengths covering us all in the leading group and I'm in no rush to make a move. It's a carbon copy of my Champion Hurdle win on Punjabi, except this time I'm on a much better horse. I have to conserve the little bit of energy that he has left and see how long we can hang on to their coattails. Then I can decide when it's time to go.

I pull him out wide on the run down the hill to the third last. We've passed a couple, moved up into fourth, and we're still in touch. Bobs Worth jumps it really well, and when Silviniaco Conti falls in front us, he skips around him like a horse that has still got a little bit left in the tank. That's the only proof I need that we still have a chance.

Before I can blink, we're eight lengths down. Sir Des Champs and Long Run take off, AP and Sam Waley-Cohen going head-to-head to try and win the race right there and then. They're at full tilt as they turn into the straight and I'm treading water behind them. I can't go any quicker, even if I want to. If I ask Bobs Worth to go before he's ready, he'll give me everything he's got. He always does. But that'll only be enough to carry us for a furlong and a half and then he'll be empty. I nurse him as the two lads rock on like there's no tomorrow and then when we finally start to chase them, it's like a slingshot effect. Sir Des Champs and Long Run bottom out as they get to the second last and we come bombing down behind them, full to the brim and ready to go.

The eight-length gap vanishes as quickly as it appeared. We pass them both on the run down to the last and jump it with a lead of a half a length. Sir Des Champs finds a second wind and comes after us. He turns it into a fight, but he can only fight for so long. With 100 yards to go, he has nothing left to give. Bobs Worth runs all the way to the line. He loves the hill. He loves this place. He's just won the Gold Cup.

It should be a moment that I'll treasure for the rest of my life. It should be up there with Moscow and Kicking King and

Sprinter and all the other great memories. I should be saluting the crowd, singing Bobs Worth's praises after the most gutsy of runs, savouring the second Gold Cup of my career. I wish I could be happy but I can't.

I feel empty. There's no joy in this moment. None of it matters. There's a photo, taken just after the finish line, of me staring into space. No smile. No nothing. Vacant. All I can think of is John Thomas and his family.

John Thomas McNamara was paralysed from the neck down as a result of his fall in Cheltenham that year. He was 41 years old when he died in July 2016. For me, he will always be a big part of that memory of the day I won the Gold Cup on Bobs Worth. May he rest in peace.

22

printer Sacre's Champion Chase is a procession. When he jumps the last, I give him a squeeze – go on if you want to, stretch your legs and show them how easy this is for you. He doesn't need to be asked twice. He runs out a winner by 19 lengths, and the rest of the racing world runs out of superlatives. Wherever the bar for all-time greatness is, Sprinter has his nose pressed up against it. And he's pushing.

He transforms from horse into rock star and we give the fans what they want with a mini-tour to finish out the season. Just two dates: Aintree and Punchestown. The Melling Chase at Aintree is a high-class race, and we're up against very good horses – Cue Card, Flemenstar, Finian's Rainbow – and he coasts through it. It's his first time running over two and a half miles, but the extra distance doesn't inconvenience him in the slightest. Running down to the last, he's still got so much energy, so much enthusiasm, that he nearly runs away on me. Five strides away I can see that he's on a long stride and I give him a fraction of rein so that he can go for it; an inch would be too much. His next stride is longer, and his next one longer again, until all of a sudden, there's a danger that we'll get in too close to the fence. I take him back and he pops up over it instead. It's a rare feeling to be on a horse that travels that well down to the last, never mind in a Grade 1 against the best of what's out there. But then again, Sprinter is a rare horse.

Punchestown is his Glastonbury and he's ready to headline the main stage. It's his third big race in the space of five weeks and we school him a week before he travels to Ireland, just to be sure that he has come out of Aintree okay. It's a gauge that Nicky often uses – if a horse schools well, they are well – and Sprinter schools perfectly. The sun shines on Punchestown and the place is absolutely heaving, a record crowd, and there isn't a question of who they are there to see. I can't ever remember a big day's racing that was so much about one horse. They're packed 10 deep around the parade ring, all elbows and tippy-toes just to catch a glimpse of him. I drink it in. I've been spoiled with good horses and big winners since taking the job with Nicky, but the vast majority of that success has been in England. And it's true what they say: there's no place like home.

Sizing Europe takes off at the front to make the running. Throw the kitchen sink at your man – that was Henry de Bromhead's parting instruction to Andrew Lynch, and that's what they do. But as we come down the back straight, I have two hands full and I'm trying to keep a lid on Sprinter. There's no reason for concern until we swing around the corner and make the turn to the fourth last. The change is instantaneous, as if the keys have been pulled out of the ignition. We hit a patch of heavy ground in the dip before the fourth last and Sprinter goes completely flat. It's like riding a completely different horse. I switch into survival mode. Even running on empty, Sprinter's still good enough to pull this one out of the fire. I don't do anything to give him a hard race. I let him move up to challenge Sizing Europe between the last two. He flies the last fence and I ride him hands and heels to the line.

If the ground hadn't been so soft in the last half mile, he'd have coasted home. Instead, for the first time in his career, he's had to dig deep and win ugly. He wasn't stopping at the line, he galloped right through it, but he's gone to the bottom of the well; I can feel it. It hasn't been the spectacular performance that people came to see. It wasn't the surgical excellence that you expect of a 1/9 shot. But it's a five and a half-length win at the end of a long season, a tenth straight win over fences, and the first horse to do the Cheltenham–Aintree–Punchestown hat-trick since the great Istabraq. He gets the champion's reception that he deserves. By the end of the year, I'm left wondering if it all might have come at a cost.

Everything's as it should be going in Kempton that day. Everything is fine.

If I'm looking for a warning sign, or even a hint, maybe Sprinter doesn't quite have the same spark that he would normally have. That thought crosses my mind briefly on the run down to the start but it's easily explained. He's had a good long break from racing. It's over eight months since his run at Punchestown. He turns eight in a few days' time. Maybe he's just that little bit more at ease with everything, a little bit more relaxed, as he gets older.

This race, the Desert Orchid Chase, is a Grade 2, but it's far from the strongest field of horses he's ever run in. Of the five we're up against, Sire De Grugy, the Tingle Creek winner, is the only one within two stone of him on the official ratings. He might be good enough to give us a bit of a workout, but for a horse of Sprinter's calibre, it's as straightforward as they come. A couple of the outsiders jump off to make the running and we leave them to it. I drop Sprinter in to get a bit of cover, our usual move in the early stages. He jumps the first couple of fences fine but then he runs right down to the base of the third and pops it on a short stride. That's not like him; it catches me a bit off guard.

Riding Sprinter is normally like a rollercoaster – buckle up and enjoy the rush. As we go past the winning post and turn away from the stands, it's not happening with the same zip, the same enthusiasm, that I've become so accustomed to. There's nothing obvious amiss but something just doesn't feel right. Everything is just … grand, which is not a description I've ever had reason to reach for in the past.

He puts in a good leap at the ditch going away from the stands and jumps up into second. That's better. Jamie Moore comes through on our inside on Sire De Grugy, joins us, and then presses on to go after the leader. I sit and let him go. I'm waiting, half-expecting Sprinter to tell me that he's sick of hanging around and that it's time for us to give chase too. He'd usually need no invitation. But he doesn't move.

The batteries are flat. I need to get him revved up a bit. I'm ready to ask him for a big one at the next fence, just to test the water and see if it sparks him to life. A few strides out I realise that I'm not going to get it from him. I leave him to do it his way and he pops it again. He lands at the back of the fence. He's flat, going nowhere. This isn't how it should be. I pull him up.

Whatever it is, there's something wrong. The way Sprinter's travelling, there's no way he's going to win the race, so the sooner I get him stopped and try to find out what's causing the problem, the better. It doesn't even enter my mind to keep going on him. The further we go, the worse it's going to get. I'd do the same thing if this was happening in the Champion Chase. A few years later, I do; he's not travelling and I pull him up before the last in Cheltenham. I'd do the same thing on any horse without hesitation. The horse comes first.

He's not distressed or in any obvious pain. He's able to walk without any problems when I pull him up, so I can see he's not lame. I stay in the saddle and turn him around so that we can trot slowly down the racecourse, back in the direction we've just come from. He's fine in a trot too. We go gently, all the way back, until we're back at the unsaddling enclosure. I meet Nicky there. I'm at a loss to explain to him what's just happened. Physically, he seems perfect to me, but I know that he's not.

The unsaddling enclosure fills with concerned looks and furrowed brows. Anybody who thinks that they might be able to help is there to try. The vets start to examine him. As soon as they listen to his heart, they discover the problem. Atrial fibrillation. An irregular heartbeat. I don't need the experts to tell me what the worst case scenario could have been if I had kept riding Sprinter, if I had fought against him rather than listening to him and pushed him to the finish. It doesn't bear thinking about.

∩

The bad days and the good aren't too far apart, as is so often the case in racing. When I go home that night, Sprinter is on my mind. The next morning, Paula gets the two girls dressed up in their Christmas best, Síofra in her navy coat, Órla in her red one, and they follow me out to Leopardstown. I'm excited to bring Bobs Worth home, back for his first ever run outside England. I'm excited for the Irish racing public to see the Gold Cup winner in full flight. More than anything, I'm excited to share the day with my family. He runs in the big race of the day, the Lexus Chase, and he wins it the way he loves to, a vintage Bobs Worth performance – chasing and chasing but never fully committed until he bombs home and snatches it at the death.

A few months later, the four of us go to Fairyhouse on Easter Monday and I win the Irish Grand National on Shutthefrontdoor for JP McManus. There has been so much success since moving to England, and a little bit of complacency as well, but there's no disguising the raw emotion of those two days. I punch the air coming back to the stands on Shutthefrontdoor. Síofra is eight. She knows how special it is for Dad to win the Grand National on the track just down the road from our house. Órla is a few weeks short of her third birthday, still too young to fully appreciate it, but that doesn't matter. What matters is that they're there with me. The photos from those two days, the memories, they're the ones that stand head and shoulders above everything else, above all the Cheltenham wins and all the trophies in the cabinet, as the most magical moments of my career.

It has been so long since I've had big wins like those on home soil. Once I get that taste of it, I realise how much I've missed it and how much I've been longing for it. It's not just about family; it's the community. I have great friends in England, and great times, but it's just not home. These are the tracks I grew up on, with the same familiar faces that have been there since I first started racing. There are plenty of occasions when I win a big race in England and I don't get time to enjoy the moment. I'm racing out the gate, in the car and on my way to the airport within 20 minutes of my last ride, and racing home; two and a half hours, door to door. I'm so grateful to have the job with Nicky but I start to feel a bit detached. My week in England is stretching out – Wednesday, Thursday, Friday, Saturday. It's too many nights to be away from my own bed. And then when I come home, I'm on the couch on so many Sundays watching good Irish racing instead of being a part of it. I feel like I'm living two lives.

Without even realising it, I put myself in the shop window for an opportunity that will give me the best of both worlds. I've been winning races for JP McManus since the late nineties, back when Go Roger Go was with Edward O'Grady and I'd only just ridden out my claim. It was JP who first quoted Tommy Carberry's line to me about being on your arse at the back of a fence, a few minutes after I ended up on my arse at the back of the last in Leopardstown riding Le Coudray for him. He has always had a few for me to ride over the years – my second-ever Cheltenham winner was on Youlneverwalkalone for him – and even after AP McCoy becomes his first jockey in 2004, there's always a chance of picking up a good spare ride in the green and gold.

That's exactly what happens at Cheltenham in 2014. JP has three horses entered in the Champion Hurdle and AP unsurprisingly picks the best of the three, My Tent Or Yours, who just so happens to be Nicky's only entry in the race. I've no other ride in the race so I'm more than happy to get back on to Jezki, Jessie Harrington's horse that I've ridden and won on a couple of times as a novice. It's a similar situation in the World Hurdle, the three-mile championship race on Thursday. Nicky has no runner in the race and JP has two, so when AP picks At Fishers Cross, I jump at the chance to get on More Of That. I'm convinced that he's the better of JP's two horses, even if At Fishers Cross is the one with a festival win already on his record. But the whole field will have a job to get past Ruby on one of the bankers of the week, the brilliant Annie Power. Both Jezki and More Of That are about 9/1 in the betting, which is definitely fair value given their chances. I put them up as a nice each-way double at a preview night ahead of the festival, an outside bet at taking around €10,000 out of the bookies' satchels and giving it a good home with a charity.

That year's Champion Hurdle is won and lost at the final hurdle. JP's third runner, Captain Cee Bee, sets a strong pace from the front and I take a lead in behind alongside Hurricane Fly, the favourite, who is bidding for a hat-trick in the race. I get through on the inside of Captain Cee Bee at the second last, still travelling nicely, and that leaves me in a position to dictate how things will shake out in these last few furlongs. I know that there's a slightly fresher bit of ground a little bit out from the rail so I edge out onto that, pushing Ruby and Hurricane Fly wider onto the older ground. I already have him beaten but this is the death knell. As I make that move, I'm aware that I'm leaving an invitation for something to come up my inner. I don't know who it is that's creeping into that gap to challenge, but when I sense them coming, I let Jezki drift back across so that the space is a little bit less inviting. AP arrives on My Tent Or Yours, but it's tight and he jinks left, looking out towards the wing. It doesn't cost him much momentum, but it's enough. He's not quite as quick over the last as we are and Jezki battles all the way to the line, just doing enough to hold him off by a head.

I saw my chance and I took it. That's enough to win the Champion Hurdle for the second time in my career, but I have to be a lot more tactical when I go out in the World Hurdle two days later. Of all the jockeys I've come up against, Ruby is always the hardest to beat. Paul Carberry was very tough to ride against because he'd arrive into a race like a ghost; AP McCoy had the strength and determination in a finish to get the best out of a horse that wouldn't have won otherwise; but tactically, Ruby is the sharpest of all. I've never been intimidated by going up against him, never feared him. I never allowed myself to. My brain never even allowed me to acknowledge his brilliance when I was trying to ride against him. Even the last ride of his career, his win in Punchestown on Kemboy, he couldn't have squeezed another ounce out of the horse; there are very few others out there who would have been capable of it. It's only when he retires that I can step back and acknowledge it – Ruby is the best I've ever ridden against.

Put him on a hotpot like Annie Power and it's nearly impossible to beat him, but it makes it all the more enjoyable when I do. I've never ridden More Of That before, so JP and Jonjo O'Neill keep their instructions as simple as possible: follow her. That's it.

Ruby is wise to me when we get down to the start. He lines up right out the back, last bar one, and he watches me settle in behind him. I doubt he's expecting that Annie Power could get beaten, but he knows that I could end up making life harder than it needs to be.

'Don't sit on my girth,' he warns me, worried that she might run keen.

'Ah yeah, of course, of course,' I reassure him.

He doesn't need to say, if you fuck me over today, I'll fuck you over tomorrow. That much is understood.

I don't usually like going out with the intention of following one horse. It's not a tactic I use. I much prefer to ride the horse I'm on, rather than trying to ride the race. But I know it's the right thing to do in this situation and I follow her. I follow her and follow her and follow her. She's a keen-going mare, and stepping up to three miles for the first time where the pace is a touch slower, she runs even more keenly.

There comes a point in the race where I have to do my own thing unless I'm planning on following her all the way to the line, and it comes after we jump the third last and start to make our run down the hill. From this point, I have to take things into my own hands. Big Buck's has got the inner, just in front of both of us, and when he gets niggled along a bit, I see where the space is going to open up for me. If I don't take it, Ruby will, so I commit on More Of That. It's the right place, right time, right decision. I get a brilliant run through up the inside and at the same time, Ruby has to pull Annie Power out wide and come around the traffic just to get back into a challenging position. He uses up a couple of lengths of her kick just to get to where he wants to be while I've got there without any effort.

AP and At Fishers Cross lead us on the long run down to the last but he's a sitting duck. Annie Power and More Of That hit the front and then jump the last together. Two good jumps. Ruby goes for it. I go for it too. And I get that little bit more in response. More Of That wins the battle of the last 100 yards and when we pull up after the line, Ruby comes to congratulate me. I'm well able to spot the difference between someone who is disappointed and someone who is completely gutted – I know both feelings well myself – and Ruby is absolutely sick. It's one of the only times that I see him like that in a race where I've beaten him.

AP's not much happier to see me either. He finishes the week with one winner but he's also got off the wrong two of his boss's horses and given them both to me. The two of us have another fight to the finish in the old Whitbread Gold Cup at Sandown a month later. AP and Burton Port lead us over the last, but I come late on Hadrian's Approach to snatch it by three-quarters of a length.

'Oh sure, who the fuck else could it be?' he says with a bit of a smile as he congratulates me.

The speculation about who will take over as JP's first rider starts as soon as AP announces his retirement. My name is mentioned straight away as a possibility. It doesn't take the most imaginative leap for people to see me in green and gold after winning two of the championship races at Cheltenham and the Irish Grand National in the colours. I have a lot of time to consider what I'll do if an offer does come my way; AP announces his retirement at the start of February 2015 but rides on until the end of April.

There's a lot to weigh up. I have a great relationship with a lot of Nicky's owners, people like Michael Buckley, Ronnie Bartlett and Simon Munir, and this would mean cutting ties with all of them. It wouldn't be a total breakup with Nicky – I'd still be able to ride any of JP's that he trains. I've had seven amazing years with him and Sophie and Corky and everyone at Seven Barrows. We've won a Champion Hurdle, two Champion Chases, a Gold Cup and the rest.

I know that the spotlight will be on if I take the job as JP's first rider. I'm not worried about that. I'm not worried about taking over from AP. None of that stuff bothers me. All I can see are the positives. I'll ride good horses in England and good horses in Ireland. It's the best of both worlds. It's what I want. There'll be fewer nights away, which means more nights at home with Paula and our family, which is about to have another new arrival very shortly; Rían, our little boy, is born in June 2015.

When I go to see Nicky to tell him, he knows why I'm coming. He understands where I am and where I want to be.

'We'll have more success,' he tells me. And we will.

Nicky was the one who took a chance on me when nobody else would, who gave me the good horses that let me fight my way back to the top. But I'm 35 years old and I know I can't go on for ever. I want to stay on top. Go out on top.

And there's no bigger job in racing than the one I've just accepted.

23

J P McManus insists on excellence. He didn't get to where he is by settling for anything less. He has been at the heart of the National Hunt game in Ireland for so many years, the biggest owner in the sport, and he applies the same principles to racing, his love, his passion, as he does to business. He invests in the best horses. He employs the best team. It's very similar for anyone involved in the Limerick hurling team, who he has supported for years; he wants people who will work hard and leave no stone unturned to deliver success.

'The difference between being involved and being committed is like when you have bacon and eggs for breakfast,' he tells me one day. 'The hen was involved but the pig was committed.'

I hear him use that one over the years. That's the level of dedication he expects from everyone who represents the iconic green and gold colours of the South Liberties GAA club in Limerick, the colours that have become the flag of the McManus family, the colours of success. Frank Berry, the former Champion Jockey, has been working alongside JP for years. Frank's official title is racing manager; unofficially, he's his right-hand man, friend, and trusted adviser. Not only is he JP's right-hand man, he's the jockeys' right-hand man too, someone who is always looking out for me and the other lads, there with a helping hand or a word of advice when we need it.

JP's involvement in racing is very much a family affair, and from the moment I take the job, myself, Paula and the children are all made to feel like we're a part of the extended family. Noreen, JP's wife, is incredibly supportive, a warm and caring person who is always interested in hearing the latest news from Paula and the kids, and the first to light a candle after any of my falls. Along with their three children, John, Sue Ann and Kieran and their families, they make sure we know that we're always welcome to their home in Martinstown House and that we're invited to all their big family occasions.

JP has won every big race there is to win, most of them on multiple occasions, but from the moment I take the job, it's clear that the little races mean just as much to him. The joy of watching a smaller trainer deliver with an unheralded horse in a midweek meeting in Ballinrobe or Kilbeggan means every bit as much to him as a big winner at the weekend. He just loves racing – watching racing, talking about racing, anything to do with racing. It's as simple as that. It's something that Kieran, JP's son, mentions to me when I first take the job.

'Give Dad a call after racing every day,' he advises me. 'He likes to hear about the horses.'

I'm nearly a little bit taken aback by the suggestion. Surely JP is too busy to be taking calls from me every single day, I think to myself, but Kieran is dead right. Whenever I need to talk to JP about racing, he is ready and waiting at the other end of the phone.

The beauty of riding for JP is that, no matter what happens, there's always another good horse to get excited about. You never have to wait for long. The days of going to big festivals with one or two good rides and the rest of my book full of half-chances – if I was lucky – are gone. JP has so much strength, depth and quality that practically all his horses are capable of winning a race on their day; most of the time, the biggest challenge is trying to figure out which of his two or three entries in a race has the best chance and making sure that I'm on the right one. The opportunities are endless, and I know that it's a privilege to be in this position.

From day one, I'm very conscious that this is the biggest job in the sport, that it demands respect. There's a certain level of expectation that comes with the position, of course – that's understandable – but I feel a responsibility to perform, to deliver, that I've never felt before. Those carefree days of my early twenties are a distant memory. I'm 35 now, soon to be 36, and nowhere near as blasé as I once was. Maybe that's what happens when you get a little bit older or start to come towards the back nine of your career. Decisions, consequences, life: they all seem to carry a little bit more weight and significance. The more I think about things, the more pressure I put on myself.

Ask JP how many winners he's had at Aintree, Punchestown, Galway, any of the big festivals, and he won't even know where to start. But ask him how many winners he's had at the Cheltenham Festival and he'll not only know the number, he'll be able to talk you through nearly every one of them, all the way back to Mister Donovan in 1982.

That week is when the expectation really comes to the boil, when the winners and losers really count. I've ridden a few of those winners over the years, but it's only in 2016, my first Cheltenham in the job, that I get a taste of what it really means to be there as JP's first jockey. We need to have a good week and there are two big hopes that I'm banking on to deliver for me. Yanworth is one of them.

The early pace in that year's Neptune is strong. Paul Townend goes fast from the front on Thomas Hobson, but I know I'm on the best horse in the race and I'm riding him like it. Yanworth is unbeaten in four starts over hurdles, ran amok in a good Grade

2 on trials day, and deserves to be the hot favourite. While Paul takes off, I keep Yanworth in a little bit of space towards the back – he doesn't like to be in a crowd – and as we turn into the back straight and the fizz goes out of the pace, I let him slowly start to creep a little bit closer.

We're all still there in a bunch coming away from the fourth last at the top of the hill and as everyone battles to hold their position, we bunch together and I'm carried wide. I never intended to have Yanworth out that wide and now we're trapped out there with nowhere else to go. I kick him at the third last, asking for a big jump that would put us in a better position, but I get the opposite result. Yanworth misses the hurdle, lands flat, and the mistake totally knocks the wind out of our sails. All the while, Ruby has been creeping into contention on Yorkhill, making good ground along the rail with minimum effort at the same time as I'm dipping into Yanworth's reserves and using him up just to get around horses and manoeuvre him into a challenging position. By the time we jump the last, we've got nothing left to chase Yorkhill down. Yanworth runs to the line for me without ever closing the gap and we finish second, a length and three-quarters behind Ruby and Yorkhill. From the moment we pass the finishing post, all I want is to go back to the start and have another go, to get the opportunity to do it all again. I'd like to think that there aren't too many races that have gone wrong on me in Cheltenham over the years, but this is definitely one that got away.

By the time Friday comes, Jamie Codd and Nina Carberry and Derek O'Connor have all ridden winners for JP, but I'm still staring down the barrel of a blank week. Everything is riding on the Triumph Hurdle and Ivanovich Gorbatov, my other big hope for the week. He's Joseph O'Brien's first Cheltenham runner as a trainer, still running in his dad Aidan's name while Joseph is waiting for the paperwork to come through on his own licence. I couldn't be any sweeter on his chances, and as far as I can tell, everyone involved feels exactly the same. When he was beaten in Leopardstown last time out, a couple of weeks before Cheltenham, I rang JP straight away after the race.

'Don't worry about it,' I reassured JP. 'He just struggled on the soft ground, that's all.'

I'm certain he'll be a different proposition on good ground, which is what we get in the Triumph. Bryan Cooper kicks off the turn for home on Apple's Jade, but I'm hot on his heels. Ivanovich Gorbatov meets the last on a long stride – not too dissimilar to the jump that I asked Yanworth for – but where one fell flat, the other comes up trumps for me. They're the percentages you're playing with in every race. You weigh up the horse you have, and the jump you need, and in a split second, you try to work out: are they up for it? Not all of them are but Ivanovich Gorbatov is. He flies the last and bursts past Apple's Jade to win.

The margins between hero and zero really are that fine. There isn't a more relieved man in all of Cheltenham. It's Friday but I finally have my winner.

24

Rule 212 – the non-trier rule – is there to protect the integrity of racing. It's there to stop horses being sent out for a run without any intention of winning the race. Under the old Rule 212, the jockey was obliged to do everything in their power to make sure that their horse finished in the best possible placing. The wording was changed in 2017, after the Noble Emperor case. Under the new rule, the horse has to be seen to be given a full opportunity in a race. *Seen* is the key word – all the emphasis is on the optics. Now you have to be seen to make an effort, even if you know that he has no chance of winning the race. Even if you're hanging on to a dying breath of a horse, you have to be seen to push him. Common sense is no longer an option or a defence.

Noble Emperor is a keen-going horse. He needs to take a lead from a horse, to get relaxed and settled until it's time to make a move and challenge. That's the instruction from Tony Martin, his trainer, when I go out to ride him in Limerick that day: get him a bit of cover without dropping him right out the back. It's a small stakes race, a seven-runner handicap hurdle worth just under €15,000 for the winner, and on paper, I'm on the best horse in the race – carrying top weight, seven pounds better than the next best horse on the official ratings, and the marginal favourite.

My plan is to settle in behind Cliff House, Brian O'Connell's horse, and that's what I do, but Barry Cash jumps out the gate on Velocity Boy and gets off to a flyer. When that happens, it's a bit like watching a solo breakaway at the Tour de France; one lad tears off into the sunset and whoever is at the front of the peloton sets the pace for the chasing pack. I need to keep Noble Emperor covered up, so I'm relying on someone else to do that job for me and tow me along behind them. But nobody sets off after Velocity Boy. By the time we jump the third hurdle, he's already 20 lengths up on us and the race has changed completely.

When a horse gets an easy lead like that early on, the ground is as good as lost. It's not as simple as going after him hell for leather to try to claw back the 20 lengths immediately. If you race too hard to get to him, by the time you get there he has taken a breather and your fractions are all wrong. You have to be patient, suffer a bit and play the long game, and hope that he's gone out too quickly for his own good and that he'll burn out quicker than you do. If he's running to stand still in the last couple of furlongs, he'll lose those 20 lengths in the blink of an eye. You have to make a call on it: if you go after a pace horse, you might catch him, but you'll also compromise your finish. If you sit it out patiently and wait for him to come back to you, he might. But he might not.

I stick to the plan and follow Cliff House. I won a Triumph Hurdle at Cheltenham with a ride like this, on Soldatino in 2010 for Nicky. He was a free-going horse as well, so much so that he needed to be raced in a hood at a time when hoods were a thing of the past. We were a distant third jumping the second last and still had about 15 lengths to make up on Barizan, Evan Williams's horse, who had turned the screw from the front and built up a huge lead. But by the time Barizan stepped through the last hurdle, he was punch drunk, out on his feet, and his lead was down to two lengths, if that. I timed my challenge to perfection on Soldatino; I hit the line running and won by a length and a quarter.

When you judge your run like that, nobody can say a word, but it's a tricky thing to do. I jump the third last on Noble Emperor and I wait and I wait. I'm going as fast as I can without sacrificing our finish. I could go all out on him now to chase Velocity Boy – nobody could fault us for lack of effort then – but it won't win us the race. He'll be in top gear for a furlong and a half and then he'll be trotting to the line as the others come from behind and pick us off. I'm looking for the biting point, the moment in the race where the distance to the line matches up with the energy that I think he's got left in the tank. When I make my move, I need him to have enough left to stay at that pace all the way to the finish line. We need to come with a consistent run.

I pass a couple of the others on the run down the hill to the second last hurdle and we move up into second. Now I'm asking Noble Emperor for everything he's got. Now we're coming with our consistent run. He's staying on strongly for me, seeing out his race the way I'd hoped and running to the line. Now it's a question of what Velocity Boy has got left after leading from wire to wire; plenty, it turns out. He quickens up again as we try to close the gap and he wins by 11 lengths.

When I go back into the weighroom, Michael O'Donoghue, the stipendiary steward, comes over to my peg.

'Barry, we might need to have a word with you about that ride,' he says.

When a race unfolds like that, the stewards are entitled to look for an explanation. They'll often stop a jockey for a quick word on the way back in just to see if there's anything to report. Maybe the horse hadn't travelled as well as expected. Maybe he was jumping a bit to the right or to the left. But this time, we're called in for a full enquiry, and it's not just me – the stewards interview all of us, with the exception of Barry Cash, who won the race. I don't think too much of it. At worst we're guilty of an ill-judged ride, of giving Velocity Boy too much rope and letting the race get away from us in the first couple of furlongs.

I've only ever been called in under non-trier rules twice in my whole career up until now. The first was for my ride on Magnus for Martin Pipe in the Coral Cup in Cheltenham for 2002, which was thrown out on appeal.

The only time I've only been under Rule 212 in Ireland was just five months ago, October 2015, and Michael O'Donoghue was the man in charge that day in Clonmel as well. I had the pick of JP's two horses and chose the wrong one. While Elegant Statesman won the race, I was scrubbing away at the back on Fever Pitch. I was a distant fourth in a five-horse race, fading away, riding him hands and heels after the last but stopping short of flogging him when I knew we had no chance of winning. Ruby was riding the only horse behind me and he came flying home with a late rattle to get up on the line and pip me by a short head for fourth. That was all that Michael O'Donoghue and the stewards needed to find me in breach of Rule 212 and suspend me for two days. That ban was thrown out on appeal as well. Ruby came in and gave evidence at my hearing in the Curragh; he could see that Fever Pitch was empty jumping the last, that he was going to get past me, and there was nothing more I could have done at that stage to hang on to fourth place. Because I never stopped riding, even when our chance was gone, they couldn't make the case that I hadn't tried to achieve the best possible position.

When I go into the stewards' room to discuss Noble Emperor's run, there's no part of me that thinks this can escalate into a problem. It didn't turn into the race that any of us expected, but in the circumstances, I know that Noble Emperor has run on his merits. And nobody can say that we haven't tried. I explain it to the stewards exactly as it happened: that Noble Emperor needs to be covered up and they were my instructions, and that when we challenged, we couldn't reel the winner in. They speak to Tony Martin too, and he confirms the instructions and tells them that he was happy with how I rode the race.

I go to get ready for my next race and I expect that will be the end of it. When I'm informed of the stewards' decision, I think I must be hearing things. They rule Noble Emperor as a non-trier and ban him from running for 60 days. They fine Tony Martin €3,000. I'm the one who bears the brunt of the punishment. They hit me with a 30-day ban. Thirty days – and that's thirty racing days, which is more like two and a half calendar months of a suspension. It's one of the biggest bans ever handed down to a professional jockey in Ireland under non-trier rules. I don't need to have heard their deliberations or their reasoning to know that they've latched on to something and gone for the jugular. It's a complete overreaction. I let it be known straight away that I'm not accepting the suspension and that I'll be lodging an appeal – not just against the severity of the penalty but against the stewards' ruling in full. I've done nothing wrong and I'll prove it.

Andrew Coonan is on the phone to me straight away. Andrew is a former amateur jockey and the head of the Irish Jockeys Association, but he's also a solicitor by trade. As soon as he hears about the ban, he's ready to fight it to the hilt. We know that the IHRB, the Irish Horseracing Regulatory Board, will do everything they can to send out a message by making this one stick, but they're not going to do it at my expense.

We have two weeks to prepare our appeal. Andrew recommends Stephen Lanigan-O'Keeffe, one of the top barristers in the country, to represent me. I sit down with Stephen to go through the evidence, and he tells me that my case is very solid. I'm not worried about losing the appeal; because I haven't done anything wrong, I presume that everything will be grand and the whole situation will sort itself out. And because I'm confident,

I don't prepare as thoroughly as I should. I don't spend much time thinking about what I need to explain and how I'm going to explain it. Andrew rings me one day to talk things through. He starts firing questions at me, the same questions I'll be asked on the day. He pushes me on my explanations, tries to poke holes and wind me up. And he rattles me. Andrew gets his point across: I can't take it for granted that I'll talk my way out of this just because I've done nothing wrong and I'm good at talking. It might not turn out to be as easy as I think.

I do my homework. I rewatch all the videos of Noble Emperor's previous races, the times when I've ridden him and the times when it was Mark Walsh or Niall Madden or someone else. I load up my first race on him, a Grade 3 novice chase in Naas, when I was struggling to keep a lid on him early on and he fell at the third. I study the replay of one of his runs over fences in Gowran, and the tape of the Galmoy Hurdle when Mark was on him, and it sums up exactly why he needed to be ridden in a certain way – he ran keen, tried to follow the pace, travelled well and then didn't get home. He finished last of five in the Galmoy, 69 lengths behind the winner.

As we get closer to the day of the appeal, I don't feel overly stressed or worried. I'm sleeping okay. I'm eating well. But when I step up on the scales, I'm as light as I've ever been. I can try to pass it off, to reassure myself that it will all be fine but subconsciously, it's obvious that it has been weighing on me.

The appeals panel hears all three cases together: mine, Tony Martin's and JP's. Mr Justice Tony Hunt, the High Court judge, sits as the chairman of panel. The IHRB fly in Louis Weston, a top sports barrister, from Britain to present the case against me on their behalf. I'm on the chair for the best part of an hour and a half, giving my evidence and then facing cross-examination. I explain how the race unfolded and my belief that, if I had gone after Velocity Boy any earlier, I would have ultimately finished further away. Justice Hunt puts a few questions to me and I can see he has a good read of the arguments and a great feel for the situation. Louis Weston comes at me from every angle in his cross-examination, tries to find a weakness somewhere, anything to cast a bit of doubt on what I'm saying and land a knockout blow, but he can't lay a glove on me.

When the panel deliver their decision, it's nothing but relief. All three appeals are granted and the cases against us are thrown out. My good name is upheld and, just as important, my 30-day ban is rescinded. I'm free to ride – just in time for the Punchestown festival, which starts next week.

The whole ordeal is still playing on my mind when I go out to ride Coney Island for JP in the three-mile novice hurdle on the second day of the festival. I feel like I'm being watched, that there's a spotlight on me and my riding, and I'm not as patient as I should be on Coney Island. Instead of sitting and biding my time like I normally would, I rush things. I start to make my move on the run to the third last, but it's too soon and it comes back to bite me. Ruby picks me off on Bellshill and wins by half a length.

It's a mistake, and it's not one that I'm going to make twice. Thirty-five minutes later, when Carlingford Lough is still a good 20 lengths off the leaders with five fences to jump in the Punchestown Gold Cup, I do it my way. I forget about the Noble Emperor enquiry, forget about the scrutiny, and I ride him the way I know I should: drop him out, follow around, wait for the right moment. Once we make our move, Carlingford Lough finishes like a train for me and the horses in front of us have no chance. We win by four and a half lengths.

The Gold Cup is the big race of the festival but when I meet JP back in the winners' enclosure, I still apologise for the one that got away.

'Sorry, I should have won on Coney Island too.'

I finish up at Punchestown with four winners and as the leading rider at the festival. There's no better way to close the book on a difficult few weeks.

25

hit the ground hard when Charli Parcs falls, bone bouncing off turf, but it's a horse's hoof that does the damage, not the impact of the fall. My body crashes and rolls out into the middle of the track, setting off a chain reaction. Harry Skelton, who rides the horse coming from behind, can't do anything to help me. Harry's horse is only concerned about the half-tonne frame on the ground in front of him. He jinks left to avoid a collision; my ribs are the collateral damage.

I feel him plant his hoof into the side of my back as I roll. When I try to take a deep breath, I can't, but I'm okay. My breathing is shallow, sharp, but I know there's no reason to panic. I'm badly winded, that's all. It will pass. I sit up first, gather myself, and then stand up and walk over to the side of the track where the ambulance has pulled up to collect me.

It's late February, a time of year that nearly every jockey hates – there's just over two weeks to go until the 2017 Cheltenham Festival and a bad fall now could easily leave you sitting on the sidelines for the most important week of the year. I'm lucky. It doesn't feel like there's any serious damage done, and that's the most important thing. The medical staff at the track beg to differ. They insist on sending me straight to hospital, no arguments. JP comes down to the ambulance room to check on me as I'm being loaded up in the back of the ambulance and taken away. I give him a thumbs up, all that I can do to reassure him – it's all fine, don't be worrying about me – although the oxygen mask strapped to my face is a dead giveaway.

Every time I take a breath, the pain comes from the exact same place. It's just one rib. When the doctors in the hospital start to examine me and ask me where it hurts, I'm able to tell them exactly: that's it there, that's the one that's fractured. When the X-ray comes back, they have news for me. There isn't one fractured rib; there are eight. It sounds like there must be some mistake. I know the feeling of a fracture and it's definitely not sore enough for eight of them to be fractured. I'm not in anything like that type of pain. A few days later, when the adrenaline and the medication start to wear off and the discomfort really sets in, I understand exactly what eight fractured ribs feels like.

The ribs have punctured my lung as well, which explains the shortness of breath and why it hasn't got any better yet. The doctors plug a tube into my side which allows the lung to inflate again. The ward that I'm brought up to is chaotic, six beds packed into a tight space with doctors and nurses and visitors all rushing in and out while trying not to fall over one another. Someone drops over a bag from the racecourse – my clothes and my wallet – and that's it. I lie there, trying to get some rest, until I realise that I have a visitor: JP. Nobody else on the ward even notices him come into the room as he spots me and sits down beside my bed. I'm delighted to see a familiar face. He hands me a bag, a few bits that he thought I might need in case I'm kept in for a couple of days: a couple of pairs of pyjamas, boxers, socks, a pair of slippers and eight or nine boxes of chocolates that I'm to give to the nurses as a thank you for looking after me. He stays for a while and we chat. I'm to give him a call when the doctors say I'm allowed to be discharged, JP says. He'll have the helicopter ready to come and pick me up to bring me home.

As far as injuries go, this is just the latest in a bad run that started with a broken leg in March 2015, just before I started riding for JP. The Downpatrick race that I was riding in was pretty insignificant, but the kick I got in the shin was anything but. A greenstick fracture, they called it, a bone that has bent and cracked from the force of the kick but hasn't broken completely. Greenstick. Hairline. Such deceptive turns of phrase, as if anything the width of a hair could cause the same pain as these two bits of bone which were never meant to be separated. For the first time in my career, the only thing that could spare me was morphine, and a lot of it. I was 14 weeks on the sidelines with that one; by the time I got back racing, I had a new job.

The injuries come thick and fast after that. Cernunnos was coming to challenge in the Summer Plate at Market Rasen in 2016, jumping the last, when he fell and pitched me up and over the top. Whether I wanted to or not, I broke my fall, and when I sat up, I saw an arm lying on the grass beside me. There was a curiosity to it – that is my arm, isn't it? I reached out and picked it up. I'd never held a loose, lifeless arm like that before. It was heavier than you'd expect, the same weight as a bag of flour maybe. I brought it back in close to my body where it belongs, put it between my legs and used my left hand to hold it in place until somebody came to help me.

Whatever way I landed, the full force of the fall was absorbed through the place where my elbow used to be, but for some reason – shock, probably – I couldn't feel a thing. Richard Johnson came into the medical room to check on me and see how I was doing, and just as he was about to go and get ready for his next ride, I sat forward onto the edge of the bed.

'Here, Dicky, look at this,' I said with a bit of a laugh and I leaned forward, letting my jelly arm hang there and swing freely, painting a picture that he really didn't need to see when he was about to get back up on a horse. Eleven weeks, six days, and one steel plate later, I was fit enough to ride again.

And now this one: eight broken ribs and a punctured lung. They keep me in hospital for four days before they're happy that I'm well enough to go home. In my head, I've still got another two weeks to make sure that I'm as ready as I can be for Cheltenham. I haven't even started to consider the possibility that riding a horse in this condition might be a bad idea. My ribs, my chest, my lung, they're all screaming at me, but I make an appointment to see a specialist in the Blackrock Clinic to get a second opinion. I'm nowhere near fit and the consultant's answer is unequivocal: there's not a chance I'll be back racing in time.

The Sunday morning before Cheltenham starts is D-Day. That's when the final declarations for the first day of the festival are made. The doctor may have ruled me out, but until that deadline passes, nothing is decided for certain. JP has three horses entered in that year's Champion Hurdle: Buveur D'Air, My Tent Or Yours, and the one that I'm still hoping to ride, the favourite, Yanworth. I have to give myself every chance. I have to ask the question. The last thing I want is to be sitting at home watching it on TV if there's a part of me that thinks that I could be right there in the thick of it. I get out of bed early on the Sunday morning and I do 10 press-ups, no problem. I'm feeling good. I ring Dermot McLoughlin, whose yard is only five minutes down the road from our house, to explain the situation and ask him for a favour.

'Have you anything that I could sit up on this morning? And maybe I'll pop a few hurdles as well. Everything feels fine but I just want to see how it is when I'm up on a horse.'

Dermot tells me to jump in the car and come down to him, but when Paula sees me grab my gear and the keys and head for the door, she's not impressed.

'Are you mad?' she says. 'This is your lungs we're dealing with here.'

I know in my heart that she's right, but Cheltenham is the only logic that I'm willing to listen to.

'It's grand, I've got two of them,' I tell her as I run out the door.

Riding out in Dermot's only encourages me more. I feel good afterwards. There's no reason at all for me to miss Cheltenham. I try to ring Paddy Kenny to see what I need to do to get cleared to ride but there's no answer. While I'm waiting for Paddy to call me back, I ring JP to get the ball rolling.

'I've just been riding out and I'm feeling fine,' I tell him. 'I think I'm going to be okay to race on Tuesday.'

This obviously isn't the phonecall that he was expecting from me. I can hear that he's a little bit shocked.

'Okay, let me think about it and I'll get back to you.'

Before I can even start to get my hopes up, the phone rings again and Paddy puts a swift end to the conversation.

'No way, not under any circumstances,' he insists. 'One, you've a serious laceration of the lung and that could collapse again under pressure, and two, you've also got eight broken ribs – that's like riding with sixteen daggers in your back. Not a chance.'

When JP rings back, he's come to the same conclusion.

'No, I can't let you ride next week. I wouldn't be comfortable watching you out of fear of what could happen.'

There's relief all round when I tell him what Paddy said. They're all dead right – Paula, JP, Paddy. It's way too much of a risk. If I fell again, I could do very serious damage, and the damage that has already been done is bad enough as it is. But I needed to hear it. I needed the decision to be taken out of my hands. Otherwise, I would have spent the next week sitting at home tormenting myself with ifs and buts.

Mark Walsh will take the ride on Yanworth in the Champion Hurdle as well as most of the other ones that I had in my book for the week.

I've always got on well with Mark. There is great respect and honesty between us. I tell him that I've been ruled out and the two of us settle in for a good long chat about everything I was due to ride. Mark knows all these horses well himself, but I've been plotting and planning for most of the season and he's stepping in at short notice, and I want to give him every little bit of help that I can. If I can't win the race myself, I want to try to make sure that it happens for everybody else involved. I lay out every little bit of detail that I have for Mark, ride the race as much as I can, and let him add it all in to his own notes. You see plenty of jockeys who are wary of sharing too much information because they're afraid to give someone a leg up in case they lose their place in the pecking order, but that's never been how Mark and I operate. If the shoe was on the other foot, he would be doing the exact same thing for me.

I miss Cheltenham for the first time since 1999, and I realise that watching the races on the telly is far more difficult than being there in the thick of the action. When you're there, you're caught up in the adrenaline and you don't see a fraction of the drama or incidents; when you're at home, you see far more than you'd really like to. Mark's festival turns out to be short-lived. I swallow hard when he takes a bad fall on the first day, and again in the opening race of the second day, both on horses that I should have been riding. Right after Mark's second fall, I'm on the phone to Kieran McManus, ringing to see if there's any news and how he is doing. He's stood down for the rest of the day and, shortly afterwards, stood down for the rest of the week. It's not easy watching from the couch, but for a man with my injuries, there's no doubt that it's a safer place to be.

I'm delighted to get back racing in time for Aintree at the start of April, but my comeback is short-lived. Eleven days later, I get a fall off Minella Foru in the Irish Grand National at Fairyhouse and end up with another broken arm. It has only been eight months since the last broken arm – it's the other arm this time, the left one, and it leaves me sidelined for another 15 weeks. The only silver lining is that with so much free time on my hands, we've the opportunity to take JP up on one of his many generous offers to come out for a holiday to his incredible hotel in Barbados, Sandy Lane. It is paradise, all golden sand and deep blue sea, and everyone that we meet out there is so warm and welcoming. Sandy Lane itself is a stunning place to stay. Myself and Paula have the time of our lives, not to mention the three kids, who love everything about our time there. Órla learns how to swim, and then gets to swim with the turtles, which is not a bad way to start out. We have such a beautiful time out there as a family. We're only sorry that we don't have the opportunity to take up JP on more of his offers over the years.

I recover from the broken arm in time to make the Galway Festival at the end of July, but before August is out, I'm back on the sidelines again with a cracked shoulder blade and another four weeks out. Whatever luck I once had with injuries has very definitely run out. This is exhausting.

Buveur D'Air's Champion Hurdle is my first ride of the week at Cheltenham in 2018. In a race with such fine margins, I make all the right decisions. He's the defending champion, odds-on favourite as he tries to win back the crown, something that only a handful of horses have ever managed to do. We hit the front just before we jump the second last and I know that we have most of our rivals beaten. But coming down to the last, Paul Townend and his horse, Melon, are right there beside me and they won't go away. I quickly weigh up my options again. I don't know what they've got left in the tank, but they're going every bit as well as us for now. Like a heavyweight boxer reaching out to touch gloves before the last round, I don't need to be told that we're in a battle here.

We jump it side by side, touch down practically simultaneously, and as we race away from the back of it, Paul and I both know that we each have one shot at this, one move, one chance to get it right. That's what's going to decide the winning and losing of it. That's the margin between victory and defeat. I get low on Buveur D'Air and I drive, pushing him to the line with my hands and heels, willing him with my mind. Paul plays his hand first and inches ever so slightly ahead of us. The finishing line will be here in a moment, but I wait, saving those last few ounces. We can't go now. It's still too early. Not yet. And 100 yards from the line, the lights turn green and I go, putting everything into one last push, letting everything ride on my instinct that this will get us there just in time but not a moment too soon. A few strides from the winning post, Buveur D'Air puts his nose in front. A few strides later, he's the champion again.

It's the result that everyone expected, even if nobody imagined it might take such a battle. Afterwards, when the replays have been watched and scrutinised, I get the same compliment over and over again: 'Jesus, there's not many would have won that on him today.'

But Cheltenham lasts for four days, not one, and although your first winner on the board each year is always your most important one, the week is never defined by one race, no matter how good the ride. Nor is it defined by one disappointing defeat, I hope, when Glenloe gets beaten by a whisker on Thursday.

He's one of our big hopes for the week and he travels like a dream for me in the Pertemps – travels a little bit too well if anything. Because he's running away with so much in hand, we get involved in the race earlier than I'd like to, and then I'm caught in two minds as we come to jump the last. I can see a long stride but the horse is not looking at the hurdle at all so I don't force the issue. He has been so clever throughout the race up until now, I trust that he's going to be clever again one last time. But no. He drags his hind legs through the hurdle, lands on the back foot, and Davy Russell gets up on Delta Work to beat us by a nose in a photo finish.

The rest of Thursday goes by without a winner. That's just how it goes sometimes, but then you close the book and go to bed, and when you wake up on Friday, you go again. I ride Apple's Shakira in the first race, the Triumph Hurdle. She's only starting out in her racing career, just four years old, but she's won all three of her races since JP brought her from France and none of her rivals have managed to get within three and a half lengths of her yet. Nobody needs to say what we're all thinking: there's no margin for error here; this one needs to go to plan.

As soon as we jump off, it starts to unravel. The two of us have two very different ideas of what it's going to take to win this race. Or rather, I'm thinking about what it's going to take to win the race, and she just wants to get on with it and run free and fast until she can't run any more. She pulls and she pulls, and I wait and I wait for her to settle, to stop fighting against me and start to work with me, to get into a nice steady rhythm and save some of this excitement and energy for the business end, when we'll need it. She pulls again and I try again to calm her, to convince her to take the foot off the pedal just for a couple of strides. Even if it takes a mile of the two-mile race before she agrees, it's better than nothing. If she just settles for a moment, she'll give herself a chance. If only she'd realise that, maybe we'd finish better than fourth.

I certainly can't afford to dwell on it. I still have a day's work to do and thankfully, things take a turn for the better. OK Corral chases home the winner to finish second with a good run in the Albert Bartlett. I latch on to something that JP says to me when I come back in afterwards.

'He could be a Gold Cup horse in time,' he suggests, impressed by the bit he had left in the tank to see out his first three-mile race.

'Well, it'll be another two years,' I say. 'Sure hopefully we're all here.'

I'm not sure why I say it. It's been a tough winter, a really wet one, and some of the horses haven't been performing in the way we know they can. Buveur D'Air and the Champion Hurdle are already starting to become a distant memory; there have been more low points this week than we would have liked. But that kind of thought wouldn't even come to mind, even subconsciously, unless there's a bit of uncertainty there.

Anibale Fly digs deep in the final yards of the Gold Cup, the big race of the week, to finish third. And then, with the last bullet left in the chamber, I go out to ride Le Prezien in the final race of the festival, the Grand Annual. I take one last look at the form before I go out to make sure that I have the tactics right. There are 22 runners in the race and – I count them – eight are front-runners. There's going to be loads of pace in the race and if I drop Le Prezien out the back early on to switch him off, let him relax and creep my way into the race, it's going to suit us to perfection.

I know Paul Nicholls will want me to ride him handy up towards the front – that's the way he likes his horses to be ridden – so I sit on the fence a bit when he asks about the tactics in the parade ring.

'What do you want to do, chap?'

'We'll go half way,' I tell him, knowing that I'm meeting him half way. But when Nicholls leaves, and Kieran McManus and Frank Berry come over for a chat, I talk them through the plan in full.

'There's eight front-runners in here. There's going to be loads of pace. I'm going to drop him out and I'll be there at the finish.'

Kieran and Frank are delighted with those tactics. They can hear the excitement in my voice. They know we've got a live one here.

I do exactly as I've told them. I sit out towards the back as the leaders race off at a million miles an hour, and I get Le Prezien jumping in a nice rhythm. With about half a mile to go, I start to move up and get a little bit closer. We're sixth as we make the turn into the home straight, but a couple of the horses in front of me have been out there since the start and they're starting to get tired. We've still got two lengths to make up as we jump the last fence, but once we're over it safely, the patient tactics pay dividends. Le Prezien picks up again for me and charges up the hill to win by four and a half lengths.

It's a huge relief to sign off on a winner. When I phone JP on the way back to the airport that evening, we have a great chat. We've had our ups and downs this week, no doubt, but the disappointments never seem quite so bad when you leave on a high. Even when things aren't going your way, I think to myself, it's always good to balance the books.

26

'Are you retiring?' JP asks me as we step out onto the balcony of his box. There's still a few hours to go before the first race of the day and Punchestown is quiet, starting to come to life.

I can understand why he's asking. I've heard the rumours too. Punchestown is the final fixture of the Irish racing season every year. I'm 38 years old, rising 39, and I've been at this a long time. The end of a campaign is a natural full stop and people have started to put two and two together on my behalf. Just the other day Warren Ewing, a good friend of mine who I own a few horses with, heard someone mention it and called me to see if there was any truth to the rumour, slagging that he'd be the last to know. I tell JP exactly what I told Warren – absolutely not, I have no intention of walking away just yet.

'No, I'm not retiring,' I assure him.

'So what's your plan for next season?' JP asks.

'Jesus, no plan.'

'Lot of talk you're going to retire,' he says.

'No, not at all,' I assure him, and that's when the bomb goes off and 26 April 2018 is drawn as a line in the story of my career.

'Some of the trainers aren't happy with how you're riding,' he tells me. 'We're not going to have a first jockey next season.'

There's only a couple of feet between us, and we're out here alone, so there's no fear of me mishearing him; as far as I'm concerned, I'm sacked. JP doesn't use that word – it's a bit more vague than that – but whatever the words, it amounts to the same thing. From this point on, I'm no longer his first jockey.

'How do you feel you're riding?' he asks me.

How do I feel I'm riding? It's only six weeks since I won the Champion Hurdle – that's what I want to say, what I should say, but I'm too shocked to answer. I can't make sense of this at all. With the exception of the two wins at Cheltenham, there's no disguising the fact that we haven't had the success that we might have liked this season. But if now's the time to start dissecting what went right and what went wrong, or if certain trainers are hanging me out to dry, I'm ready to fight my corner. I'll either back the decisions I've made in a race and defend them to the hilt or, if I know I'm in the wrong, I'll hold my hands up, apologise and move on. That's always been my way.

I ask JP if this has anything to do with the horses that I've pulled up but he assures me it doesn't. That's the most obvious criticism that I've had to deal with from punters and pundits over the last few months. Every time I pull up a horse, it seems to become a talking point. The stewards called me in to explain one of my rides in Fairyhouse at Easter. It was noted again in the media during Aintree when I pulled up Le Prezien. It's a stick that's been used to beat me for as long as I've been riding – Geraghty pulls them up too easily – but I've no problem with that. When we're out there in the thick of it and it's just the two of us, I know the horse I'm sitting on. Everybody else might think they know better, but they're working from incomplete information. They're only guessing. But I know. I've never been that insecure, that cold or uncaring, that I'd need to give a horse a hard race, beat him through the last half-mile, so that I can come back into the parade ring and wash my hands of it. There has to be a duty of care there too; a horse deserves better than that. If we're not going forward, if he's not able to race competitively any more, I'll pull him up.

Only yesterday, I pulled up Demi Sang, and nobody can tell me that it wasn't the right thing to do. He got the life frightened out of him at Cheltenham and as soon as we jumped off yesterday, I knew that he still wasn't over it. He panicked at the first fence, dived out to the left, and my saddle slipped. After that, the best I could do was to forget about winning the race for the moment and concentrate on getting him back jumping to build up a bit of confidence. I got him back onto some kind of an even keel and then, rather than run the risk of undoing all the good work when he was tired late on, I pulled him up with three fences left.

I ducked out before the bumper, the last race, to beat the traffic and I phoned JP from the car on the way home. It was a quick call. I only had a handful of rides, and only two for him, Demi Sang and one other. There wasn't much to say so there wasn't much said. I didn't think anything of it as we finished our call and he asked me to call up to his box before racing for a chat. There's certainly nothing unusual in the two of us having a cup of tea and a chat, but it's obvious now that this isn't one of those chats.

Some of the trainers aren't happy with how you're riding. Those words hang in the air. That's the crux of it. Whether I'm retiring or not is immaterial, it seems.

'I want to give the other lads a chance next season,' JP explains, but my head is spinning. Where does all of this leave me? He indicates that I can still ride some in England, keep going with Buveur D'Air and five or six others that Nicky trains for him, but beyond that, I don't really know where I stand any more.

I'm sure JP is expecting me to put up a bit more of an argument but I'm stunned and all I can manage is silence. I put down my cup and turn for the door.

'Prove them wrong,' he challenges me before I leave. 'Prove them wrong.'

'I don't know what to say to you,' I tell him. 'A cup of tea at Punchestown is a dangerous thing.'

I don't know where to go. If I go down to the weighroom, it won't take a second for somebody to notice that my head is gone. I don't want to speak to anyone. All I want is to be left alone, and the best way to do that is to hide in plain sight. I walk out onto the track and ring Paula. I muddle my way through the story of what happened, try to make sense of what JP said by reconstructing it for her. I hit the key points: I've just been sacked and I don't know what I'm doing or where I'm going. In all the time we've known each other, she's watched me glass-half-full my way through whatever problems came our way. This time, she can hear the hurt.

I tell her what JP said about retirement, and that he seemed surprised to hear that they were rumours and nothing more.

'Maybe I should just retire, should I?'

There's a part of Paula that would love me to retire, but more than anyone, she understands that it has to be my decision, that I can only retire when the time comes and I'm happy to go and ready to embrace life after racing, uncertainties and all. It has to be on my terms; retiring like this would be anything but.

'If you're happy riding, keep riding,' she tells me. 'You can retire in a month's time or you can retire in six months' time, whenever you want.'

She's right.

Instead of retiring, I go back into the weighroom and I do what I've done a thousand times and more over the last three years: I get dressed in the green and gold and I go to work. Even today – especially today – I can't ride an emotional race. I can't ride the ride of an angry man. At least I'm thinking clearly enough to realise that, to know that it would hurt me rather than help me. All I want is to win and, by winning, to prove my doubters wrong. Twice that afternoon I think I have the horse, sitting with plenty in hand as we go down the back straight only to come up short on both occasions. I finish third in the first race and again in the second and, as I dismount, I know that I couldn't have done a thing differently in either case.

Mark Walsh and Fish – Mark Enright – are the only two people I tell about what's after happening. I don't really want to talk about it, but I'm shaken and I have to tell somebody. I know I can trust the two lads, but I don't say a word to anyone else. People talk; the story will filter out in time. Unless it's already out there, that is. Before I can even get home on Thursday evening, someone shouts over to me that I'm wanted outside when I'm ready, that a couple of journalists are waiting outside the weighroom looking for a chat. I haven't had a winner yet this week so they're definitely not looking for a few quotes on how well things are going. They must know.

I can't figure out why this has all kicked off so suddenly. It doesn't make sense. I start to panic. I don't want to do this now, but I can't stay in here all night either. I'm going to have to go out there at some stage. I ring Paula first and then I ring Frank Berry to see what he thinks I should do. Frank has always looked out for me.

'Someone must have got wind of what's going on,' I tell him. 'There's journalists outside looking to have a word with me. What the hell am I supposed to say to them?'

'Just say nothing,' Frank advises me. 'Say nothing, it'll be grand.'

Frank's right. I say nothing.

Much as I'd like to, I can't just want my way to a win. The following day, Friday, hammers home that point with no small measure of irony: a stride from the line in a race that I so badly want to win, Katie Walsh gets up to beat me by a short head and announces her retirement right there on the spot. When Saturday comes, Paula and the three children are with me. It looks like they're putting on the big show because it's the last day of the season; only we know any different. As far as the outside world is concerned, there haven't been any changes to JP's riding arrangements. I haven't said much over the last few days, so there hasn't been much said to me. The small circles of Irish racing don't have space for too many secrets though, and Paula doesn't have to read too much into the sympathetic looks and apologetic semi-smiles being offered in her direction the whole day. That evening, I try to get dressed so quickly and get the hell out of there that I end up ripping my shirt. Tony O'Hehir from RTÉ catches me and asks for a quick word.

'Have you any news, Barry? Have you anything to tell us?'

I try to play it cool.

'No, no news, Tony. Nothing, sorry.'

I'm so wrapped up in the fear that this is spreading like wildfire that I completely misread the story that they've been looking for over the last few days. Last day of the season. The whole family here with me. They're all outside the weighroom because they're waiting for me to come out and announce my retirement.

I meet Paula and the kids outside, and we walk back to the car with Frank and Claire, his wife. Frank's trying to reassure me that this might not need to be as catastrophic as it seems.

'There's plenty of horses there for you,' he says. 'It'll be okay, we'll work something out. If anyone is asking questions, keep the head down and say nothing.'

Before we run off to Alicante to get away from everything and everyone, I ring JP again. It's the lack of clarity that's tormenting me. I can't get my head round the situation I'm in when I don't even know what that situation is. I hate knowing that I stood there on Thursday and barely said a word; that all the imaginary arguments have been stacking up since but abandoned me when I had the chance and will only be heard now by the audience of one in my head; that I never made it hard for him. I talk it through with Paula before I ring him, a rehearsal, her opportunity to screen the hurt and prevent me from saying something that I might regret.

'What are you going to say?' she asks me.

'I just need to find out exactly what the problem is. That's all I want to know. I don't think I've been riding badly, do you? I know they didn't all come off for us at Cheltenham but we got some big results as well. I need to know what this issue is with the trainers so that I can sort it out. I'll just ask him that straight out.'

But whatever script there is, I rip it up as soon as he answers the phone. I don't mean to. It just happens, logic and reason replaced by the desperate, unthinking flailings of a wounded warrior. In a haze of ignorance, I speak my mind in a way that I never intended to. Before I can stop myself, I'm off the phone, and the shaken look on Paula's face is enough to let me know that that wasn't the approach we discussed. I text JP quickly to apologise. 'Sorry, I've had sleepless nights over this, but I shouldn't have spoken to you like that.'

By the time we come back from Spain four days later, word is as good as out. Eagle eyes have noticed that Mark Walsh is booked for a few of the horses that I'd normally be riding, and my phone is red with the glow of a thousand unanswered calls. I'm still none the wiser as to where I fit into the new plan. I'm not expecting a lifeline, but when Ciaran O'Toole, my agent, rings me with one, I don't need a second invitation.

JP gives me the chance to prove myself. I'm needed to ride a few of his horses in Killarney and my ears prick at mention of one of them, Ballyoisin. I'd been on him in Punchestown, starved myself to get my weight down to 10st 4lb, and we finished eighth. I'm expecting to be jocked off him too and for Mark to get the call to replace me, but Ciaran tells me that I'm down to ride him. This fella is made for me. I know him and know what he's capable of. If ever there's going to be a chance to force the door open again and show what I can do before it's too late, this is it.

I ride him like he's stolen and I haven't a care in the world. We rip around Killarney together, having the time of our lives as we ping every fence. There isn't a horse out there that can lay a glove on us as we win by nine and a half lengths. Frank is there to meet me in the parade ring and congratulate me. The phone is glowing again, except this time it's with strings of 'well dones' and 'attaboys'.

When I call out to the house to visit JP a few weeks later, the riding arrangements are still the same but the mood music feels very different.

'There's a good team of horses in England for you,' he says. 'Hopefully we've a good year with them.'

Words like 'we' and 'this year' are all I need to hear.

'Hopefully,' I say. 'Hopefully.'

27

'Do you need to be riding in the Topham?' Paula asks me when I tell her that I've been booked to ride Peregrine Run at Aintree. This particular race is a bit like running the gauntlet: two miles five furlongs over the Grand National fences, the day before the big one itself, with a huge field gunning for a decent prize pot. She sees the dangers that I don't.

'It'll be grand,' I tell her. 'He's clever as a fox.'

Almost a year has passed since my conversation with JP in Punchestown, and although I've still been needed to ride some of his horses in Ireland, Mark is getting the lion's share and the other lads – Niall Madden, Luke Dempsey, Jody McGarvey – are picking up most of the rest. I still carve out some opportunities for myself in Ireland. I keep tabs on the possible spare rides for anything that might have a bit of potential, and horses like Peregrine Run, who has all the hallmarks of a good summer horse, is exactly the kind of ride I want in my book.

Paula's right, there's always an added risk riding in a race like the Topham, but when Roger Loughran retires, I ask about getting on Peregrine Run and the offer is there. If I don't ride him at Aintree I can't exactly expect Peter Fahey, his trainer, to give me the call for Killarney or Ballinrobe or Galway later on in the year.

I'm dead right about Peregrine Run's potential. He wins his next five races in a row after the Topham. It's little consolation to a jockey stuck at home recovering from a broken leg.

The nights are every bit as bad as the days.

By the time ten o'clock comes, I'm exhausted. As soon as my head hits the pillow, I'm out like a light. I don't even need to dream; not being awake, a few peaceful hours where I'm not aware of this torture device bolted into the bones of my leg, is more than enough. But then two o'clock comes, or three o'clock, and as soon I try to turn in my sleep, I can't. My right leg is lifeless, weighed down by the frame, and now I'm awake again. And once I'm awake, the night becomes very long.

At least my leg is elevated when I'm lying in bed. When it's propped up like that, I nearly forget about the pain, but I can't stay there for ever. It's when I give up on the illusion of a few more hours of sleep, when I roll my legs over the edge of the bed to start a new day, that's when the agony really begins. The blood rushes back down to the tips of my toes, the pressure builds and my leg swells as it tries to push through the frame until the metal buckles. It happens in an instant, a flood. It takes all my effort just to get up and get down the stairs, and by the time I get there, all I can manage is to get to the couch and lie down so that I can get my leg back up again and relieve the pressure. I position it so that it's resting on the back of the couch. The blood drains away just as quickly; it's bliss.

I turn the TV on but it's barely a backing track for my mind as it races from one pity to the next. I can't sit still. I want to be better already, even if it has only been a couple of days since the operation. And if I can't be better, I want to be able to function at the very least. After a half an hour of lying on the couch, I'm fed up. I need to get up and do something, but everything is hell. I try to challenge myself, to dial into my competitive side and use it, but even the simplest task – something as straightforward as hobbling the few yards from couch to dishwasher and helping to unload it – takes me the best part of 40 minutes.

For the first few days, the cycles are short: I can stand for two minutes but then I need to lie down again for 15 or 20 minutes. Every day it gets a little better. That two minutes becomes five and then 10 and then 20, and I have the confidence to put a bit more weight on the leg. When they were sending me home, the doctors said that I could walk out the door on my own two feet, that I didn't even need crutches because the fracture is bypassed through the frame. Gradually, my brain starts to allow me to trust what I've been told.

Paula double-checks the sheet of paper, just to be sure that she is looking at the correct part of the frame, and then she gently twists the metal spoke into its new position. She reads the instructions again and finds the next step in the sequence. As well as all the screws and wires in different places, there are six adjustable spokes on this contraption, each one marked with a number or a letter. When the frame was first fitted, there was no way of making sure that everything was lined up as precisely as it needed to be. That's where the computer came in: once the frame was on, the doctors took another X-ray and ran the information through a piece of software that calculated the instructions that Paula is following now. There's a very specific sequence for every day; it all has to be so precise. Every adjustment she makes rotates the frame and helps bring the bone back into line. We do this every day for 12 days and then we go back to the hospital for another X-ray. The fracture has realigned as well as could be hoped for. Now all I have to do is wait for it to heal.

This one is the worst break of my career, no doubt. It's also the one that is affecting me the most. The lack of sleep. The lack of mobility. My age, too, if I'm being honest. I might be 39 but

I'm not ready to retire yet; a bad break like this could easily take that decision out of my hands. The first week is a rollercoaster. The phone is hopping. All the lads are ringing, jockeys and ex-jockeys, and it's non-stop. As a community we're brilliant at banding together to support each other. And when I'm on the phone, everything is fine. I have a great laugh and a joke with whoever is on the other end, brush it all off – ah yeah, I'll be fine, don't worry – never even hinting at the fact that I'm finding this one tougher than anything I've been through before. All my positivity, all my energy, goes on the phone call, goes on keeping the sunny side out. When I hang up, there's a low. And when the phone stops ringing, it's even lower. I don't even notice it happening, but Paula does.

I deal with the emotional pain and the physical pain in the same way. I block it out. It's the only way I know how. I don't want to talk about it. The best I can hope for is to cope with the day and get through it and forget about it. I try to have a bit of fun, to make the most of the time at home with Paula and the kids, but I'm like a robot. Everything has to be done at a snail's pace. It's obvious that I'm struggling, but talking about it, trying to explain why I'm finding it all so hard, will only make it harder. And when I start to block it out, there's no subtlety or nuance. I block everything out. I become very quiet and detached. I start to live life in my own head. When I do that, my struggle becomes a struggle for everyone. My mood drags everyone else down with me. It starts to have a very negative effect on the whole family.

I convince myself that if we go away for a few days and get a change of scenery, we'll all get a bit of a break from this. We go down to Kerry for a week at Easter. While we're down there, my right foot goes numb. I get this strange sensation in the sole of my foot, as if there's a ball in my shoe under the front part of my foot, and then I lose all feeling in my big toe and across the top half of my second and third toes. Because of where the fracture is in my leg, there was always a possibility that there could be some nerve damage too. The feeling in my big toe comes back eventually but the second and third toe don't quite feel the same as before.

If I can't be active, I at least need to be functional, for my own headspace if nothing else. I force myself to push through.

The frame has been on for about seven weeks when I fly over to France for a day at the end of May to buy a yearling. Coming back through Lourdes Airport that evening, the man waves me through and I shuffle towards him as quickly as I can. In my head, I hear the noise –

BEEP BEEP BEEP BEEP

– and then a second later, I hear it for real as it fills the little security area. It falls silent again just as quickly. Its work here is done. I look down the frame and I look back at the bemused French security guard, scanner in hand, and I think: at least this is an obvious one, surely.

On the other side of the X-ray machine, he starts from the top down. He scans one arm, and although I'm expecting the beep again this time, it catches him by surprise. If I had a word of French, I'd try to explain, and from what I can tell, he doesn't have much English, so we resort to the universal language of showing and pointing.

I signal to him to give me a moment while I open the top few buttons on the neck of my shirt and move it to one side to show him the scar that matches his machine, a convenient shorthand for the steel plate that it hides. His curiosity satisfied, he turns his attention to the other side and has a bit of a laugh to himself when the scanner goes off again. Different arm, same story.

I'm sure he's well used to situations like this. I am too. There's a screw in my knee that I've had since I was a kid. It went unnoticed for years, but time moves on and technology gets better and now it's no surprise if that childhood memory flashes up on the airport computer screen. There's a scar for that one too, if I need to explain; the same for the plate in my arm. They all have their stories. But in the absence of being able to explain any of them to my new friend, all we can do is have a bit of a laugh as I do up the buttons of my shirt and shuffle off again to pick up the rest of my bits.

The five of us go to the Bloom garden festival in Dublin on the bank holiday Monday at the start of June: me, Paula, Síofra, Órla and Rían. I haul the frame round the Phoenix Park as we cover the length and breadth of the festival. It's exhausting, but I keep pushing. I can only push so far, though, before I start to aggravate the wounds and the skin tears open again. That's the greatest discomfort. There are two wires drilled into my leg just above the ankle. The little hole in my skin is barely noticeable at the start, no more than a couple of millimetres wide, but even the smallest movement in the wires is agony. They settle into place overnight while I'm in bed and the skin starts to knit back together around them, but then as soon as I get up and start forcing myself to move around, it tears again.

I shouldn't even be considering going to see George Ezra play in Malahide Castle in June, but we have tickets and I'm determined. Before we go to the concert that evening, I go back in for a check-up and David Moore, my orthopaedic consultant, decides that he can take one of the pins out of the front of my ankle. Whatever it is about that particular pin, it has always given me trouble; as soon as it's taken out, I'm like a new man. The transformation is unbelievable, in every sense. It feels like the entire frame has come off, not just one small pin. That night is the first bit of fun I've had in 10 weeks, the first time I've started to feel like myself again and not the quiet, withdrawn shell I've been since this happened.

By pure chance, we bump into a few people we know: Jennifer Walsh is there with her husband Killian and their kids, and so are Sue Ann McManus and her family. We have a brilliant night. I'm singing and dancing with the kids, and I even manage to put Rían and Órla on my shoulders. It's complete happiness and I haven't felt this way in a long time.

I'm desperate to get the frame off completely. Once I'm rid of it, it's the most obvious milestone on the road back to normality. Nobody could ever really say for certain how long it would need to be on, but 12 weeks was the best guess and the timeline that I've had in mind all along. I push to get it off even quicker than that. At 11 weeks I go in to see Mr Moore and ask if I still need it.

'I can see from the X-ray that the fracture has done really well,' he tells me, 'but the report from the radiologist says that it's still not fully healed and I can't overrule that. We'll have to leave it on for a few more weeks.'

Report or no report, Mr Moore has me well sussed out. I'd have been trying to get out of the frame after four weeks if I thought I had half a chance. When I do finally get it removed three weeks later and I feel how weak and vulnerable my leg still is, as if it could snap in a strong breeze, I know he's saved me from myself. I arrive for my appointment at eight o'clock in the morning only to discover that it has been pushed back until the afternoon. I'm fasting, starving, but if I'm told that I'll have to sit here for another 24 hours, I couldn't care less. Whatever it takes, the frame is coming off.

The Galway Races come and go without me. All I can do is laugh at my optimism, but it doesn't bother me in the slightest to miss it. That first weekend when I broke my leg, my only concern was to get out ahead of the retirement rumour and kill it stone dead. It was far more important to be decisive, to set a comeback date quickly, than it was to be fit and riding again by the end of July. I'm still nowhere near ready to go back racing but I've come a long way in the last four months. I've made so much improvement. I've got some semblance of normality back in my life. That's reason enough to be happy, even if there's an awful lot more still to do. The Listowel Races start in five weeks' time; that's the new target.

We book a few days away in Portugal, right down south in Alvor, a nice quiet little fishing village in the Algarve, lovely and laid back. We're only there for five days, but everything about it is simple, and it's perfect, precisely what we need. I'm still moving like a man with a recently broken leg, but nothing can stop us enjoying ourselves. I give Rían a piggyback as we go for a walk down through the town. Before they know it, Paula and the two girls are 150 yards ahead of us. I'm coming but I'm coming at my own pace; there's no rush. Another day, we rent a pedal boat and take it out for a spin around the marina. It's a bit choppy as we bring it back in to dock it afterwards, and the owner is roaring at us as we try to get out of it –

'Now. Jump. Go. No.'

I can see the kids are starting to get half-panicked by all the shouting so I jump off the back of it to see if I can help to bring it in that way. I land on my feet just as the undercurrent goes out from underneath me and lifts the pedal boat up and away from the shore. I'm standing four or five feet from it now and I know what's coming next. I try to dive out of the way before the next wave carries the boat right back in on top of me. It's a pretty weak effort – 14 weeks in the frame hasn't left much power in my foot – but it gets me out of the way. I'm hobbling and holding my leg as I get back to my feet. There are a few bystanders who've stopped to watch what's happening, and when they see my leg swollen up as big as a balloon, they think I've hurt myself jumping out of the way of the boat. 'It's fine, it's fine, it was like that already,' I reassure them. I'm as lame as a dog for a week or more afterwards, but nothing can spoil these few days.

I'm glad Enda King isn't around to see that feeble attempt at a dive. Enda was one of the first people I called for advice from Aintree Hospital and, now that the frame is off, he's the man looking after my rehab. A bit like Mr Moore, I get the feeling that Enda might be managing me as well as managing my rehab. The programme he has me on demands so much discipline; I manage to do about two-thirds of it every day before I get fed up and lose interest. But when I go to see him in the Sports Surgery Clinic for my check-ups, he seems happy with the progress I'm making. I've a strong suspicion that he knew I wouldn't do all the exercises he was giving me, and that he loaded up on me and gave me a programme and a half in the first place.

Anything is easy after the frame, but working through rehab is mind-numbingly slow. It's the monotony of it all that kills me. Enda gives me two different programmes to work on, alternated day by day, but even at that, it doesn't take me long to get bored. There are so many repetitions and the exercises, these tiny little flexions, they're so small that you wouldn't even notice the movement. I can feel it, though, and if it's taking all this energy and attention just to get my foot to move in this very basic way, that's the whole reason why I'm sitting here doing them. Enda is brilliant at keeping me motivated. He keeps reassuring me that every rep I do today will pay dividends down the line when I get back riding.

'When you start to get movement back in the foot, you'll know why you've been doing this,' he tells me. 'Put in the hard yards now and when you get going, you'll really feel the benefit of it.'

I stick at the physio work and I start to add in some sessions on the exercise bike as well. By the time I'm ready to get back up on a horse, I can't believe how fit I feel. When I went back riding after both of my broken arms, I was nowhere near as fit as this because all my recovery work was focused on my upper body. I'd done nothing for my legs, and your legs are the part of you that are working hardest when you're riding a horse. Enda was right. This time round, the hard yards have all been worth it.

I go down to Gavin Cromwell's on a Tuesday morning in late August to ride a couple of lots for him. I've known Gavin for as long as I've been racing, and his yard in Danestown is only 15 minutes away, so it's the perfect place to ease myself back into things. I try to force my foot into my riding boot for the first time in months and I burst it; the swelling on my leg does part of the damage and the rotten zip takes care of the rest.

It feels good to be back riding out again. I get into a routine, riding out a couple of days a week, and it's all systems go for Listowel until I go back to see Mr Moore for one last check-up. He's delighted with how everything has healed.

'What are your plans now?' he asks me before I leave.

'Listowel is next week so I'll be back racing then,' I say.

'Do you know what, you might be better to give it another month. If something happens and you twist your leg, you'll find the weakness in the bone.'

As soon as he says that it might not be a good idea, that's the decision made; I can wait another month. I'm not taking any risks. The last five months have been a hell that I never want to go through again. I'm not going back to the start again.

28

The phone rings on a sleepy Sunday morning in west Kerry.

'Ballyoisin runs in Tipperary this afternoon. You're up.'

I race outside to start packing the car like a kid taking the stairs two at a time on Christmas morning. The rest of the Dingle Food Festival will have to wait until some other time; I'm going back to work.

I thought today would never come. The ground has been drying out all week and I thought it was only a matter of time before Ballyoisin was scratched from the race. But the decision is left right up until the last minute on Sunday morning and when the ground comes up with a little bit of give still in it, I get the phone call and the green light.

Paula looks at me and sees the excitement, the certainty in me. There must have been times over the last six months when she looked at me and wondered if, mentally, I really wanted this as much as I thought I did. Was I really up for it again – up for all of it, the hard luck and the near misses and the falls and the scrutiny as well as the good horses on the big days? Now that it's here, there isn't a hint of doubt in my mind. When it felt like the four walls of life were closing in on me, this day, the thought of finally being able to go back racing again, was always there at the end of the road. I kept going forward towards it, one step at a time. My leg feels good. I feel good. I'm ready to go.

It couldn't go much worse. Ballyoisin is a free-going horse, he likes to make the running, but there's another front-runner in the race which makes things a bit more complicated. Rachael Blackmore rides Petit Mouchoir and I know that they'll go out flat to the boards.

'Jump out to make it and see,' Enda Bolger, who trains the horse for JP, suggests. 'And if you're going too quick, just sit second and follow him.'

But Petit Mouchoir goes off like a shot and when Ballyoisin tears off after him, I can't put the genie back in the bottle. By the time we jump the first hurdle, we must be 10 lengths clear of the horse in third, but after a mile, he's empty. Petit Mouchoir bottoms out a couple of furlongs later and finishes fourth, but my lad is barely able for much more than a canter as we cross the line last of six, 70 lengths behind the winner. Ruby's working for Racing TV, doing the live analysis, and he doesn't mince his words when it comes to how my horse and Rachael's set the race up for the rest of the field.

'They completely cut each other's throats,' he says. 'It was crazy to watch.'

It's not the comeback I was hoping for. After six months of torture, fighting to get back, all it takes is one ride to remind me that this won't be easy. I've no doubt that I can still ride at the top level but I still feel that I need to prove it. I'm not worried about my leg. I'm not worried about my bottle. I've seen lads who get shaky, afraid, as they get into the latter years of their career, thinking about falls, wondering if one more bad one could stick with them for the rest of their days, afraid to go all out in the same way that they used to. That's not me. All I want is to be swinging in with two to jump and a chance, coming along upsides a lad and saying to myself, right, what have you got left? That's where the buzz is. Even at 40, it's still unbeatable.

A few of the good English horses get out for their first runs of the season at the start of November and that helps me to get things back on track. Sporting John carries great expectations; Philip Hobbs starts him at two miles one furlong for his debut over hurdles and I get a first look at what seems to be a promising engine when he finishes strongly to win in Exeter.

Champ goes to Newbury a couple of days later for his first run. His defeat in the Ballymore at Cheltenham was the only twist in the tale of last season and before he even has a run over fences, he's already on top of the shortlists for the RSA Chase next March. He wins by an easy three and a half lengths; it was just about as perfect as you can get, Nicky tells the press afterwards.

I go on to the November meeting in Cheltenham and I've a good weekend there too. I do everything right bar win on Brelan D'As, who is just touched off, beaten by a neck in the BetVictor Gold Cup, and then Defi Du Seuil, another of the superstars of this year's team, gets his first one on the board for the season by winning a small but competitive renewal of the Shloer Chase.

By the time I get back to Newbury at the end of the month with Champ, the conveyor belt of good races and good horses is rolling. Champ is giving us every indication that he wants the full three miles, and that's the plan for him eventually, but Nicky is in no rush for now. He keeps him at two and a half for the Berkshire Novices' Chase; he's still full of running as he crosses the line, but that's only part of the story.

We make it as far as the third fence without incident. It's an open ditch, and as Champ jumps it, a loose horse jumps right across our path and we crash into the back of him. We come down heavy and for a second, I'm hanging on to his neck, just to steady myself so that I can get back into position. The next time round, that same open ditch is the third last, and again, it causes us problems. It's shaping up as a three-horse race – Johnny Burke has Black Op going along nicely out in front and while I come at him on one side, Tom Cannon and Deyrann De Carjac are getting into position on the other. Champ guesses at it, far from his tidiest jump, and now we have a bit of work to get back on terms with the others. I get stuck into him and give him a couple of smacks on the run down to the last and we touch down a half-length behind the other two.

We're in a fight to the finish and I put my head down and go for it. That's the natural posture when you're riding a finish. You can't drive a horse properly if you're looking all round you. You have to get down on him and push. If you need to take a peek, you have to make it a quick one because every time you look up, you stop pushing for a split second. When you're in a fight like this one, you can't afford to give away too many of those split seconds. You need to keep maximum pressure on as much as possible.

There's a rail that splits the middle of the run-in at Newbury – right for the finish line, left for the water jump and to head back out into the country again. I take Champ off the inside when we jump the last and line him up towards the right-hand side of the rail. I drop my head, drive, and then take a peek to make sure we're still on course for the finish line. I drive again and as we pass Johnny Burke on Black Op, I take a quick look up again – and oh fuck, I'm gone. I grab a hold of the right rein with both hands and I pull, just before we smash straight into the rail in the middle. There are so many horses that would resist and fight against you but as soon as I pull, Champ works with me. I see it late, but when I do, he reacts quickly enough to dig us out and save us. We swerve back to the right side of the rail just in time and Champ straightens up, barely breaking stride, to run on to the line before Black Op can punish us.

I turn it into a laugh and a joke in the interviews afterwards: 'He just wanted to go round again,' I explain. I'm lucky that we won the race and that I'm able to pass it off with no big fuss; a split second later and it could have been a very tricky one to try to explain away. It wasn't a lack of concentration on my part, just circumstances. I had my stick in my left hand and I was doing all the right things, but it's my responsibility to make sure we're on the right line and the buck stops with me. If I hadn't looked up when I did, we'd have ended up in big trouble. The bruised ego would have hurt as much as the bruised bones.

The following day, nobody blames Buveur D'Air either. His record speaks for itself: eight Grade 1 wins over hurdles so far including two Champion Hurdles, soon to be three if this season pans out the way everyone's expecting. He starts what will hopefully be another championship campaign on familiar territory: the Fighting Fifth in Newcastle, a race he's won in each of the last two seasons, against opposition that shouldn't cause him too much trouble.

The danger when you're sent off a 2/13 shot against mere mortals is that the horses that you're up against have nothing to lose. If they come home from a race like this with one of the minor placings and some nice prize money, that's a good day's work, but if they're feeling brave, they've a free shot at you. If they take a risk and it doesn't pay off, the worst that can happen is that they'll end up getting beaten in a slightly different way.

That's exactly what Cornerstone Lad does. It's the first Graded race of his career and, after a bit of shadow boxing down at the start line, Henry Brooke decides that he'll make the running and earns himself a healthy lead over the first couple of hurdles. We keep a nice pace in behind him, but nobody makes any attempt to chase him down until we turn into the straight and jump the third last. Buveur D'Air is a heavy horse whose fitness always improves for his races. But this is his first run of the season and when I feel him give a couple of blows during the race, I decide it's best to wait and play our cards late rather than run the risk of giving chase too early and getting tired. But Cornerstone Lad already has a couple of runs under his belt and he's fit as a flea. He's not coming back to us as easily as we might have hoped and Buveur D'Air still has eight lengths to find as I set him off in pursuit on the run down to the second last.

We meet it on a great stride but Buveur D'Air doesn't pick up. He raps the top of the hurdle with his front legs and lands on his heels. It's a mistake when we really didn't need to make one, but there's no need to ring the alarm. We're not done yet. Buveur D'Air finds plenty more for me on the run down to the last. The distance to Cornerstone Lad is getting smaller and smaller. We're getting there. Twenty yards before the last, I can see that it's coming up on a nice stride. He measures it perfectly, slick and at speed, and jumps it like a winner.

We're right up on Henry's boots. He's all out on Cornerstone Lad, desperately trying to hang on, but this is meat and drink to Buveur D'Air. He draws up alongside Cornerstone Lad and then heads him, sticking his nose into the narrowest of leads with 100 yards or so to race. Once we've passed him, the rest should be a formality, until it's not. Buveur D'Air fades just a fraction on me. It's so unlike him. He goes from being up by an inch to down by an inch, and before he can turn things around again, we hit the line; Cornerstone Lad wins the Fighting Fifth by a short head.

I know how this will look: misjudged at best, careless at worst. It will look like I gave Cornerstone Lad too much rope, both underestimated him and overestimated my own horse; and then, as I tried to claw it back, I fired Buveur D'Air at the second last. That's the only mistake he made and that's what cost us. If you look at someone like Ruby, or Noel Fehily, lads who would be very quiet riders; they don't ask for the big one as much. But that's not my way. That's not my style. I ride a horse in my hands so that he takes me down to a fence, and I know that he's more likely to meet it on a forward stride. For me, it gets a horse jumping quicker. It's more economical. They learn to be more accurate.

I'm sure some would disagree, but there's no right or wrong answer. It's a style; it's personal. It's the way I've been riding Buveur D'Air for the last two miles. It's the way I've been riding since I was a teenager. If that stride is there and he's on it, and I change my mind and don't go for it, he's very likely to go for it anyway. And if he's committed to doing things one way, and I'm caught in two minds, that indecision is what's going to do more damage than anything else. But we've just been beaten by a horse that, with the greatest respect, shouldn't have been within 20 lengths of us, so I'm not in a strong position to be splitting hairs over racing techniques and who's right and who's wrong.

I pull Buveur D'Air up after the winning post and we turn down the chute back towards the parade ring. As soon as he hits the walkway, as soon as he gets off the soft ground onto the firmer surface, I can feel that he's lame. I jump off him straight away. I look at his hoof and see the problem – there's a splinter driven into his coronary band, where the hair meets the hoof. It must have come off the second last hurdle when he clattered through it. If there's damage done, it's all below the surface. All we can see is the splinter. We won't know how serious it might be until the vets come to take a look. When Nicky sees it, he tells me he's never seen anything like it in all his years. It's a freak accident, but it's a nasty one, and I'm immediately fearing the worst.

A bad result is one thing. A bad result with a question mark over the ride is worse again. Add in an injury to the Champion Hurdle favourite and I start to worry that, after six months on the sidelines, the last 24 hours haven't exactly been a brilliant advertisement for my ability. I need a win.

⌒

The first time I meet Francis O'Toole is in his practice in Slane. Going to see him is Paula's suggestion. She's the one who finds him. I need help trying to find a better balance between work, home and family.

To begin with, I see Francis once a week for six weeks in the run up to Christmas in 2017. I connect with him straight away. From the moment I meet him, he puts me at ease. He's a really warm, engaging, kind person. There's no judgement from him. He's not jumping to conclusions. Instead of telling me what I'm doing wrong, he's trying to encourage me to do right. I can talk and try to explain and he listens and we figure things out together. He just gets it.

There was a time when I would have dreaded facing any of these thoughts myself, and dreaded having to share them with a stranger. Hilary Kearns laid a lot of the groundwork in that respect, long before I ever started going to see Francis. Hilary is an acupuncturist based in Dunshaughlin. The first time I met her was in the summer of 2015, the first time I broke my leg; the swelling inside the cast was causing me all sorts of problems and I desperately needed someone who could help, give me any sort of relief. I'd go in to see Hilary and I'd be in bits, my leg stuck into the inside of the cast. She'd work away, needling my other leg, and when she was done, the cast would be loose on me again.

But Hilary is also a human givens counsellor, which is a holistic framework for mental health. As she's working on my leg, she's also having a chat, trying to get me to open up. Without even knowing it, you're having a counselling session too – mind and leg, two for the price of one. Hilary loves racing, and I thought she was just a very chatty, curious person. I didn't realise what she was trying to achieve, that she was trying to help me with these conversations as well. But by the time I started going to see Francis, I was much more open to thinking about myself and talking about myself. A lot of that is Hilary's doing.

Francis focuses on mindfulness. The importance of taking a second, of being in the moment. Awareness. Awareness. Awareness. One of the first things he teaches me about is the dishwasher. It's the one job I do around the house a lot; I'm no good at washing clothes, but filling the dishwasher and emptying it, I can take care of that. But I do it and I'm thinking about a million other things, firing knives and forks everywhere as my mind races, instead of concentrating on what I'm doing. That's where Francis starts. It's not about the dishwasher. It's about being present and giving your attention to what you're doing right there and then, not worrying about the past or trying to anticipate some unknowable future.

Francis puts it to me that those occasions when I have too much of a good night out are wrapped up in the same behaviour; it's a lack of control caused by a lack of awareness. I put it down to poor tolerance or bad habits that I didn't have the maturity or the tools to address. When Francis links it all back to my lifestyle, my pace of life, it clicks and starts to make sense with me. It's adrenaline. I live for the high speed of racing, but I'm not leaving it at the racecourse; I come back in after a busy day and everything is still pumping. It's the same travelling home from England – win the 3.15 p.m. in Kempton, get on the 4.20 flight from Heathrow, charge in the door at home at 6.15, and think it's brilliant. I've no outlet for the adrenaline, no way of dealing with it. That constant fight or flight mode is what Francis works on getting me out of. Don't always be in such a rush. Take my time. Take a few deep breaths. Slow everything down.

Francis helps me with work too, to deal with the pressure that I'm putting myself under. For the most part throughout my career, I've been good at taking the ups and downs in my stride, not riding the highs too high, not dwelling on the lows. That laid-back, level-headed approach wasn't an act. That's who I am, and it brought out the best of me when I was riding.

But as I've got older, there are times when I'm distracted. I might be talking to Paula but not engaging with her. Or there can be days when the kids rush over to say hi when I come in the door. They're so delighted to see me and I'm delighted to see them too, but 30 minutes later, I'm back thinking about horses. I'm so absorbed in my own world that I've no time for theirs, to listen to the stories they want to tell me. I'm sitting there beside them but my mind is somewhere else. I create a vacuum, a bubble around myself. Instead of addressing the problem and trying to deal with it, I just block it all out, and by blocking out the pressure, I end up blocking out everyone.

I feel the benefit straight away of the time that I spend with Francis. I learn not to hang on to things, not to harbour them and let them build up, which is when they really start to cause issues. It's something a lot of jockeys – a lot of men in general – struggle with, not being as open and as able to talk as they should be. When I'm with Francis, I learn to switch off. I come out afterwards and ring Paula and I feel brilliant. Calmer, more relaxed and at ease, if nothing else.

Even though it's not that long ago, I grew up in a very different era, a very different Ireland, to the one in which we're raising our children. I was a sensitive child, but 1980s Ireland had a very straightforward approach to dealing with emotions: when something bad happens, you forget about it and move on. That's just how society was back then. But I want our children to be able to talk to us if they're upset or if they're worried just as much as

I want to hear about their hopes and dreams and the things that make them happy. In order for that to happen, I've realised that I have to work on myself, too. By spending time with Francis on mindfulness, my head is clearer when the kids have something they want to talk about. I'm more aware of what they're trying to tell me, and I have the space to empathise and try to help them understand and deal with whatever is going on. I learn the importance of asking open questions. When I'm dropping them to school, rather than asking, 'Are you looking forward to school today?' and getting a yes or no answer, I see how much better it is to ask, 'What are you looking forward to in school today?' and then listening to the answer.

Racing is a tough lifestyle. It's dog eat dog. Races come thick and fast and you need to be able to block out the bad moments and disappointments so that you can focus on the next race. But what works on the racecourse doesn't work when you're a husband and a father. I'm trying to draw a line under that cold, sometimes self-centred person that I became in my twenties, and to reconnect with the more sensitive kid of my childhood. I haven't gone full circle yet but I'm in the process of it.

∩

It takes a few days for the full severity of Buveur D'Air's injury to reveal itself. I'm praying for good news. I'm on the phone to Nicky constantly, waiting for the latest. Sophie, his wife, rings me with real-time updates any time she gets any sort of information. She knows I'm shaken by the whole thing. There is some good news: the injury hasn't become infected and there's no damage to his coffin bone, which is right in behind the hoof. But when the vets get a proper look at it, it's clear that there's only one way to take the splinter out. They'll have to operate on his hoof and cut it open. His season is over. The Champion Hurdle is gone.

I'm relying on Defi now. He's one of those horses – a Macs Joy, a Bobs Worth – that I've always loved from the start, that I've had a great connection with since the first day I sat up on him. Philip Hobbs, his trainer, is one of the gentlemen of racing too; I love riding for him. Saturday is the Tingle Creek, a Grade 1, a National Hunt classic. Saturday is the day that will help us to understand if Defi is good or if he's great, that will show us if he really has the class to be a Champion Chase contender this season. He's up against some top-level horses: Un De Sceaux, who is still the biggest threat in the race, even at the age of 11; Politologue and Sceau Royal were second and third in the Champion Chase just gone. There's already enough pressure on the situation without me heaping it on myself. It's on my mind all week and I build it up and build it up. I convince myself that I have a lot riding on this one race, that I simply cannot afford to lose.

Paula wishes me luck as I get ready to head for the airport that morning, and then she gives me a very important perspective at the moment when I need it most:

'It's only a horse race,' she says. 'Don't worry about it.'

All the anxiety disappears the moment we jump off and start racing. The saddle gives my head peace; I can't afford to think about anything except what I'm doing. I park my demons for those four minutes and my mind goes completely blank. Paul Townend plays his hand first as we run down to the third last, the pond fence, and Un De Sceaux takes up the running. He might be the veteran but he's here today to win. Defi moves up on to his tail as we turn into the home straight. Un De Sceaux jumps the second last two lengths in front and as we hit the ground running behind him, I give Defi a squeeze. We hit the front as we jump the last, right on cue and not a moment too soon. I ask Defi to go, to find a finish, to shake off the challenger but Un De Sceaux won't go away. He's going to make us fight all the way to the line. We're a length clear but Defi doesn't like being out in front alone. He likes the company. He likes to be in a race. He starts to idle, and just in my peripheral vision I can feel Un De Sceaux right there beside us, snapping. It feels like the line will never come. I give Defi one last push, all I've got, and it's enough. He holds on to win by a neck.

This one means everything. The spotlight was on, the pressure was on, I needed to deliver, and I have. Just to get back racing after the injury was one thing; to win another Grade 1 is as good as it gets. It's 16 years since I first won the Tingle Creek on Moscow Flyer, the first of our battles against Azertyuiop. Sixteen years is a long time, but the buzz, the thrill, the complete unbridled joy of this particular moment right now before life moves on to the next winner or loser has never changed in all these years. I love it. I'll need a few minutes to start to go through the text messages, but there's one moment that stands out and I'll always remember: a chance meeting with Arthur Moore at the sales in Goffs.

'Well done,' Arthur says to me. 'That justified your return.'

Arthur's right; every bit of the struggle, it has all been worth it now. I don't think people doubted me. I don't think they had written me off. But for anyone who wondered how I'd be when I came back from the broken leg, if I could ever really be the same again, they have their answer now. The big race, the big day, there's never been anything quite like it to get me focused. It has always been my bread and butter. It still is. Job done.

29

When I wake up on the morning of St Stephen's Day, I know I have a chance. If there's a potential star among the 10 horses that will line up for the Christmas Hurdle at Kempton, it's the one I'm on: Epatante.

I go in hope rather than expectation. The last time I rode her on a racecourse, at Cheltenham nine months earlier in the mares' novices' hurdle, she was like a rag doll afterwards, completely lifeless. Nicky was billing her in interviews beforehand as his best chance of the meeting – a meeting where he was sending out Altior as the 4/11 favourite in the Champion Chase – so we were at a loss to explain how she ended up running so flat and finishing ninth. I thought she boiled over going down to the start; Nicky put it down to the after-effects of the vaccination that all the horses needed following an outbreak of equine influenza in the weeks leading up to the festival. Either way, it wasn't a true run or reflection of her ability. I'm happy to put a line through it. It's of no concern to me at all.

I was in Newcastle riding Buveur D'Air when she had her first run of the season, a handicap hurdle at Newbury where she won by a very impressive six lengths for Aidan Coleman – and went up nearly a stone in the official ratings as a result. On that basis, she still has a bit to find with the others in the Christmas Hurdle, but most of them are exposed. We know what they'll bring to the table. With a horse of Epatante's profile, a five-year-old mare coming from Nicky's, there's always a chance that the best is yet to come.

Not in my wildest dreams do I expect that we'll uncover a Champion Hurdle contender. When Buveur D'Air goes down for the season, so does my chance of winning the race for a fourth time. There's no replacing a horse of that calibre and quality; you don't just pick the next one off the production line and slot them in to fill the void. Unless you're JP McManus and you're always a few steps ahead, shopping for next year's champion before this year's one has even been crowned. Then there's always a possibility that something could blossom come March. By the time I leave Kempton that afternoon, the bookies have a new favourite at the top of the market for the Champion Hurdle. They like what they see in Epatante. So do I.

The soft ground is my only worry. If it's going to bite, I'll know it sooner rather than later, but five furlongs in, as she turns down the back straight, she's travelling like a dream for me. She still has two or three in front of her but she cruises up around their outside as we come off the bend into the home straight. We've still got two to jump, but even as I keep a hold of her, she's chewing up the ground. She's slick over the second last and as soon as I give her a squeeze to turn up the heat on the others, she quickens up nicely. We jump the last in front and when she hits top gear, that's when she really puts her name in lights. If she's still full of this much running, still has such a lethal turn of foot, on soft ground on St Stephen's Day, how good could she be in March? I don't need to say much to Nicky when we come back in.

'What do we do now?' he asks me.

'Win the Champion Hurdle.'

The last year has been the toughest of my career but, finally, the future is looking bright. I've won a Grade 1 and now I'm on the favourite for the Champion Hurdle, and, in Defi, close enough to the favourite for the Champion Chase as well.

I don't need to be reminded of how quickly things can change in racing; it's been more than 20 years, and I've seen it all. Within a week, everything is upside down again.

I spend New Year's Eve at Punchestown. I only have one ride but one is more than enough on this occasion, because Sizing John is back. The 2017 Gold Cup winner hasn't raced in more than two years because of injury. There have been setbacks, there have been false dawns, but 733 days later – if you're keeping count – Jessie Harrington is happy that he's finally ready to ring in the new year and start 2020 with sights firmly set on a second Gold Cup.

When Jessie rings to ask if I'm available, I jump at the chance to ride him. Robert Power, her first rider, needs a few days off to recover after falling at Leopardstown over Christmas, but I'm thinking longer-term. JP doesn't have anything being aimed at the Gold Cup, which means that I'll have no ride unless I can force myself into the picture somewhere else, and I know that Puppy is going to have a decision to make when the time comes. He rides one of the big English chances, Lostintranslation, as well, and it would be a huge call to get off him on Gold Cup day, particularly when there are still so many question marks over Sizing John after such a long layoff.

But December isn't March, and we need to get him there first. Burrows Saint and Rachael Blackmore make all the running and get a decent lead, but Sizing John runs well towards the head of the pack. He moves up into second place as we turn out of the back straight and come down to the third last hurdle. He doesn't hit the hurdle; he jumps it perfectly, pings it, but after two years off the track, he's a little bit out of practice and not quite concentrating as much as he needs to be. He comes over it like a novice, not like a Gold Cup winner, and he's a little bit slow and unsure of himself as he tries to get his legs out on landing. His momentum carries him forward for a stride before he knuckles and goes down in one slow stumble and that's the end of it. True to form, Jessie doesn't have as much as a cross word when I come back in.

'He stumbled, the bloody eejit,' she tells me, and that's all that's said. That's Jessie. She has never changed over all the years.

Sizing John doesn't make it back to the Gold Cup after all, although it's not because of the fall at Punchestown. The plan unravels a few weeks after that; Jessie brings him to the Curragh for a piece of work and discovers afterwards that he's not quite right. It's incredibly frustrating for everyone in Commonstown who has worked so hard over the last two years to get him back, but there's no sense in taking a chance and risking him. Jessie calls a halt to his season on the spot.

If I'm waiting for the new year to bring good fortune, it certainly doesn't happen on day one. Champ goes to Cheltenham for the Dipper Novices' Chase, his last run before Nicky wraps him up in cotton wool and puts him away for 10 weeks until Cheltenham. Our scare on the run-in at Newbury is a distant, irrelevant memory now.

He's the 4/9 favourite, which is a fair barometer of the expectation that's surrounding him, not just today but for the rest of the season in general. He's two from two over fences but he's only learning and I can still see plenty of room for improvement, a couple of moments where he hasn't been as natural with his jumping as he could have been.

The Dipper is another two and a half-mile race, and we know he won't be short of stamina, so Nicky is happy for me to tag along with whatever makes the early pace. Paint The Dream, one of the outsiders, plays that role and Champ settles in behind him in second early on. I let Champ move up on the outside and take over as we pass the stands and head back out into the country. So far, so good. He gets in a bit close to a couple of the fences down the back straight but then puts in a monster leap at the open ditch, letting me know that he's still with me. He travels beautifully down the hill, five lengths clear, and into the home straight. The noise level rises as we turn within earshot of the crowd of 30,000 packed into the stands. Galloping down to the second last, he's distracted. His mind starts to wander, possibly wondering who all these people are and why they're shouting when all he wants to do is go for a run and jump. That can be the problem if you're out in front on your own on a novice; they don't know where to look when they're approaching the stands. There's a novice's naivety to him too; he doesn't realise how vital it is that he concentrates on what he's about to do, that I can't do it all for him.

The longer I can wait without making any rash decision, the better. I'm waiting for him to prick his ears and look at what he's doing but he never does. His head bobs left and right and I'm still waiting for him to lock on and look at the fence. He's on a longish stride and I give him a squeeze to let him know to go on, go for it. He shapes to jump it but then puts down into the fence and skids crashing to the ground as soon as his front hooves hit the ground.

Champ gets up and gallops away. I pick myself up and quickly give myself the once-over; I'm okay too. That's all that Nicky's worried about, that both of us are fine. It's an easy fall to explain – the horse wasn't concentrating, he didn't look at the fence, and he paid the price. There's very little I could have done differently in the circumstances.

Thank God for Defi Du Seuil; at least I know that he won't let me down. The glare of the spotlight is as strong as ever when

Defi goes to Ascot for the Clarence House Chase in the middle of January. With two months to go until the Champion Chase, the top of the two-mile division is starting to take shape and three horses are head and shoulders above the rest. Try to split those three, though, and everyone's got their own favourite. Altior, the two-time champion in 2018 and 2019; a record 19 wins in a row, unstoppable, until he was stopped by Cyrname in November and the streak came to an end. Chacun Pour Soi, Willie Mullins's French import, who was very impressive when he beat Defi at Punchestown at the end of last season. And then Defi, undisputedly the best novice in training over two and a half miles last season, now out to prove that he's every bit as imposing over the shorter trip in open company.

Today is about Defi and Defi alone. Chacun Pour Soi is taking the Irish route to Cheltenham with a run at the Dublin Racing Festival in a few weeks' time, and although the Clarence House was pencilled in as the curtain-raiser between Defi and Altior, his connections decide to give it a miss when the ground comes up heavy. That leaves us and Un De Sceaux to go at it again, to either frank the Tingle Creek form or to turn everything on its head.

Defi copes with heavy ground, but Un De Sceaux excels on it. That's why, even though Defi is five years younger, there was only a neck between them at the line in the Tingle Creek. He jumps off in front again but this time he sets a much steadier pace than he did in Sandown. Defi stalks him in behind, never letting him more than a couple of lengths clear. When Un De Sceaux puts in a good jump, Defi responds. When he ups the pace, Defi goes too. It's automatic. He leads us the whole way around and we have everything else well covered. It's a two-horse race on the run down to the second last. Defi jumps it and as he lands, he takes off on me. Within a few strides, he's pulled three lengths clear of Un De Sceaux and is bounding down towards the last in the lead.

It's frighteningly effortless, but this wasn't the plan. I've hit the front on him early in other races – in the Dipper against Lostintranslation for one – and it came back to bite me. I wanted to hold on to him for a little bit longer now, but he's got his own ideas about how we're going to win this race and I'm not going to argue. I'm looking back through my legs at Un De Sceaux and I know that all we have to do is jump the last safely. All it took was one quick burst of acceleration from Defi and this one went from fight to formality in an instant.

We both jump the last well, but I don't even need to give Defi a squeeze to get him to see out the race. He cruises home in my hands, and Un De Sceaux runs on bravely behind us as Defi eases down. A little less than three lengths separates us at the line, but it's the performance, not the winning distance, that will make the headlines in tomorrow's papers.

30

stop to watch the TV in the weighroom at Cheltenham. It's tuned to one of the news channels and Leo Varadkar, Ireland's Taoiseach, is making a speech.

The COVID-19 virus is spreading rapidly across the world with over 100,000 confirmed cases of the disease in more than 100 countries. Yesterday, Wednesday 11 March 2020, the World Health Organization officially described the disease as a pandemic for the first time; by the end of the week, they declare Europe to be its epicentre. Schools and colleges are to close, the Taoiseach explains. Offices too, with people advised to work from home. Any large gatherings in Ireland, whether they're indoor or outdoor, will be cancelled.

Nobody knew whether Cheltenham would go ahead but as it got closer, it became clear that it would. When the festival begins, I'm very aware of it. We're advised not to shake hands and to take other precautions. Phil Taylor, one of the jockeys' valets, mentions to me that there's a strong possibility that spectators could be prohibited, that we could be racing behind closed doors by the end of the week. The situation is changing every day. I hear snippets of information from Paula, who's getting updates from people at home, but I don't have much time to fully take in all the latest news at it happens. Standing in the weighroom watching the Taoiseach's speech, it's clear that all of our lives are about to change in a way that we could have never foreseen; for how long, nobody knows.

By the end of the month Ireland, like a lot of the world, will be in lockdown. But for now, racing goes on.

Every cloud gets me worried. Epatante can beat anything that lines up against her in the Champion Hurdle, but she can't beat the weather. The rain comes again on Monday night into Tuesday morning. Officially the going is soft for the first day of the festival, but by the time I ride Chantry House in the Supreme Novices' Hurdle and feel how dead it's riding in places, I'm forced to accept that her chance is probably gone.

Sometimes you notice things at the racecourse, in the minutes before a race, that you'd never notice at home. As Epatante is led around the parade ring, I can see a difference in her. She was always slight but she has really filled out behind and bulked out in her back end. She looks like a stronger horse, which can't do any harm. When we get out onto the track, I'm tuned in as she skips up over the first couple of hurdles and passes the stands. The ground is soft in the back straight, more of a slog than she'd like, but she travels away without showing any ill effects. This isn't too bad – the longer she can keep it up, the less chance that the fuel light will start flashing in the last few furlongs and she'll flounder up the hill.

When we get to the fourth last, my biggest worry is that she'll go on too soon and get away from me; that's how well she's travelling. Petit Mouchoir's been out in front for most of the race and Darver Star, Gavin Cromwell's horse, is next. I use him as my shield so that I can take cover and try to conserve her. I'm sitting on a rocket and the last thing I want to do is light the fuse, which is exactly what will happen if she moves up alongside him or they go eyeball to eyeball. I park her on his tail, knowing that she'll have to slow down without me doing anything to disrupt her, and let him act as my handbrake.

It's the same at the third last. I don't want a big jump from her because she'll kick into top gear and take off and leave her finish at the bottom of the hill. I sit quietly to let her pop over the hurdle but she hits it – not a bad mistake but enough to kill the head of steam that she's building up, which inadvertently works in her favour. It just takes the rush out of her, forces her to slow down for a second before she goes again. She switches off and relaxes and when she jumps the second last, she's on a great stride and pings it. It's perfect.

Petit Mouchoir starts to fade on the rail as we make the turn into the home straight and Darver Star leads the Champion Hurdle down to the last. Twenty-four years of experience tells me that I've done everything right until now. We haven't gone too quick, I've ridden the right race for her, and I can feel that I've saved plenty for the finish. If that isn't enough to win it from here, I can't have done much more. Because she's still full of running, we have options at the last hurdle; we can go long or we can go short. I want Epatante to take it on, to use it as our springboard. I ride her into the hurdle so that she gives me a big one, joining Darver Star and then passing him all in one fluent move.

Now we start the long run to the line. We've taken care of everything that was in front of us. I throw an eye towards the big screen and check to see if anything else is coming from behind. All I want to see is that there's nothing near us. I don't notice Sharjah finishing strongly, passing Darver Star and running on well into second, but he's not going to get to us in time.

You can't feign the emotion. It's joy. It's relief. It's everything and more. It has been the most exhausting, draining, demanding, challenging year of my life. The broken leg. The retirement talk. The rehab. The days when things just wouldn't go right. The belief, the certainty that I could come back from it all, that I could be as good as I was before. The tiny, unspoken fear that maybe I wouldn't get a chance. I've done it now. I'm here. Epatante wins her first Champion Hurdle and I win my fourth. Tim Molony and Ruby, they're the only jockeys to have ever won four and now I have too, taking my share of the record. It doesn't get any sweeter than this.

Fitzy is on interview duty for ITV at the finish line and he's one of the first over to congratulate me. I'm giddy with the happiness. Where do I start?

'I want to say hello to Síofra, Órla and Rían who are at home watching this with their nana,' I tell him. 'This one's for them.'

Every time I've said it over the years, I've meant it: your first winner at Cheltenham each March is your most important. I believe it now more than ever. Nothing can match this feeling. If it's as good as it gets for the week, it's more than enough. It's so special and it's only right that I dedicate it to three very special people. I don't know if I'll get the chance again.

JP rings at eight o'clock the next morning. It's a new day and we need to talk about Champ.

'It might help to keep him out a bit wider,' he suggests. 'Keep him on the better ground.'

It's music to my ears. We're racing on the old course again today, same as yesterday, which means that all the ground on the inside will still be chewed up. Once the damage is done, there's no way to fix it overnight, but the further wide you go, the better the ground. Now that I've got the green light from JP, I can push it as far as I need to. It can make all the difference.

Champ hasn't run since his fall on New Year's Day. Initially, the plan was to get him out again and let him get a clear round under his belt before Cheltenham. Nicky weighs up a couple of options for him in the middle of February, nothing too strenuous. There's a card in Wetherby and one in Kelso too, either of which he could go for until Storm Ciara sweeps Britain and forces both meetings to be abandoned. In the end, Nicky decides that he doesn't even need another race; that pressure to get in one more run, you're only either trying to please the public or please yourself. Nicky's happy to give him a racecourse school and leave it at that, and I tend to agree. Moscow Flyer won the Arkle on the back of a fall, and there's no reason why Champ can't do the same in the RSA.

By this stage we've already been putting him through his paces at home, trying everything we can think of to get him to sharpen up and show his fences a little more respect. I suggest to Nicky that we try schooling him over showjumping poles and then take him out over fences afterwards; he won't fall or hurt himself if he clips a pole, but it will come down with a bit of a clatter and it might just give him the fright he needs. Nico de Boinville, Nicky's first rider, does a brilliant job with him over the poles, and when I go over the following day I take him for a spin over fences. It definitely helps. Champ jumps much, much better, but that carelessness, that lack of self-preservation, still hasn't gone away completely.

A week before Cheltenham I do a preview night in the Moyvalley Hotel in Enfield, and Robert Power is on the panel with me. Puppy comes from a showjumping background – Captain Con Power is his father – and I pick his brain on the work we've been doing with Champ over the last few weeks.

'He's not really jumping fluently,' I tell Puppy, 'not as quick through the air with his hind legs as you'd like him to be.'

We chat it out, and when the mics come on and Puppy's asked for his lay of the meeting, his best bet for a horse that won't win, he doesn't bat an eyelid.

'Champ,' he says.

It's a strong race, and Puppy might not have fancied him anyway, but I have to stop myself laughing. And as they work their way along the line to me and I'm asked for the one horse to back above all others, I give the exact same answer –

'Champ.'

I'm deadly serious. He's the best horse in the race. He won't have any issue with the ground. I don't think he'll fall. I don't think he'll make a bad mistake. And even if his jumping is not as good as I know it can be, I think a consistent round of average jumping will be good enough on the day. It'll certainly give him a better chance than if he's good at five fences and then ploughs through the sixth. That's how his schooling has been shaping up. When it comes to his jumping, I'm happy enough to hope for average.

After JP calls me on the morning of the race, I have a good chat with Frank as well before I go out. It's not just Champ. The two of them have been discussing every one of our runners from every possible angle for weeks; that's how meticulous they are. When it comes to instructions, they deal in the general rather than the specific. They give me their read on things, but then they want me to ride the race as I see it and they trust me to put the finishing touches on the tactics.

'What do you plan on doing?' Frank asks me.

'Probably sit fourth or fifth,' I say. That's how I've visualised the early parts of the race.

'Or do you want to drop him in a bit?' Frank asks. 'Have a think about it.'

Within five minutes, I've come round to Frank's way of thinking. He's dead right – drop him in, get a rhythm and let him find his feet and get comfortable with his jumping – and that's exactly what I do. Allaho and Minella Indo, the two Irish horses at the top of the betting, jump off out in front, and between them, they make the running the whole way around. I've only got two behind me as I jump the first but it's a long way around, 19 more fences to jump, and for most of it, there's only a handful of lengths separating first and last.

I keep Champ out wide, hunting for the freshest ground. It's the long way round – we're four wide at times – but if the ground on the inner is as bad as I think, it'll grind down anyone who's taking the short route. He jumps the way I expect him to: average. He drags his legs through the back of a few, which is no surprise given the way he's been schooling at home. He gets in close to a couple as we go down the back straight for a second time. It stalls his momentum, but never for too long, and within a couple of strides, he's done enough to hold his position.

Paul Townend and Allaho lead us down the hill on the run to the third last, but Rachael Blackmore has been marking him every step of the way on Minella Indo and she's not giving him a moment's peace. The rest of us bunch up in behind – four or five lengths covers all of us as we jump three out. We've all got work to do to catch the front two, but I know it's still too soon for me to challenge and chances start dying around me very quickly. When we come off the bend into the straight, Champ is not just at the head of the chasing pack; he is the chasing pack. He could be slicker at the second last, but he just nods as he lands and I'm still nursing and nursing, waiting for him to fill up and come alive as we make the run down to the last. Rachael Blackmore jumps it in front on Minella Indo, but it's a tired jump and she leaves the door open for Allaho. By the time I get over it on Champ, they've already gone eight lengths clear up the run-in.

The RSA is not done after three miles – there's another half a furlong to go. In those last 110 yards there's still time for one last plot twist and a grandstand finish. Like a boxer pulling himself bolt upright from the canvas to beat the count, Champ comes back from the dead. From nowhere, he finds a bit more as he starts to come up the hill. When I look up, I see two tired horses in front of me. Champ is the only one who's not on his knees already and the gap is closing. Rachael knows she's got Allaho covered, so when she hears the pitch of the course commentator's voice rise, I know exactly how she's feeling. I've been in that seat before, hanging on to hope and nothing else. Champ is six lengths down. Four lengths down now. When he moves to within three lengths of the front two, I know I'm going to get there. He's flying, they're finished, and the line isn't going to come quickly enough for either of them. Allaho's on the rail, Minella Indo is out towards the centre, and I drive Champ into the space they've left between them. He gets there in the nick of time, with only a couple of strides to spare; by the time he hits the line, he's already pulled clear by a length.

Rachael pulls Minella Indo up alongside me to congratulate me. 'I know where you are,' I tell her; I've never forgotten Native Dara in 2000, that sinking feeling as I felt the race slip through my fingers and knew that I was powerless to stop it. Davy Russell hands me the red tartan armband of the festival's top jockey. There's still a long way to go in the week, but it's nice to wear it one more time, no matter how briefly. My 40th winner at the Cheltenham Festival is one I don't think I'll ever forget.

Forty could become 41 very quickly. I've still got Defi to come in the Champion Chase in an hour's time but before that, Dame De Compagnie is favourite in the next race, the Coral Cup. It's not just market talk or a green and gold magnet; she has a great chance. I wouldn't have been quite so positive a fortnight ago when she did a fairly average piece of work in Kempton, but when Nicky brought her back out at home last week, she sparkled. She has enough pace, she has won around the track, she'll stay – she ticks all the boxes. But the Coral Cup is a craps shoot, 25 horses handicapped to within an inch of their lives, and there's no guarantee. Make a plan, go in with an open mind, and see how it all unfolds.

The plan here is simple: get into a good position and sit there. I've marked up my card and I know that there's no real pace in the race, so it won't cost me anything to have her handy up in the first half of the field. Even if they've done their homework, a lot of lads go out assuming that a bit of pace will come from somewhere, that something will go to the front and take us out at a clip. It doesn't always happen like that. In 2006, I won the Coral Cup on Sky's The Limit doing the exact same thing – sitting handy in a race with no pace and then quickening in the last mile before running away. It's hard to quicken past a horse that's quickening from the front. You're hard at work but not making a dent; for every bit of ground you make, you're losing the same amount.

Position is everything, and we give it away at the very start. There's a false start and when we eventually jump off from a standing start, Dame De Compagnie is slow to go with them. We need to be in the front half rather than the back, and unless we can get out quick and take our ground, someone else is going to take it. The rest of the field will bunch together and there'll be no way through. There's a gap in front of us and we get there in time, jump up into it before it closes. We haven't even gone a furlong yet, but all those little things, all those moments, they make a difference.

We move up into the middle of the pack and I let her take a tow off Nico on Burrows Edge, another of Nicky's runners. We have the position; now it's a constant assessment – where are we as regards pace, ground, danger? How fast are we going, how slow are we going? Ending up out of position in a race like this, too far forwards or too far back hits you like an allergic reaction.

We get a perfect run round. I leave her to track Nico most of the way, and then as we run down to the third last, we inch a little bit closer, so that we're sitting in behind Dicky Johnson's horse, Honest Vic, who's up there disputing the lead. We're close, a little bit too close maybe; Honest Vic jumps slightly right at the third last and we nearly land on his heels at the back of it, but there's no harm done. Dame De Compagnie is exactly where I want her to be. Davy Russell comes up the middle to challenge on Black Tears. Kevin Brouder has the rail on Charles Byrnes's horse, Thosedaysaregone. But we've done everything right until now and I know she's not done yet. Dame De Compagnie hits the front as we jump the last and runs away up the hill to win. It's turning into one of those weeks.

I've played out the Champion Chase over and over in my head, but never quite like this. The big screens, the bookies' boards, they all say the same thing: Defi Du Seuil is the 2/5 favourite. It's ours to lose.

It's only the middle of the second day and the week has already far surpassed anything I could have ever hoped for. But if you'd given me the choice beforehand to win just one race all week, it would be this. The Champion Chase is the race of the meeting: Altior, Defi, Chacun Pour Soi. The superstar clash, the one that has been on everyone's lips for the last few weeks, the one that the entire racing world has been waiting for – and then it all falls apart in the space of 72 hours and Defi is the last man standing.

The news on Altior first broke on Sunday. Nicky found him lame that morning, struggling with a problem with a splint in his leg. They go to work straight away, ice packs, cold water, anything to try to help him along. By Monday morning, he had made huge improvements and was moving well enough to be left in the race at the 48-hour declaration stage. But by Tuesday, it's obvious that he won't be ready in time. Nicky knows he has no other option; the two-time champion is out of the race.

It's a huge disappointment for racing, but it's a big weight off my shoulders – not just because he's the best two-mile chaser of his generation, has proven class, and is the presumptive favourite, but because it's a hell of a lot easier to keep tabs on one good horse than on two. Chacun Pour Soi likes to go from the front, Altior will want to drop in a bit, and Defi is going to be somewhere between the two. When you've a good horse in front of you and a good horse behind you, it leaves you with a lot of decisions over the course of two miles. You need to get them right.

When I get to the course on Wednesday morning, I take a quick scan of the non-runners board in the weighroom. They have two non-runners marked down for the Champion Chase: number one, which is Altior, and number three as well. Is that right? I'm pretty sure three is Chacun Pour Soi's number. I run back into the weighroom to grab my copy of the paper and check it. It is. He's out too. When he trotted up that morning, the vets found he had an abscess in his foot. Racing has been robbed of a classic, but you only savour the classics and the great finishes when you're on the winner. I'm not too worried about that right now; I've just been gifted a penalty kick to win the Champion Chase for a sixth time and I can't quite believe it.

Defi is ready. Our expectations were high anyway, quietly confident that we could handle whatever Altior and Chacun Pour Soi threw at us, but now anything less than victory will be a disaster. Now we're the ones with the target on our backs. I turn my attention to the four other horses that are left in the race. Politologue will be handy. Sceau Royal will be dropped in. The script is ripped up. The plan is flipped on its head. Instead of plotting what I need to do to win on Defi, now I'm thinking about what I need to do so that he doesn't get beaten. The instructions boil down to the basics.

'I'll keep out of trouble,' I say to Frank.

That's all he wants to hear. That's all I need to do. But by the time we jump the fence away from the stands, that's already becoming an impossible ask. That fence, the fifth, is on a turn. When a horse is switched on, he'll take the corner, enthusiastic, racing, staying with the pack. Defi doesn't do that. He jumps it straight and lands out to his right. He's flat.

I don't panic but I have to react. Plan A is gone out the window. This is a different Defi, and the race is not just going to fall into our lap in the way we might have expected. I try to coax him along down the back straight, keep him out wide on the fresh ground, anything that might just help him to save a bit. I know what I have to do. I've been here before. If I can just get him to hang in, to get himself into a challenging position, if he sparks to life and picks up, we'll still have a chance.

It doesn't happen. We're only a couple of lengths down as we jump the third last but Defi's not travelling like a 2/5 shot. Harry Skelton has barely moved a muscle on Politologue out in front. He's got the rest of us strung out behind him, on the rack, and he's starting to turn the screws. I give Defi a squeeze, ask him if he's able to make a chase of it, but he's not finding anything. It's over.

There's no explanation for it. While the crowd fills in around the winners' enclosure to salute Politologue, the new champion, we bring Defi to the stables to get him checked out. The vets can't see any obvious issue. He's fit and he's well, which is the most important thing, even if it makes the last 15 minutes even more of a puzzle. There isn't a lost shoe or a bad jump or a tactical mistake or anything else that we can point to. He was well beaten in the end, tailing off into fourth more than 13 lengths behind the winner. There was nothing we could have done differently. He just didn't run the way we know he can. That's the real disappointment.

It's easier for me to put it to bed – I've already ridden two winners today, and the Champion Hurdle winner yesterday. It's Philip Hobbs I feel for. It's 18 years since he trained Flagship Uberalles to win the Champion Chase; I wanted to win it for him as much as anyone else. That the stewards decide to call us both in for an enquiry into the running and riding of Defi afterwards only makes matters worse. Anyone who knows the first thing about horse racing could see at every stage that he wasn't going. At best, it's out of touch; but in the circumstances, it's insensitive more than anything else.

It's the only disappointment of an unforgettable week. Sire Du Berlais carries top weight, 11st 12lb, in the Pertemps Final on Thursday but it still leaves him with a chance. It's three pounds more than he had when we won this race last year, but he never got a run at all that day; I was scrubbing and scrubbing, got the benefit of a little bit of space when I needed it on the run down to the second last, and just got him up on the run to the line to win by a neck. I'll happily take the extra bit of weight if we get a clear run round this time.

Davy Russell rides Gordon Elliott's other horse in the race, The Storyteller, and knowing the form that Gordon has my lad in, I suspect he'll be our biggest threat.

We're side by side the whole way around, silently sizing each other up, waiting for any sort of tell. We both know that we have a chance and we both know that the other is the biggest danger. I don't say a word, and Davy says less. Every ounce of focus is on winning the race. As we turn into the straight, there's just enough of a gap on the rail for me to squeeze Sire Du Berlais through, space for one horse but definitely not for two. This is the run that I didn't get from him last year. Davy is forced to sit and then pull The Storyteller out wide in the straight. Tout Est Permis, one of Noel Meade's, leads until we join him to make it three in a line jumping the last. The Storyteller touches down first but Sire Du Berlais is only a step behind. Top weight doesn't bother him. He won't be beaten today.

I'm running out of words. David Casey joked about me one year that if I was going out on the saddle horse at Cheltenham, I'd fancy my chances. He's probably right. I've always been quick enough to make a case for one in my own head, and it doesn't take much to get a reputation in the weighroom. I knew that my book of rides this year was as strong as ever, I knew I had a lot of chances, but I never expected this. As assistant trainer to Willie Mullins, it's David who gives me a leg up for my last ride of the week, Saint Roi in the County Hurdle.

'He has plenty of pace,' David tells me.

'Ride him like a good horse?' I ask.

'Ride him like a good horse.'

It has always been my privilege to ride good horses for good people. I'm lucky that I have enough good memories to fill scrapbooks from front to back a dozen times over. Lucky too that most of the bad days have long since been forgotten. More than anything, it has been fun. I came here content that if I left with one winner, it will have been a good week; Saint Roi makes it five. Crossing the line there's a part of me that knows that, no matter how I try to dodge the question in the post-race interviews, I'll never be back here again. If this is it for me and Cheltenham, for me and racing, I couldn't have asked for a better goodbye.

You'd be afraid to dream this much.

Epilogue

'A're you going to give somebody else a chance this week?' Mick Fitzgerald asked me as we did a quick TV interview before Saint Roi was led back to the winner's enclosure.

'I'm done now, Mick,' I told him with a laugh, 'so they can do all they want.'

There was no hidden message in my answer, nothing more to be read between the lines. Saint Roi was my final ride of the festival and after that, my week's work was done. But what I didn't say, what I couldn't quite bring myself to say just yet, was that it wasn't just my last ride of the week. In my heart I knew that this farewell was the beginning of the end, that I wouldn't be back. I had already made up my mind that my twenty-fourth season as a professional jockey would also be my last, and so this was it, my final Cheltenham. I was ready to retire.

I never wanted to retire. I always felt that as long as I was enjoying myself, and I was fit and healthy, I'd keep going. I never lost my love for racing: the rush, the buzz. Even as I got older, and my mid-thirties turned to late-thirties and then crept into forties, I accepted that I was well down the back nine of my career, but there was always another big race to win, always another good horse to ride, always something to keep me coming back. But as I fought my way back from that horrible double leg break in 2019, it brought a new perspective and new focus. I knew I couldn't take it for granted that I would be able to get back to full fitness and get back up on a horse again. I had no divine right to expect that I would be allowed to go out on my own terms. From that point on, that became my only goal: to get back racing, to finish the job my way. I knew how I wanted to bow out.

'I might call time at the end of the season and hopefully sign off on a Grade 1 winner,' I told JP after I made my comeback. I didn't plan to finish up after Cheltenham. There were still too many big days left in the season that I was afraid I'd miss out on. Fairyhouse, our local track, at Easter on the 150th anniversary of the Irish Grand National would have been a fitting occasion for me to announce my decision. So too would Punchestown, the grand finale of the Irish calendar. But global pandemics aren't interested in our plans.

'Will I do it now?' I asked Paula when I came back into the parade ring after Saint Roi's win. Maybe the time was right. There was still so much we didn't know about the devastating impact that COVID-19 would have on the world, and there was already so much uncertainty about whether or not sport would be allowed to continue. Would Aintree go ahead? Would it take place behind closed doors? Nobody knew for certain. I was in no rush back to the weighroom after Saint Roi's win. I was happy to stand and chat, savour every last moment and let it all sink in, sure in the knowledge that I would never have this opportunity again.

'I thought you might go another year,' Frank Berry said to me when I asked his advice on making the announcement that day.

'No, I'm done,' I assured him.

'Don't rush into it. Do you not want to ride in the Grand National?'

'I do.'

'Sleep on it.'

Frank was right; he usually is. If I had called it quits there and then, and had to watch Aintree from the grandstand or the couch, it would have been a challenging start to retired life. As it happened, I didn't have to worry about it. Within a week of Cheltenham finishing, the Aintree Festival had been called off, the Grand National was cancelled for the first time since the end of World War II, and racing in Britain had been suspended across the board. By the beginning of April, Fairyhouse, Punchestown and the remainder of the Irish national hunt season had been cancelled too. Sport, and life as we knew it, was shut down by the pandemic. In the end, there was no racecourse goodbye, no final dismount, but we didn't need the big crowd or the cameras to make the night of my retirement a special one. Instead, we invited family and some of our closest friends over for a garden party. The sun was shining, the kids loved being right there in the thick of the action enjoying the whole evening with us. For me, it was the perfect way to mark the occasion. I made a short speech to announce my retirement and then, at 10.59 p.m. on a Saturday night in July, I put out a short message on Twitter to tell the rest of the world.

It wasn't how I planned it, but I couldn't have asked for a better way to sign off than with five winners from 11 rides at Cheltenham. Through the injuries and the bad days, whenever the little bit of doubt and insecurity started to creep in, I always kept believing that when the big day came, I'd still be able to deliver. And at Cheltenham, I did. I've always loved the big day and the big occasion — the best going up against the best with the whole racing world watching. Throughout my career, that was always what excited me, what motivated me. That was when I thrived. I cherished my success but I never dwelled on my defeats; I was comfortable with the fact that someone had to finish second and that there'd be plenty of occasions when that someone would be me. Most important, I never lost sight of the fact that I was lucky to be doing something that I loved. Arriving at the course, getting ready for a day's racing, getting stuck into the craic in the weighroom and giving as good as I got: it brought me so much enjoyment. When the spotlight was on, I was at my best, but I took the rough with the smooth and never took myself too seriously. If my career is to be remembered for anything, I'd like it to be that.

For every great day I've had, there was a great horse with me all the way. The special ones were always more to me than just a horse that I had to ride for work. They were friends, characters that I got to know and love and build a connection with over the years. I knew their personalities, their strengths and their quirks. They were my pets. The only question that I can't answer is which horse was the best I've ever ridden. For me, Moscow Flyer and Sprinter Sacre are still impossible to split, and that's the highest compliment that I can pay to either of them.

When Moscow died in 2016, I was sick with the sadness. He meant the world to me and I know that my career wouldn't have been the same without him. The only small consolation was that myself, Paula and the children had been down to visit him in the National Stud before he died. It had been on our to-do list for so long before we got around to it, and it would have been such a shame if we never got the opportunity. Síofra, Órla and Rían are all too young to remember him at his superstar best, but it was so important to me that they got a chance to meet him – that Moscow was more than just a photo on the wall or a replay on the television – and that we spent that day together as a family. I was able to introduce them to Kicking King as well, another of my old pals, who is enjoying his retirement in the National Stud. We made the trip back to Conna on another occasion to say hello to Jimmy Mangan and Monty's Pass, my first time back there since the night of that unforgettable Grand National celebration. Monty is well into his late twenties now, and thankfully still fit and well, and we have a lovely photo of Rían sitting on his back, just as I did in Aintree back in 2003. After I announced my retirement, JP invited us to Martinstown to mark the occasion. It was a fantastic day – we went for lunch and ended up staying for dinner – and the kids were delighted to get a chance to meet Buveur D'Air as well as Epatante, Champ, Dame De Compagnie and Sire Du Berlais, four of the five horses that had made my final Cheltenham so special. I've memories to last a lifetime, and these magnificent horses have been at the centre of it all.

None of it would have been possible without the support of my friends and family and, in particular, without Paula. I know that being married to a professional jockey isn't easy. The racing year is long, there are a lot of nights spent on the road away from home, and weekends, Christmas and Easter are all earmarked for work. But no matter what the challenge was, Paula was always right there by my side. I couldn't have done any of it without her love, her support and her guidance, and I can't wait for the next adventures that life after racing brings us. I know how fortunate we are to have been able to share some very special memories with our three wonderful children in the last few years, at an age when they were all old enough to remember and appreciate them. All I wanted going to Cheltenham in 2020 was to have one last winner so that I could dedicate it to them. When the time came to announce my retirement, it didn't really matter to me where or when or how it was done, as long as my family were by my side.

Above all, I'm grateful – grateful that I've had such a good career, grateful that I've been able to enjoy so much success for good people who placed their trust in me, grateful that I've been able to share it with the people I love most. Life has been good to me, and I've enjoyed every second of it so far. Whatever bad days there were, they're distant memories now, but the good ones will live on for ever. I got the opportunity to live my dream, and I've achieved all I ever wanted and more.

More than anything, it's been fun.

Leabharlanna Poiblí Chathair Baile Átha Cliath
Dublin City Public Libraries

Acknowledgements

I would like to thank my beautiful wife Paula, who has supported me and my dreams for so long. I would never have made it this far without her help. To our amazing children: Síofra, so thoughtful and caring; Órla, always smiling and kind; and Rían, active and loving.

To my parents and family for all of their help and for giving me the opportunity to immerse myself in a life of horses.

To Paula's family for all of their care, support and fun over the years.

To the lads in the weighroom, who always looked out for me and others. Thanks for the great times we had.

To the owners and trainers, who trusted me with their horses.

To all at Gill Books, from Deirdre Nolan, who brought me around to the idea of writing this book, to Catherine Gough, Ellen Monnelly, Teresa Daly and Laura King for helping to put it all together. And, of course, Niall Kelly, who patiently sat with me going through my life story for days and days in person and on Zoom.